Transformational Entrepreneurship

To achieve progress in society and business practices, more entrepreneurship is needed to encourage action and enhance social capital in society, and transformational entrepreneurship may be the key. Transformational entrepreneurship offers a way of integrating sustainability practices whilst focusing on sustainable future trends.

This book discusses how transformational entrepreneurship uses novel business practices to reduce inequality in the marketplace and how it transforms society through creative solutions that enable change. The book provides useful insight into better understanding this emerging concept.

Vanessa Ratten is Associate Professor at La Trobe University, Australia.

Paul Jones is Professor at Coventry University, United Kingdom.

Routledge Frontiers of Business Management

For more information about this series, please visit www.routledge.com/Routledge-Frontiers-of-Business-Management/book-series/RFBM

Transformational Entrepreneurship

Edited by Vanessa Ratten
and Paul Jones

Routledge
Taylor & Francis Group

LONDON AND NEW YORK

First published 2019 by Routledge

2 Park Square, Milton Park, Abingdon, Oxfordshire OX14 4RN
52 Vanderbilt Avenue, New York, NY 10017

Routledge is an imprint of the Taylor & Francis Group, an informa business

First issued in paperback 2020

British Library Cataloguing-in-Publication Data
A catalogue record for this book is available from the British Library

Library of Congress Cataloging-in-Publication Data
A catalog record for this book has been requested

ISBN: 978-1-138-48475-7 (hbk)
ISBN: 978-0-367-50410-6 (pbk)

Typeset in Galliard
by Apex CoVantage, LLC

Contents

vi *Contents*

Figures

Tables

Foreword

Our understanding of transformational entrepreneurship is in its infancy at best. However, we recognize its potential for socio-economic value creation. This concept can advance if we answer two basic questions – the what and how of transformational entrepreneurship. While the answer to the first question concerns its goals and objectives, the second relates to influence-mechanisms through which transformational entrepreneurship creates value.

Self-employment and small businesses ensure low to moderate economic impact with lesser focus on societal impact. High-growth entrepreneurship maximizes economic impact, yet its societal impact may be moderate. Social entrepreneurship concerns obtaining long-term societal impact with moderate economic impact. Transformational entrepreneurship is that form of entrepreneurship that seeks to maximize both economic impact alongside long-term societal impact. Hence, its role in maximizing economic impact as well as sustaining societal impact sets it apart from previously conceptualized forms of entrepreneurship, something which we are only beginning to understand. Transformational entrepreneurship entails approaching problems systematically, addressing and treating root cause, unlocking human potential and seeking to empower people, improving people's relationships, ensuring that people learn from each other and, in doing all these, creating more value than it can capture. In this sense, transformational entrepreneurship has close semblance with yet another emerging concept – that of collaborative entrepreneurship – synergistically combining each other's resources to create socio-economic value.

In as much as the benefits of transformational entrepreneurship are desirable, it is contingent upon the entrepreneurs' context. What is transformational will vary by societies, depending upon the priorities, norms, desirability and feasibility of bringing about change. A society driven by technological changes will have impacts different from one that is driven by subsistence. Regardless of the motivations, transformational entrepreneurship is productive by definition and embedded within a context. When conditions are right, and as we would begin to see more and more entrepreneurs channelling their efforts and resources for the greater good, transformational entrepreneurship would become synonymous to institutional entrepreneurship and consistent with Baumol's notion of productive entrepreneurship. Here it is important to note that cultures therefore will play a

significant role. Transformational entrepreneurs as leaders would be more acceptable, even endorsed, in societies where cultural leadership ideals are supportive of leadership styles that are participatory, humane-oriented, team-oriented
and charismatic. These styles are key elements of yet another emerging field of
research in leadership – that of collective leadership. Cultures that are open to
embracing collective leadership styles are the ones that would create the most
socio-economic impact via transformational entrepreneurship.

The chapters of this book have been able to capture a lot of these themes and
is a great start for research in transformational entrepreneurship. I congratulate
the editors and the participating authors for looking into this important topic
and advancing entrepreneurship research in a new direction. It was an honour
to write a foreword and I wish great success to this book and everyone involved.

Thanks.

Saurav Pathak
Kansas State University

Contributors

Mário Augusto is Assistant Professor at University of Coimbra, Portugal.

Vitor Braga is Associate Professor at Porto Polytechnic, Portugal.

Alexandra David is Assistant Professor at Institute for Work and Technology, Westphalian University, Germany.

Elisa Baraibar-Diez is Assistant Professor at University of Cantabria, Spain.

Antonio Duarte is a PhD Student at University of Tras-de-Montes, Portugal.

Carlos López Hernández is Assistant Professor at Universidad Panamericana, Mexico.

Paul Jones is Professor at Coventry University, United Kingdom.

Cynthia Laurin is a researcher at Deakin University, Australia.

Macarena Lopez-Fernandez is Associate Professor at University of Seville, Spain.

Stephanie Juliette Moreno Hernández is Assistant Professor at Universidad de Ciencias Aplicadas y Ambientales, Colombia.

Carla Susana Marques is an Assistant Professor at University of Tres-de-Montes, Portugal.

Jesus Barrena-Martinez is an Assistant Professor at University of Cadiz, Spain.

Ethan Samuel Miller is a researcher at La Trobe University, Australia.

Jessica Rubiano Moreno is Assistant Professor at Universidad de Ciencias Aplicadas y Ambientales, Colombia.

Waleed Omri is Assistant Professor at Paris Business School, France.

Maria Odriozola is Assistant Professor at University of Cantabria, Spain.

Joanna Poyago-Theotoky is Professor at La Trobe University, Australia.

Vanessa Ratten is Associate Professor at La Trobe University, Australia.

Pedro Romero-Fernandez is Professor at University of Cadiz, Spain.

Ladislao Luna Sotorrio is Assistant Professor at University of Cantabria, Spain.

Judith Terstriep is Assistant Professor at Institute for Work and Technology, Westphalian University, Germany.

Anne Tjønndal is a researcher at Nord University, Norway.

Pedro Torres is Assistant Professor at University of Coimbra, Portugal.

Connie Zheng is Senior Lecturer at Deakin University, Australia.

1 Transformational entrepreneurship

An overview

Vanessa Ratten and Paul Jones

Introduction

Transformational entrepreneurship is a distinct kind of entrepreneurship and has an interdisciplinary nature with linkages to anthropology, economics, sociology and regional planning. Entrepreneurs involved in transformations encourage positive action that has a flow on effect, which enables business ventures to deliver outcomes that change the surrounding environment by viewing things in a different way (Ratten et al., 2017). Transformational entrepreneurship is related to the concept of challenge-based entrepreneurship, as it is an important and socially significant type of entrepreneurship that transcends cultural barriers (Anggadwita et al., 2016). Transformation is a popular term used by entrepreneurship practitioners to indicate major changes in society and when combined with entrepreneurship it is presumed to have superior competitive capabilities that influence market performance (Moscardo, 2014). This means that transformational entrepreneurship has a practical, social and theoretical component, which makes it an interesting field of research.

The field of transformational entrepreneurship is exciting due to its relatively recent emergence and the need to assess the results of innovative behaviour. Transformational entrepreneurship offers a way to understand the causations and implications of entrepreneurship in terms of how innovation flourishes in society (Alvord et al., 2004). This enables valuable insights to be learnt from transformational entrepreneurship and it is an interesting research field with useful practical results. The exploration of transformational entrepreneurship opens up unique research opportunities that can help guide policy initiatives. As such, the chapters in this book provide a good starting point for scholars to further enrich management practice by focusing on transformational entrepreneurship. From this book researchers should be able to contemplate the opportunities around the topic of transformational entrepreneurship, as it is an exciting area of research that will continue to capture the interest of researchers. This chapter examines the role of transformational entrepreneurship in society by introducing the concept and current approaches. Increasingly, scholars, entrepreneurs and policy makers recognize entrepreneurship as having transformational powers and societal facets. Thus, this book adds another perspective to the current debate about the effects of entrepreneurship by placing attention on the transformations that have the biggest effect on society. This chapter explains the role of transformational entrepreneurship in the global economy so as to make recommendations on how the former can help improve the state of the later. In this chapter, the term 'transformational entrepreneurship' is introduced as well as the significance of the topic.

Entrepreneurship and social change

Entrepreneurship is a dynamic process that involves unforeseen events that are often unpredictable (Ferreira et al., 2017). The uncontrollable nature of entrepreneurship means individuals need to cope with the changing realities (Ratten et al., 2017). Hall et al. (2010, p. 439) states 'entrepreneurship is increasingly recognized as a significant conduit for bringing about a transformation to sustainable products and processes'. There is no one type of entrepreneurship, as it is a diverse field with both profit and non-profit motivations (Leal et al., 2016). Therefore, to understand entrepreneurship the context is important in understanding differences in behaviour (Ferreira et al., 2017).

Entrepreneurship is the key to achieving change but depends on the significance of institutional factors influencing business structures. This is due to entrepreneurship being a strategic decision making process that incorporates individual and firm behaviour (Ramadani et al., 2017). Research on entrepreneurship has in many respects been dominated by a corporate perspective with only recently emphasis being placed on social and environmental issues. This is despite there being a positive association between competitive orientation and amount of transformation. The field of entrepreneurship has a multidisciplinary approach that necessitates a better understanding of social tensions requiring solutions (Ratten and Ferreira, 2017). Research based on traditional entrepreneurship theory may not apply to recent and emerging social innovations that are responsible for transformations in society (Tajeddini et al., 2017). Thus, there is much to learn about how entrepreneurship transforms society.

There are different ways to define and conceptualize entrepreneurship. Schumpeter (1934) was one of the first academics to discuss the role of entrepreneurs in society. He suggested that entrepreneurs are those who create new combinations of distribution systems, markets or products (De Bruin et al., 2006). This definition of entrepreneurship is still used by many and is considered one of the more traditional approaches. Another perspective of entrepreneurship is by Kirzner (1985) who viewed it as those with an ability to filter information in order to discover opportunities. This approach has become popular particularly with the knowledge economy and strategic use of information for competitive reasons. A broader approach to entrepreneurship is taken by Aldrich (1999) who views it as the initiation of new activities. This includes an emphasis on the achievements needed to conduct or start a business venture.

Entrepreneurship can be an elusive topic due to its range of definitions and ways it is applied. There is now more emphasis on entrepreneurship in the economy due to its influence on business growth rates. In the past, entrepreneurship was associated with negative connotations but this has changed with more people viewing it in a positive light as it impacts global well-being due to its ability to change society. Entrepreneurship captures a range of activities, attitudes, behaviours and motivations (Schoar, 2010). This means that entrepreneurs have diverse personality characteristics that range from being risk taking, proactive and interested in innovation. The core element of entrepreneurship is adding a form of value. Entrepreneurs are different to managers, as they focus on creating or discovering opportunities that have a degree of novelty. Managers on the other hand focus on existing businesses rather than seeking new opportunities. Thus, transformational entrepreneurship provides a way for managers to be strategically relevant, as it outlines practical examines that facilitate societal change (Tassabehji et al., 2010). The effective utilization of transformational entrepreneurship for business and management studies needs to further address social inequalities in society. Technological innovation has altered the way people live but this has brought about inequalities that can be partly solved by transformational entrepreneurship.

The demand for entrepreneurs increases when there is more diversity in technology, business and consumers (Crecente-Romero et al., 2016). Entrepreneurship involves the use of resources in a productive or destructive way and is viewed as a productive resource because it enables businesses to develop that create jobs, which contributes to societal development. However, entrepreneurship has also been viewed in a destructive way when it hurts the environment or changes society in a negative way. The environment for entrepreneurship is impacted by adverse conditions that require new ways of thinking (Ling et al., 2008). Market environments that are unstable provide opportunities but at the same time require risk. The deregulation of many economies has created market niches. This is more evident in transition, emerging and developing countries that are opening up new markets and require the injection of money into the economy.

Transformational entrepreneurship involves looking at opportunities in new markets to evaluate changing conditions (Matzler et al., 2008). The competitiveness of markets can increase when new businesses enter the market. To get better results there is an emphasis on big changes from entrepreneurship, as information communication has opened up many markets providing ways for companies to compete that were previously hard to do due to geographical factors. In addition, the rise of the knowledge and service economy has demanded entrepreneurs to think about innovative ways to have market penetration. To improve synergies between different sectors of the economy it is important to encourage collaboration. This can influence the launching of potentially transformative products and services that overcome current market barriers.

There are also contextual facts that influence individuals to become transformational entrepreneurs. This includes individuals who are driven to become entrepreneurs because of opportunities compared to those who need money to survive and thus are called necessity entrepreneurs. There are also differences in entrepreneurs because of other factors such as location, gender, age and occupation. Therefore, when we discuss transformational entrepreneurs there also needs to be an acknowledgement of their different characteristics. This helps in understanding the complexities of being a transformational entrepreneur.

Social changes are the result of innovation and improvements to current conditions that enable better collective empowerment. This helps reconfigure better social practices that can help build better community relations. Certain social contexts are characterized by more innovation that influences transformational entrepreneurship. Not all social innovation leads to transformational change due to the more incremental forms of entrepreneurship that take a longer time to process (Yuki, 1999). There is value in the variety of change incorporated within transformational entrepreneurship due to the context impacting the form of transformation. Thus, it is important to understand entrepreneurship by considering which major forms of change are influencing the environment.

Game changes are part of an entrepreneurial society and have been utilized to transform the way business is conducted. Transformational entrepreneurs change the rules of current business practices by incorporating different forms of behaviours. This helps society keep up to date with current trends and technological developments. Social innovation involves new ways of organizing relations that involve change but also a non-profit or altruistic component (Tajeddini et al., 2017). The framing of social relations is built on the practices of how people act together. Transformational change involves social innovation, as it encourages more community-oriented decisions. This is important in altering people's decisions about business practices.

Because entrepreneurship is a societal phenomenon its antecedents and outcomes lead to transformations in communities. Entrepreneurial behaviour that goes beyond current expectations is considered transformational. The context of entrepreneurship matters in explaining whether there will be transformational change due to the impact of cultural, political and economic influence. Knowledge transfer is necessary for entrepreneurship due to the role communication plays in disseminating ideas. There are a variety of dissemination channels that entrepreneurs can use to transfer knowledge about their findings, including word of mouth, marketing and internationalization.

The question in entrepreneurship arises of whether there is a transformational change from the impact of ideas in society. A desirable achievement for entrepreneurs is to change taken-for-granted assumptions and have disruptive innovation. To do this requires a deepening effect of the entrepreneurship that combines ideas with practical approaches. It is worth looking at transformational entrepreneurship to find mechanisms that ensure the dissemination of knowledge because it offers a way of implementing radical ideas that reasonably questions the current state of affairs.

In entrepreneurship research there is a tendency to emphasize positive personality and environmental factors without taking into account negative circumstances such as economic, emotional and socio-cultural factors (Miller and Breton-Miller, 2017). The challenges people face in their lives can be a source of inspiration for transformational change. This is due to people overcoming adverse conditions that lead to resilient behaviour. People who become effective entrepreneurs may have experiences that lead to better risk tolerance and creative behaviours. In addition, social skills formed through adverse circumstances can help in obtaining business networks for entrepreneurship. Social skills are important in facilitating transformational entrepreneurship as they enable the tapping into other individual's abilities. Sometimes it is necessary for entrepreneurs to work with and rely on others as part of their business model.

To build transformative change requires the aid of others in order to complement and extend existing capabilities. Entrepreneurs create networks of relationships in order to exchange information. Moreover, in the interconnected global business environment there may be a need to have a team approach that involves multiple business partners. Entrepreneurs with similar goals may utilize networks to help develop their businesses and share ideas. Thus, entrepreneurs can unite with others who share similar goals in order to overcome challenging experiences. Given the risk associated with entrepreneurship it may be essential to partner with others.

Defining transformational entrepreneurship

Research on transformational entrepreneurship is currently under active in the entrepreneurship literature. To further develop the field there needs to be more focus on the extent and need for entrepreneurs to behave in a transformational way. This chapter provides an understanding about transformational entrepreneurship but there remains considerable opportunity for further research. Once an entrepreneurial venture has been launched, individuals can work with others to make their businesses successful. The difference between transformational and non-transformational entrepreneurs is a function of individual, environmental and cultural factors. Individuals with a need for achievement can have a personality that motivates them to launch transformational business initiatives. To support these businesses, often individuals will have a need for autonomy and self-regulation. The co-presence of other factors such as intuition and originality is also important.

Transformational entrepreneurship tries to reconcile the economic and social disparities in society (Newey, 2017). To do this there is a need to change the existing socio-economic strategies. This helps to reconceptualize and alleviate social inequalities that were creating problems in the past, as transformation can take a variety of forms and differs in context (Newey, 2017). Part of the process for transformational entrepreneurship involves changing economic systems so they provide better services to marginalized groups of society. There is an increasing interest in transformational entrepreneurship due to more concern about social and community issues.

There are continual technological innovations that are utilizing entrepreneurship to bring about change. The value of transformational entrepreneurship is in how it becomes a strategic decision to contribute to societal development. The concept of transformational entrepreneurship is evolving due to changing notions about how to define transformation. Organizations need to be supported in their efforts to be transformational entrepreneurs. In order to act in a transformational way there needs to be an awareness of change and how it can be nurtured. Thus, organizations need to permit new ideas in order to have a transformational vision.

Transformational leadership

Transformational leadership focuses on the way leaders influence their organizations through visionary activity (Mittal and Dhar, 2015). Leaders can transform organizations by motivating people and forecasting future demand. It is important that leaders encourage growth by facilitating an innovative attitude in their organizations. This enables an organization to extend its current capabilities by visualizing future changes. By having a collective vision of innovation, leaders can transform current thinking patterns into more beneficial outcomes. This helps change employee thinking from being self-involved to being more collectivist in nature. Mittal and Dhar (2015, p. 906) states 'transformational leadership is the best way for leaders to develop the creative skills of their employees and consequently to develop effective solutions to their problems'. In today's globally competitive world, there is a need for transformational leadership that involves creativity and innovation. Leaders that have a transformational style are likely to build a more innovative organizational culture that fosters change. Organizations that share knowledge can improve their information flows and increase overall performance.

The key element of transformational entrepreneurship is universal, as it reflects substantial change that benefits society. Entrepreneurship that serves to benefit the social environment and is economically viable is considered transformational. Increasingly, there is consideration about the environmental effects of entrepreneurship for future generations. It is critical that the global economy becomes more sustainable and engages in transformational entrepreneurship.

Sustainable entrepreneurship involves focusing on how to find more novel ways to be sustainable in the marketplace. There is increased interest in bringing sustainable development strategies into entrepreneurship in order to be more transparent and to manage ecological initiatives (Provasnek et al., 2016). Miles et al. (2009) suggested that the main components of sustainable entrepreneurship are being accountable in terms of long-term environmental management. These components are linked to the presence of innovation in business that integrates environmental initiatives. More organizations are interested in sustainable entrepreneurship due to the emphasis on renewal or improvement in products that are also socially responsible (Provasnek et al., 2016).

Transformational entrepreneurship is an emerging topic of inquiry but has been used in vague terms. Entrepreneurs need to rise to the challenge of finding transformational changes that will help solve global problems and utilize market imperfections to find opportunities that bring about change. This enables information asymmetries to yield opportunities that bring about new economic behaviours as entrepreneurs find solutions to environmental problems. There needs to be a fundamental transformation in the way energy and resources are consumed (Hall et al., 2010). This is due to there being more interest in environmental issues that require transformational entrepreneurship. Business and policy analysts are more focused on sustainable development and transformational entrepreneurship because it provides a conduit between sustainability and environmental issues. This is the result of entrepreneurship acting as a panacea for pressing social issues due to the need for innovative thinking.

Transformational social innovation

Avelino et al. (2017, p. 2) defines transformational social innovation as 'the process through which social innovation challenges, alters and/or replaces dominant institutions'. There are societal challenges that require the capacity to solve problems in an innovative manner. To mobilize organizations there needs to be more creativity amongst employees in organizations. This can be accomplished by empowering individuals with the ability to think outside the box. Organizations need to have shared expectations about the challenges they face and how to solve problems. This is a complex process, as the challenges are interlinked and need to be understood in a systemic manner. Therefore, there needs to be a systemic process approach to entrepreneurship that goes beyond linear casualties to include complex configurations. Transformation often needs time to implement, as there are changes with an evolutionary trajectory that come in different degrees from minor to major depending on its impact. System innovation involves transformations that influence societal processes such as water, energy, health, transport and welfare (Avelino et al., 2017). This means system innovation influences structures in society that are modernized to develop better adaptive management processes. It is important to develop systems to provide for better social policies that anticipate market need.

Social innovation as a field of study is characterized by conceptual ambiguity despite its frequent usage in academic and policy circles. There is a diverse array of settings that social innovation can be studied in and its relevance depends on the environmental context. The trend towards citizens and organizations engaging more in discussions about society has led to the increased popularity of social innovation. The perception of innovation as being not just about technology but also linked to policy interests has led to more studies focusing on social innovation. The literature on social innovation is still fragmented due to the diverse ways innovation can be applied in a social context.

Social innovation relates to new forms of interactions between society and business. The social component of social innovation refers to society but can also include political and cultural dimensions. There is an increased interest in changing society by deriving new social policies that lead to innovation. This is an important way of promoting social practices that disseminate new forms of behaviour in society. As more organizations are focusing on sustainability and social responsibility, social innovation provides a way to design better processes. Sustainability is a dynamic concept that refers to thinking about the present without compromising future needs. The ability of future generations to live well depends on humans preserving the environment. Cultural sustainability is part of transformational entrepreneurship, as it enables the longevity of behaviours across generations. The ability to transmit culture is an important way entrepreneurship can transform society and address social needs. Innovation transcends cultural, organizational and social structures to bring about change (Swanson and De Vereaux, 2017). Cultural capital is important in explaining how entrepreneurs take action (Henry et al., 2017). Bourdieu (1986) suggests that there are three forms of cultural capital: the embodied, objectified and institutionalized state. The embodied state focuses on the thoughts and feelings people have that affect behaviour. An entrepreneur's mind is an important part of their being and influences decisions. The objectified state examines the cultural elements of society, such as languages and artefacts (Henry et al., 2017). Objects that are associated with a culture provide a way to link heritage to business pursuits. The institutionalized state refers to more government-related entities, such as educational providers, that impact regulations in society. Institutions provide the more formal way of understanding roles that are needed in order for entrepreneurs to act efficiently in the marketplace.

System innovations are reconfigurations in socio-economic conditions that involve both collective and individual values. This means innovation enables institutional and organizational change that takes into account alternations in knowledge and lifestyle. Some innovation needs to be morally interpreted for its affect on different segments of society. System innovation can involve profound change depending on the level of societal segment it involves. In addition, the type of innovation will have different affects on society and involve different institutional stakeholders.

The systems of innovation approach is relevant to studies on transformational entrepreneurship due to its focus on dynamism from institutional changes. There is a process of interactive learning embedded in entrepreneurship that is impacted by institutional structure. Institutions operate at different levels of society from local and community orientated ones to more regional and internationally active organizations. Institutions can help or hinder transformation depending on the context. The innovation process develops better when there are institutional structures in place that enable the flow of information. Most institutions take a formal structure in terms of promoting innovation through education and training. However, there can be other mechanisms utilized by institutions to help transform society, such as research, funding and regulatory support. The way institutions influence entrepreneurship is based on societal needs but also depends on the environmental context. Informal institutions such as these that form network groups can help support the psychological development of ideas. Thus, an institution does not need to have a strict set of rules but can instead include more supportive ways to encourage change. In transformational entrepreneurship there can be a need to realign the change with practice so that it can be implemented into the market more easily. To do this institutions can provide the stability of concentrations in order to facilitate transformational entrepreneurship.

Social capital is useful for entrepreneurs to access resources that enable transformations in the economy to occur. Social capital is defined as the 'sum of the resources, actual or virtual that accrue to an individual or group by virtue of possessing a durable network of more or less institutionalized relationships of mutual acquaintances and recognition' (Bourdieu and Wacquaint, 1992, p. 119). The growing impact of transformational entrepreneurship can be attributed to more emphasis on social and sustainability issues in business. The changing nature of business to incorporate more social responsibility has led to increased interest in entrepreneurship.

Entrepreneurship has a social role to play that is often overlooked in contemporary research studies due to the emphasis on firm behaviours rather than societal implications (Zahra and Wright, 2016). Welter et al. (2016) describes entrepreneurship as a way to create organizations using social technology. Entrepreneurship is a way for individuals and organizations to pursue myriad goals that can increase social equality. There is a broad array of reasons why entrepreneurship occurs, but the most important are in terms of empowerment. The increasing social emphasis within economic systems means more businesses are focusing on transformative strategies as part of their development. For regions, transformational entrepreneurship provides opportunities to create positive change that will benefit future generations.

Entrepreneurship provides a way to alleviate social problems and connect business to pressing issues. Cultural capital is needed for transformational entrepreneurship due to the need to access societal expectations about appropriate behaviour. De Clercq and Honig (2011) states that cultural capital includes objectified, institutionalized and embodied dimensions. Objectified cultural capital refers to tangible goods that are associated with a role in society. This includes the use of buildings for business purposes that have a history of housing entrepreneurs. Depending on the context, the objects can range from minor such as dress codes to more substantial such as mode of transformation. Institutionalized cultural capital involves the qualifications needed to conduct business. This includes certifications or expertise needed to signify trust in a person. Embodied cultural capital refers to the characteristics in a person that involve knowledge.

Social entrepreneurship is part of transformational experiences in the context of new business creation. The difference between social and transformational entrepreneurship is that the former focuses on non-profit issues that solve social problems but the later goes beyond this to produce fundamental changes in society. Entrepreneurs have an effect on society, which means there is a relationship between business activity and the sustainable use of resources. Cunningham and Lischeron (1991) suggest that entrepreneurs are more ethical and socially responsible than non-entrepreneurs due to their innovative and forward thinking capability. This is an interesting claim, as entrepreneurs have traditionally been considered as hedonistic and profit orientated.

Entrepreneurs have a moral compass that means they need to behave in an ethical and responsible manner. Weber (1930) in a seminal book suggested that entrepreneurship involves an ethical obligation. This means that entrepreneurs have a propensity to engage in moral behaviour due to the psychological factors associated with certain behaviour. Colonomos (2005) suggests that entrepreneurs take on-board a moral view of capitalism by including an ethical perspective. Entrepreneurs need to work towards both financial and social profitability by being efficient with the use of resources. Thus, entrepreneurs are the cause of transformation due to their ability to distinguish between incremental and radical innovation.

Social entrepreneurs devise innovative business models that are often overlooked by other businesses. This is due to social entrepreneurs being socially conscious individuals that are motivated to provide benefits to society. Often business and government cannot solve all social issues so social entrepreneurs help fill unmet needs. Social entrepreneurship is important for improving quality of life for disadvantaged segments of society. Social forms of entrepreneurship focus on creating purposeful forms of business creation that tie into a way of life. This helps business create social change by implementing focused changes. Marginalized groups of society often have less attention paid to them that requires intervention by other sources. Local economic development is a useful way to serve groups of society that need special attention.

Social capital can be considered from a community or regional perspective, which involves focusing on processes and outcomes. There is a sense of unpredictability in entrepreneurship, which gives way to transformational change. Venture creation is a creative process that leads to improvization of new developments. Some events unfold and force entrepreneurs to engage in exploratory behaviour. Social entrepreneurial initiatives have received more recognition from both the public and private sectors. This is the result of social entrepreneurship covering more unconventional entrepreneurial initiatives due to its emphasis on innovation and change. Increasingly, social entrepreneurship is used as a way for business to yield non-profit benefits; thus, providing a way for social initiatives to incorporate a profit-orientated purpose. Social entrepreneurship can have a broad meaning in terms of being a mindset but also a narrow definition by being involved in non-profit activities.

Entrepreneurial ecosystems

Entrepreneurial ecosystems provide the human, financial, professional and social resources needed when facilitating change. To facilitate the exchanging of knowledge, ecosystems are needed. This enables the use of networks to provide access to information in order to facilitate interaction with stakeholders (Foss et al., 2018). In an entrepreneurial ecosystem there are interconnected elements that provide a supportive environment. In order to facilitate new venture creation and growth, ecosystems provide a way to use stakeholder interactions. Entrepreneurial ecosystems are characterized by voluntary and open relationships that evolve over time.

Foss et al. (2018) distinguish between hard and soft components of entrepreneurial ecosystems. The hard components refer to the more tangible resources needed for entrepreneurship. These include physical buildings and equipment needed to build business ventures. In addition, resources such as finance and funding are included in these components due to their ability to be measured. The soft components are more intangible and include education and social networks. Entrepreneurship education is viewed as an important part of ecosystems due to new knowledge and skills about business being learnt. In addition, social networks facilitate the exchanging of ideas that is helpful in gaining access to markets.

The entrepreneurial experience is a creative one as it involves events with different outcomes. Cognitive approaches to entrepreneurship focus on explaining why it occurs within an ecosystem (Henry et al., 2017). Often it is unknown how entrepreneurship occurs in terms of why entrepreneurs make decisions and behave in certain ways. Thus, understanding entrepreneurial behaviours is a way to assess the knowledge and information behind entrepreneurship assessments. There are major changes affecting society that require transformational entrepreneurship and this includes climate change, the ageing population and the increased use of information communications technology. The increased life span of individuals has led to demographic developments and political challenges. There is a need for governments to plan better for individuals with a longer work life but also need for increased health services.

Climate change has meant biodiversity concerns and social movements to protect the environment. The perception of climate change is environmentally constructed and based on contested ideals. European countries have been pioneers in the use of renewable energy as a result of environmental crisis and political pressure. The European Union in particular has redefined how to deal with climate change by altering societal orientations towards the environment. Moreover, the internet has resulted in digital transformations that have included game-changing developments about climate change. Social relationships are being conducted in more online environments and this has resulted in socio-technological change that influences transformational entrepreneurship.

In the 2000s research on social entrepreneurship gained momentum and it is expected that transformational entrepreneurship will have the same trajectory. We believe it is time to advance the literature and debate about transformational entrepreneurship. Transformational entrepreneurship suggests that there is an alternative to the current economic system, as more social and ethical guidance is needed. The emphasis in transformational entrepreneurship is on changing the current status quo to bring new benefits for the greater good of society. The entrepreneurship literature focuses on the role of uncertainty in society (McCaffrey, 2017). Uncertainty refers to knowledge not known due to risk and changes in the marketplace. Transformational entrepreneurs respond to uncertainty by overcoming doubts to boldly enter new markets. This helps entrepreneurs to overcome barriers in the existing economic systems by facilitating positive actions. In order to exploit opportunities, entrepreneurs acknowledge the uncertainty but use it in a positive way by focusing on market niches within communities.

Communities in society

A community refers to the common sense of identity formed by belonging to a group that has a familiar feel to it. Communities enable people to share ideas and act in a collective manner. Communities have common cultures, identity, laws and forms. This enables communities to be analysed based on a common characteristic. Communities develop a special form of entrepreneurship due to their population, markets and locations (Lumpkin et al., 2018). This facilitates community-based entrepreneurship that leads to transformations in society. Lumpkin et al. (2018) suggests that there are four main types of community: geographical, identity, interest and intentional. Geographical communities refer to a specific location or land area and are characterized by their distinct contextual factors, such as proximity to other locations and land features. This enables the location to be marketed by tourism authorities based on specific features. In addition, government entities can promote social change by focusing on policies for the location. This includes promoting social change such as revitalizing deprived neighbourhoods. In addition, locations can be compared based on educational levels and level of entrepreneurship activity. Geographical communities are easier to distinguish and measure compared to other types of communities due to their naturally occurring demarcations, which are evident in maps (Lumpkin et al., 2018). Other distinct types of communities include educational, ethnic, religious and socio-economic and sport groups.

Communities of interest share a focus on a specific issue or concern (Lumpkin et al., 2018). Sharing an interest brings a sense of solidarity to a community and encourages group efforts to petition for a certain cause. There is a sense of bonding in communities that encourages a sense of connection amongst group members. The rational for starting some communities is a desire to change things and being in a group can facilitate this change. Community-based enterprises that share a common concern often are interested in issues pertaining to the environment. This helps build an argument for initiating certain actions related to the concerns and encouraging related projects to take share. Communities that cultivate a sense of purpose amongst members have a positive effect on society. Some of these communities start small but through word of mouth grow into larger global movements. Therefore, communities of interest are not necessarily bound by geography but rather are open to membership regardless of location (Lumpkin et al., 2018). Communities of interest often focus on social issues such as the alleviation of poverty. Community-based entrepreneurs utilize strategies to make members feel connected at a local and global level (Lumpkin et al., 2018).

Intentional communities are characterized by the methods they use to help address a certain issue (Lumpkin et al., 2018). As communities have different objectives and motivations it is important for them to focus on ways to achieve their goals. This means that some communities voluntarily live in a certain way because of their membership. The level of commitment to an intentional community differs depending on the belief systems of its members. The type of intention in a community can include a certain activity like reading or worship. Thus, often the intentions of individuals to be part of a community are because they volunteer to help. Communities are a way for people to express their intentions to contribute to a certain cause.

Communities of identity are those that share a cultural affinity (Lumpkin et al., 2018). Increasingly, individuals are wearing certain clothes or participating in events in order to associate themselves with a community. These communities have a social identity that derives from their sense of belonging. This is a way individuals can derive value from identifying with a group. By perceiving a common sense of identity, a person can be emotionally involved with a cause. Examples of communities of identities include nationality, sport team and religious affiliation (Lumpkin et al., 2018). By associating their identity with a community an individual can receive support.

Overview of chapters

This first chapter of the book has provided an overview of transformational entrepreneurship. The second chapter, 'Disclosure of social impact in agrifood entrepreneurial initiatives' by Elisa Baraibar-Diez, Maria Odriozola, and Ladislao Luna Sotorrio, focuses on the role of transformations in the agricultural industry. This helps to understand the environmental effects transformations have and the role of entrepreneurial ecosystems. The third chapter, 'Sustainable transformational entrepreneurship at Arouca UNESCO geopark, Portugal' by Vanessa Ratten, Antonio Duarte, Carla Susana Marques and Vitor Braga, focuses on the role of social and sustainable entrepreneurship in transformational change. This is important in the tourism industry, which needs transformational entrepreneurship in order to progress. The fourth chapter, 'Development of transformational social entrepreneurship through innovation determinants in the handicraft industry of the Wayuu community in Colombia' by Stephanie Juliette Moreno Hernández, Jessica Rubiano Moreno and Carlos López Hernández, discusses the role of artisan entrepreneurship. This chapter helps to understand how developing countries utilize transformational change for societal benefit. The fifth chapter, 'Innovation of informal ethnic entrepreneurship: a result of the opening of the EU's borders?' by Alexandra David and Judith Terstriep, analyses the role of minorities in transformational entrepreneurship. As informal entrepreneurship is an important part of societal change, the chapter helps to address the role of regional trading blocs. The sixth chapter, 'Exploring the excellence in socially responsible human resource practices: a case study from Spain' by Jesus Barrena-Martinez, Macarena Lopez-Fernandez and Pedro Romero-Fernandez, analyses the role of corporate social responsibility in transformational entrepreneurship. The seventh chapter, 'The post-mining boom: what next? the innovation agenda of Fortescue Metals Group: a qualitative case study' by Ethan Samuel Miller and Joanna Poyago-Theotoky, discusses the role of social responsibility and social innovation. This is an important component of transformational entrepreneurship that relies on companies to change the way they perceive the environment and social issues. The eighth chapter, 'Individual innovativeness, entrepreneurial creativity and religious capital: the role of transformational entrepreneurship in Tunisia' by Waleed Omri, highlights the need for creativity in entrepreneurship. The ninth chapter, 'Cultural leadership ideals and cultural practices leading to women's participation in transformational entrepreneurial leadership' by Pedro Torres and Mário Augusto, analyses the role of women in societal changes. The tenth chapter, 'Open innovation, knowledge creation and capability building: the case analysis of transformational entrepreneurship at Alibaba and SHOP.COM' by Connie Zheng and Cynthia Laurin, analyses an emerging market context for entrepreneurship. This helps to understand the role multinational corporations play in the transformational process. The eleventh chapter, 'Collaborative innovation: a viable strategy to solve complex transformational social issues in sport?' by Anne Tjønndal, focuses on the sport context for transformational entrepreneurship.. The last chapter, 'The future for transformational entrepreneurship' by Vanessa Ratten and Paul Jones, concludes the book by suggesting future research directions and policy initiatives.

Contributions of book

The field of transformational entrepreneurship is still ambiguous due to its lack of consolidation in terms of meaning and theoretical development. Scholars and practitioners need to continue to push transformational entrepreneurship as a way to address challenges in society. This book highlights the following lessons: 1) transformational entrepreneurship is an important and emerging area that links with the literature on social and sustainable entrepreneurship, 2) transformational entrepreneurship can be facilitated by focusing on innovative behaviours in communities and 3) different stakeholder perspectives must be considered in studies about transformational entrepreneurship. In this book we discuss a relatively under-researched area of transformational entrepreneurship that requires the use of entrepreneurial ecosystems and is continually expanding as a topic.

This book contributes to theory in two main ways. First, it links to the emerging field of transformational entrepreneurship by integrating social and sustainable forms of innovation. Second, it views transformational entrepreneurship as having a societal impact on the environment. This means understanding the nature of transformational entrepreneurship will provide deeper insights into how contextual forces affect strategy. The rationale for this book comes from the recognition that there is a need to go beyond the current forms of entrepreneurship to bring about transformations in society. This book plays a valuable role in the continued exploration of transformational entrepreneurship. Entrepreneurship itself incorporates change, but there are different forms of transformation.

This book is motivated by observations from current entrepreneurship research that there is a trend towards going beyond incremental innovation change and instead focusing on transformational change. New theories about transformational entrepreneurship are needed to explain how it differs to social and sustainable entrepreneurship. Most discussions of transformational entrepreneurship focus on its importance whilst disregarding its role in entrepreneurial ecosystems. Thus, transformation as a construct in entrepreneurship is still under-researched.

This book plays an important step in exploring the role of transformational entrepreneurship.

Conclusion

The chapters in this book provide ways that transformation is conducted through entrepreneurial endeavours. There is still significant work to be conducted on transformational entrepreneurship. Collectively, the chapters in this book elucidate the role of transformational entrepreneurship in society. The chapters demonstrate the value of taking a transformational perspective to entrepreneurship. Hopefully this book will draw more attention to the role of transformational entrepreneurship.

References

Aldrich, H. (1999). *Organizations Evolving*. Thousand Oaks, CA: Sage Publications.

Alvord, S., Brown, L.D., and Letts, C.W. (2004). Social entrepreneurship and societal transformation: An exploratory study. *The Journal of Applied Behavioural Science*, 40(3), 266–282.

Anggadwita, G., Ramadani, V., Luturlean, B., and Ratten, V. (2016). Socio-cultural environments and emerging economy entrepreneurship: Women entrepreneurs in Indonesia. *Journal of Entrepreneurship in Emerging Economies*, 9(1), 85–96.

Avelino, F., Wittmayer, J.M., Pel, B., Weaver, P., Dumitru, A., and Haxeltine, A. (2017). Transformative social innovation and (dis) empowerment. *Technological Forecasting and Social Change*, In Press.

Bourdieu, P. (1986). The forms of capital. In: J. Richardson (ed.), *Handbook of Theory and Research for the Sociology of Educated*. New York: Greenwood Publishing Group, 241–258.

Bourdieu, P., and Wacquaint, L.J. (1992). *An Invitation to Reflexive Sociology*. Chicago: University of Chicago Press.

Colonomos, A. (2005). The morality of belief in the profits of virtue. *International Social Science Journal*, 57(3), 457–467.

Crecente-Romero, F., Gimenez-Baldazo, M., and Rivera-Galicia, L.F. (2016). Subjective perception of entrepreneurship differences among countries. *Journal of Business Research*, 69, 5158–5162.

Cunningham, J.B., and Lischeron, J. (1991). Defining entrepreneurship. *Journal of Small Business Management*, 29(1), 45–61.

De Bruin, A., Brush, C.G., and Welter, F. (2006). Introduction to the special issue: Towards building cumulative knowledge on women's entrepreneurship. *Entrepreneurship Theory & Practice*, September, 585–593.

De Clercq, D., and Honig, B. (2011). Entrepreneurship as an integrating mechanisms for disadvantaged persons. *Entrepreneurship & Regional Development*, 23(5/6), 353–372.

Ferreira, J., Fernandes, C., Peris-Ortiz, M., and Ratten, V. (2017). Female entrepreneurship: A co-citation analysis. *International Journal of Entrepreneurship and Small Business'*, 31(2), 325–340.

Ferreira, J., Ratten, V., and Dana, L. (2017). Knowledge based spillovers and strategic entrepreneurship. *International Entrepreneurship and Management Journal*, 13(1), 161–167.

Foss, L., Henry, C., Ahl, H., and Mikalsen, G.H. (2018). Women's entrepreneurship policy research: A 30 year review of the evidence. *Small Business Economics*, 1–21.

Hall, J.K., Daneke, G.A., and Lenox, M.J. (2010). Sustainable development and entrepreneurship: Past contributions and future directions. *Journal of Business Venturing*, 25, 439–448.

Henry, E.Y., Dana, L.P., and Murphy, P.J. (2017). Telling their own stories: Maori entrepreneurship in the mainstream screen industry. *Entrepreneurship & Regional Development*, In Press.

Kirzner, I. (1985). *Discovery and the Capitalist Process.* Chicago: University of Chicago Press.

Leal, C., Marques, C., Ratten, V., and Marques, C. (2016). The role of intellectual capital and corporate strategy on sustainable value creation. *International Journal of Foresight and Innovation Policy*, 11(4), 215–224.

Ling, Y.A.N., Simsek, Z., Lubatkin, M.H., and Veiga, J.F. (2008). Transformational leaderships role in promoting corporate entrepreneurship: Examining the CEO-TMT interface. *Academy of Management Journal*, 51(3), 557–576.

Lumpkin, G.T., Bacq, S., and Pidduck, R.J. (2018). Where change happens: Community-level phenomena in social entrepreneurship research. *Journal of Small Business Management*, 56(1), 24–50.

Matzler, K., Schwarz, E., Deutinger, N., and Harms, R. (2008). The relationship between transformational leadership, product innovation, and performance in SMEs. *Journal of Small Business & Entrepreneurship*, 21(2), 139–151.

McCaffrey, M. (2017). Exploring the economic foundations of entrepreneurship research. *European Management Review*, In Press.

Miles, M.P, Munilla, L.S., and Darrock, J. (2009). Sustainable corporate entrepreneurship. *International Entrepreneurship and Management Journal*, 5(1), 65–76.

Miller, D., and Breton-Miller, I. (2017). Underdog entrepreneurs: A model of challenge-based entrepreneurship. *Entrepreneurship Theory & Practice*, January: 7–17.

Mittal, S., and Dhar, R.L. (2015). Transformational leadership and employee creativity: Mediating the role of creative self-efficacy and moderating role of knowledge sharing. *Management Decision*, 53(5), 894–910.

Moscardo, G. (2014). Tourism and community leadership in rural regions: Linking mobility, entrepreneurship, tourism development and community well-being. *Tourism Planning & Development*, 11(3), 354–370.

Newey, L. (2017). Changing the system: Compensatory versus transformative social entrepreneurship. *Journal of Social Entrepreneurship*, In Press.

Provasnek, A.K., Schumid, E., Geissler, B., and Steiner, G. (2016). Sustainable corporate entrepreneurship: Performance and strategies toward innovation. *Business Strategy and the Environment*, In Press.

Ramadani, V., Bexheti, A., Rexhepi, G., Ratten, V., and Ibraimi, S. (2017). Succession issues in Albanian family businesses: An exploratory research. *Journal of Balkan and Near Eastern Studies*, 19(3), 294–312.

Ratten, V., and Ferreira, J. (2017). Future research directions for cultural entrepreneurship and regional innovation. *International Journal of Entrepreneurship and Innovation*, 21(3), 163–169.

Ratten, V., Ferreira, J.J., and Fernandes, C.I. (2017). 'Innovation management – Current trends and future directions. *International Journal of Innovation and Learning*, 22(2), 135–155.

Ratten, V., Ramadani, V., Dana, L.-P., Hoy, F., and Ferreira, J. (2017). Family entrepreneurship and internationalization strategies. *Review of International Business and Strategy*, 27(2), 150–160.

Schoar, A. (2010). The divide between subsistence and transformational entrepreneurship. *Innovation Policy and the Economy*, 10(1), 57–81.

Schumpeter, J. (1934). *Theory of Economic Development: An Inquiry Into Profits, Capital Credit, Interest and the Business Cycle*. Cambridge, MA: Harvard University Press.

Swanson, K.K., and De Vereaux, C. (2017). A theoretical framework for sustaining culture: Culturally sustainable entrepreneurship. *Annals of Tourism Research*, 62, 78–88.

Tajeddini, K., Altinay, L., and Ratten, V. (2017). Service innovativeness and the structuring of organizations: The moderating roles of learning orientation and interfunctional coordination. *International Journal of Hospitality Management*, 65, 100–114.

Tajeddini, K., Denisa, M., and Ratten, V. (2017). Female tourism entrepreneurs in Bali, Indonesia. *Journal of Hospitality and Tourism* Management, 31, 52–58.

Tassabehji, R., Hackney, R., and Popovic, A. (2010). Emergent digital era governance: Enacting the role of the institutional entrepreneur in transformational change. *Government Information Quarterly*, 33(2), 223–256.

Weber, M. (1930). *The Protestant Ethic and the Spirit of Capitalism*. London: Allen and Unwin.

Welter, F., Baker, T., Audretsch, D.B., and Gartner, W.B. (2016). Everyday entrepreneurship: A call for entrepreneurship research to embrace entrepreneurial diversity. *Entrepreneurship Theory & Practice*, October, 1–11.

Yuki, G. (1999). An evaluation of conceptual weaknesses in transformational and charismatic leadership theories. *The Leadership Quarterly*, 10(2), 285–305.

Zahra, S.A., and Wright, M. (2016). Understanding the social role of entrepreneurship. *Journal of Management Studies*, 53(4), 610–629.

2 Disclosure of social impact in agrifood entrepreneurial initiatives

Elisa Baraibar-Diez, Maria Odriozola and Ladislao Luna Sotorrio

Introduction

Entrepreneurship initiatives tend to focus on the creation of new products/ services that cover market needs where they are unsatisfied or when they can produce them under new different approaches: they fulfil environmental or social requirements, the production process is innovative, or they are addressed to different market segments. This has led to rethinking the role of entrepreneurs in organizational innovation and the relationship of these organizations with society.

Transformational entrepreneurship is defined by Miller and Collier (2010, p. 85) as "the creation of an innovative virtue-based organization for the purpose of shifting resources out of an area of lower into an area of higher purpose and greater value under conditions requiring a holistic perspective". Social entrepreneurship is a subcategory of firms with a prominent "social stream" within transformational entrepreneurship. Social entrepreneurship is born with the aim of addressing social issues above purely economic purposes. In this sense, academic literature has been focused on the definition of social entrepreneurship and social entrepreneur. Abu-Saifan (2012, p. 25), for example, discusses the boundaries of socially oriented entrepreneurial activities and defines social entrepreneur as "a mission-driven individual who uses a set of entrepreneurial behaviours to deliver a social value to the less privileged, all through an entrepreneurially oriented entity that is financially independent, self-sufficient, or sustainable". In addition to social entrepreneurs, social entrepreneurship can be also promoted by non-profit organizations by themselves or in association with other companies, in order to develop "innovative, mission-supporting, earned income, job creating or licensing, ventures" (Pomerantz, 2003, p. 25). Social entrepreneurship is therefore an engine of change to develop the society, led by the social entrepreneur, whose goals are "the social and environmental sustainability, as well as a very strong ethical component" (Céspedes, 2009). Previous studies have analysed the links between social entrepreneurship and sustainable societal transformation, such as Alvord et al. (2004), who examine initiatives that have transformed the lives of thousands of poor and marginalized people around the world.

Social entrepreneurship projects created with the aim of respect and minimization of the impact on the environment are related to the Circular Economy

(CE) stream coming from Asia, and are increasingly widespread in Europe. Circular economy is expected to lead a more sustainable development and harmonious society, as it contributes positively to "reconcile all the elements" (Ghisellini et al., 2016). It also supports ecological production forms in which there are business links for the use of raw materials in the production process, minimizing the consumption of virgin raw materials and increasing the reuse of waste production of an industry as input of another production cycle. This approach is more respectful with the environment and it will lead to new business models further away from the "linear economy", which is based on the extraction of raw materials to manufacture products, use them and eliminate their waste.

The agrifood sector is a source of actions under the umbrella of messages such as "Save food" (promoted by Food and Agriculture Organization – FAO) or "Zero waste", which aim to reduce food waste among the population, increase the recycling of waste (especially organic waste) and give waste a possible reuse. There are initiatives in this sector coming from non-profit and profit organizations, business associations, social institutions . . . that not only fulfil an environmental objective, but also ethical or social objectives. These initiatives propose a redistribution of the produced foods, taking them from places where there are surpluses to places where there is a deficit of food, and finally they can feed a larger number of the population.

One of the main challenges that these social initiatives face (not only in the agrifood field, but in all fields of social economy) is accountability. The disclosed information is "essential for assessing the social impact of these projects" (Epstein and Yutha, 2014, p. 14). The measurement and reporting of social impact is still one of the weak points in this type of social initiative, which, despite being created with a social purpose, weaken in the dissemination of this social information.

The aim of this chapter is to analyse the disclosure of the social impact of four cases of social enterprises (SE) in the agrifood sector, embedded in the category of transformational entrepreneurship, having both economic and social purposes. The chapter is structured as follows. In the first section, there is a brief introduction to agrifood entrepreneurial activities and their social impact, reviewing the different methodologies for measuring it. Then, the holistic methodology SIMPLE is adapted to a disclosure checklist to assess the dissemination of social impact information in agrifood initiatives, which is presented in the following section. After analysing the agrifood entrepreneurial initiatives through content analysis, results, discussion and conclusions of the study are presented.

Agrifood entrepreneurial initiatives and their social impact

Several countries adopted in 2015 a set of goals to "end poverty, protect the planet and ensure prosperity for all as part of a new sustainable development agenda" (United Nations, 2018). Two of the so-called Sustainable Development Goals (SDG) are related to zero hunger (goal 2) and responsible consumption and production (goal 12), and one of the targets is "by 2030, halve the per capita global food waste at the retail and consumer level, and reduce food losses along production and supply chains including post-harvest losses" (FAO, 2018). Food and Agriculture Organization of the United Nations (FAO) is very active in the achievement of these objectives and, for that, it works not only in the definitional framework (see Table 2.1) but also invest resources on the measurement and reduction of food loss and food waste.

In addition, FAO also highlights initiatives around the world that have been created with the aim of reducing food waste, e.g. Save Food, Zero Hunder Challenge, The Global Food Banking Network, Food for the Cities, Think Eat Save, etc. However, these social initiatives tend not to specifically disclose their social impact on food waste reduction.

Social impacts are "the societal and environmental changes created by activities and investments" (Epstein and Yuthas, 2014, p. 15) and can be both positive and negative, intended or unintended. There are certain advantages for organizations derived from the disclosure of social impacts. Social impact measurement and reporting by social and hybrid organizations "has been found to be used strategically to improve their performance, access resources, and build organisational legitimacy" (Nicholls, 2009; Barraket and Yousefpour, 2013, p. 448). Also it is seen as "a requirement to gain access to resources and as a means to satisfy stakeholders based on a minimal level of compliance" (Arvidson and Lyon, 2014, p. 883), constituting an essential strategic tool for organizations in building and maintaining relations with stakeholders (Lyon and Arvidson, 2011).

However, social impact disclosure is sometimes considered as an additional burden rather than useful for non-profit organizations (Arvidson and Lyon, 2014). Academic literature mentions problems that explain why the companies are not carrying out an efficient and systemic disclosure of their social impact. Social impact is commonly understood as a social construction, because there is no clear definition of what is meant by "social" (Arvidson and Lyon, 2014), so there is discretion when social impact is assessed (Arvidson and Lyon, 2014). In addition, there is a common problem when disclosing these social impacts, and it is that, commonly, success is defined "in terms of what the organization produces rather than the impacts that result" (Epstein and Yuthas, 2014, p. 3) (see Table 2.2).

Table 2.1 Definitions of terms related to food waste

Term	Definition
Food loss	All food produced for human consumption but not eaten by humans. It is defined as "the decrease in quantity or quality of food".
Food waste	Discarding or alternative (non-food) use of food that is safe and nutritious for human consumption along the entire food supply chain, from primary production to end consumers.

Source: FAO (2018)

Table 2.2 Goals based on outputs and goals based on impacts

Goals based on outputs	Goals based on impacts
We want to deliver meals to 10,000 homeless people.	We want to reduce hunger by 5%.
We want to provide 1 million insecticide soaked bed nets.	We want to reduce malaria by 5,000 cases.
We want to convert 10,000 families from cooking with wood to cooking with gas.	We want to reduce residential CO_2 emissions by 50%.
We want to teach reading to 500 primary school students.	We want to increase literacy in the village by 10%.

Source: Epstein and Yuthas (2014), p. 4.

The lack of consensus in defining social impact (Maas and Liket, 2011) leads to the appearance of different methodologies in order to measure it, but also to audit it. There are attempts to collect these methods in academic literature, for example by Maas and Liket (2011), who categorize thirty contemporary social impact measurement methods, and outside the academic literature, where there are guidelines and recommendations to measure and improve that social impact. For example, Epstein and Yuthas (2014) have published the book "Measuring and Improving Social Impacts. A Guide for Nonprofits, Companies and Impact Investors". In addition, there are institutions like Social Impact (https://social-impact.com/), Knowhow Nonprofit (https://knowhownonprofit.org), Inspiring Impact (https://inspiringimpact.org) or Social Impact Tracker online (www.socialenterpriseni.org) that help companies, especially non-profit, to measure and report their social impact. The goal of Inspiring Impact is, for example, "working towards a world where high quality impact measurement is the norm in the non-profit sector" (Inspiring Impact, 2018).

The following methodologies have been identified to measure and report social impact: Social Return on Investment (SROI), Social Impact Assessment (SIA), Social Cost-Benefit Analysis (SCBA), Social Polyhedral Model (SPOLY), Social Accounting and Audit (SAA), Balanced Scorecards (BSC), Triple Bottom Line (TBL or 3BL), Social Life Cycle Assessment (S-LCA), Blended Value (BV), Soft Outcome Universal Learning (SOUL), Common Good Matrix, and SIMPLE. They are summarized and briefly described in Table 2.3.

Other authors such as Epstein and Yuthas (2014) have proposed the Social Impact Creation Cycle to describe "the five most fundamental questions faced by companies/non-profits/investors seeking to maximize their social impact: 1) what will you invest? 2) What problem will you address? 3) What steps will you take? 4) How will you measure success? And 5) How can you increase impact?" (Epstein and Yuthas, 2014, p. 5). These questions make clear that the social impact is not something concrete, but rather it is necessary to have a general vision of it, providing both qualitative and quantitative information. McLoughlin et al. (2009) propose a holistic methodology that allows a

Table 2.3 Summary of methodologies to measure and report social impact

Measurement	Description
Social Return on Investment (SROI)	It aims to mirror the private sector model of assessing return on investment with the reporting of a ratio of investment to financial values of social benefit (Nicholls et al., 2008; Arvidson and Lyon, 2014). Social Impact Tracker online states that SROI aims to put a financial value on the key impacts identified by stakeholders and it is often used to show how investment in a project will save the government money in a long-term.
Social Impact Assessment (SIA)	Burdge (2004) defines SIA as the systematic appraisal of "impact on the day-to-day quality of life of persons and communities whose environment is affected by a proposed policy, plan, programme or project" (UNEP, 2009, p. 32).
Social Cost–Benefit Analysis (SCBA)	It is concerned with social welfare but introduces distributive impacts, and sometimes other social objectives: inclusion, participation of women in the decision-making process, etc. (Azqueta and Montoya, 2017).
Social Polyhedral Model (SPOLY)	SPOLY calculated the monetary value of social value based on the six steps of the Polyhedral Model: identification of the working team and the setting of the timetable, strategic and management documents of the organization and the stakeholder map, value variables perceived by stakeholders, outputs generated by the organization for each value variable and seeks potential proxies, quantification of the calculations, and review of the process (Retolaza et al., 2015).
Social Accounting and Audit (SAA)	More "conventional" mix of narrative and quantitative disclosures (Gibbon and Dey, 2011). Social Accounting and Audit (SAA), created by Social Audit Network, "helps you prove, improve and account for the difference you are making. It uses eight key principles to underpin its process, ensure verification is effective and deliver continuous improvement, that are: clarify purpose, define scope, engage stakeholders, determine materiality, make comparisons (benchmarking), be transparent, verify accounts, embed the process" (SAN, 2018).
Balanced Scorecards (BSC)	Kaplan and Norton (1992) created the Balanced Scorecard including "financial measures that tell the results of actions already taken and operations measures on customer satisfaction, internal processes, and the organization's innovation and improvement activities" (Kaplan and Norton, 1992, p. 71).

(*Continued*)

Table 2.3 (Continued)

Measurement	Description
Triple Bottom Line (TBL, 3BL)	Companies should prepare three different bottom lines: the traditional measure of corporate profit, people account and planet account (The Economist, 2009).
Social Life Cycle Assessment (S-LCA)	It is a method that can be used to assess the social and sociological aspects of products, their actual and potential positive as well as negative impacts along the life cycle (Life Cycle Initiative, 2018). The United Nations Environment Programme has published the Guidelines for Social Life Cycle Assessment of Products.
Blended Value (BV)	Blended Value is "simply a conceptual framework for advancing a vision of value creation which is not based upon a bifurcated understanding of the nature of value (either/or), but rather a unified, holistic understanding of value as 'both/ and', integrated and non-divisible" (Blended Value, 2018). The Blender Value Proposition (BVP) "integrates and affirms the greatest maximization of social, environmental, and economic value within a single firm (whether for-profit or non-profit)" (Emerson, 2003, p. 38).
Soft Outcome Universal Learning (SOUL)	SOUL is "a flexible and effective toolkit for measuring progression in soft outcomes and provides evidence in a graphical format for individuals and groups" (SOUL Record, 2018). Arvidson and Lyon (2014) evidence that this method is widely promoted.
Common Good Matrix	The Common Good Matrix is the heart of the Common Good Balance Sheet (Ecogood, 2018). It describes twenty common good themes and serves as a guide for evaluating contributions to the common good. It is formed by rows of stakeholders (suppliers, owners, employees, customers and business partners, social environment) and columns of values: human dignity, solidarity and social justice, environmental sustainability, and transparency and co-determination (Ecogood, 2018).
Social impact measurement of social enterprises (SIMPLE)	The SIMPLE impact model, developed by McLoughlin et al. (2009), adopts "a five stage approach to impact measurement, helping managers to conceptualise the impact problem, identify and prioritise impacts for measurement, develop appropriate impact measures, report impacts and to integrate the results in management decision-making and the culture of the organization" (McLoughlin et al., 2009, p. 160).

Source: Authors.

complete vision of the activity's impact developed by the company. SIMPLE methodology is designed to ease impact measurement, considering an integrated management tool.

Methods

The objective of the SIMPLE methodology proposed by McLoughlin et al. (2009) is more ambitious, offering a "practical methodology for developing impact measures specific and relevant to their own organization" (McLoughlin et al., 2009, p. 174). In this chapter, however, we will adapt it as a checklist to assess the level of disclosure in a sample of four agrifood entrepreneurial initiatives (see Table 2.4). As an exploratory study, methodology is not as rigorous as in conclusive studies and sample sizes may be smaller (Nargundkar, 2003). The items obtained will be assessed (YES/NO and how) in each of these initiatives through content analysis methodology. This methodology is widespread in many contributions related to sustainable development, corporate social responsibility, communication and quality of disclosure.

Sample of case studies

The initiatives included in this chapter are embedded in the movement against food waste, directly related to the transformation of the environment and society. However, many of them have additional social purposes that help even more to generate positive change, such as the employment of workers at risk of exclusion or the promotion of awareness against waste.

1   *Huertos de Soria (Spain)*. It is a social economy project promoted in 2012 by the NGO Cives Mundi, with the aim of creating jobs for people at risk of exclusion from the labour market (Huertos de Soria, 2018).
2   *Espigoladors (Spain)*. It is a non-profit organization that fights against food waste while empowering people at risk of social exclusion in a transformative, participatory, inclusive and sustainable manner. They transform the rest of recovered foods into delicious natural and artisan preserved jams, creams, sauces and patés. They are marketed under the brand name "EsIm-perfect" (It is imperfect) (Espigoladors, 2018).
3   *Rubies in the Rubble (UK)*. After seeing the amount of discarded produce at fruit and veg markets across London, the promoter of this company started working directly with UK farmers to cook a range of preserved relish and ketchups with fresh fruit and veg from the surplus produce that would otherwise be discarded (Rubies in the Rubble, 2018).
4   *D.C. Central Kitchen (USA)*. It is a community kitchen that develops and operates social ventures that break the cycle of hunger and poverty: Culinary Job Training, Community Meals, Healthy School Food, Healthy Corners, The Campus Kitchens Project.

Table 2.4 Adaptation of SIMPLE

Stage 1 SCOPE IT: Conceptualizing impact and understanding the drivers (McLoughlin et al., 2009)		Disclosing item (adapted)
Mission/Objectives	What is the site for? Whom is it serving? Whom should it serve? Why is it being funded?	I.1.1. Does the Social Initiative (SI) disclose its mission/objective?
Stakeholder-driven impact drivers	Who and how do they influence the impact context? Who and how do they influence the mission and the objectives? Who and how do they influence management decision-making?	I.1.2. Does the SI identify the major stakeholders? I.1.3. Does the SI disclose the perceived/desired impacts?
Internal drivers – organizational context	Where is the SE positioned now? Where does the SE want to be positioned? How can this be achieved?	I.1.4. Does the SI disclose something about governance?
External drivers – SE impact context	Influences on: economic, political, funding, demographic, legal, competition, infrastructure, changing demand trends in the sector, etc.	I.1.5. Does the SI disclose its transforming potential?

Stage 2 MAP IT: Identifying impacts for measurement (McLoughlin et al., 2009)		Disclosing item (adapted)
Impact categorization: moving from the triple to the 4BL		I.2.1. Does the SI disclose a triple bottom line or a 4BL?
Mapping impact – applying the logic model	Activities. What are the products, projects or processes that allow your SE fulfil your objectives?	I.2.2. Does the SI disclose its activities?
	Outputs. What is produced as a direct result of these actions?	I.2.3. Does the SI disclose its outputs/outcomes?
	Outcomes. What benefit or change is accomplished, in the short-term, as a direct result of the output?	I.2.3. Does the SI disclose its outputs/outcomes?
	Impacts. What your organization is able to achieve over the long-term as a result of combined outcomes	I.2.4 (same as I.1.3). Does the SI disclose its achievement of impacts?

(Continued)

Table 2.4 (Continued)

Stage 3 TRACK IT. Developing measures and systems (McLoughlin et al., 2009)	Disclosing item (adapted)
Step 1. Determine the outcomes and impact the SE will measure.	I.3.1. Does the SI disclose evaluation of impact dimensions (ESG, financial)?
Step 2. Design indicators that will allow the SE to collect pertinent impact data.	I.3.2. Does the SI disclose the design of indicators?
Step 3. Develop a data collection strategy.	I.3.3. Does the SI disclose the data collection strategy?
Step 4. Implement the data collection strategy.	I.3.4. Does the SI disclose the implementation of data collection? (responsibility, training, process. . .)
Stage 4 TELL IT. Reporting on impact (McLoughlin et al., 2009)	*Disclosing item (adapted)*
Before/after data showing change, comparative data, benchmarking, targeted reporting to stakeholders. . .	I.4.1. How does the SI report impact?
Stage 5 EMBED IT	
Guidelines: raise awareness of why change is needed, foster desire to support and participate in the change, show knowledge of how to change, provide ability to implement new skills and behaviours, and undertake reinforcement to sustain change.	I.5.1. Does the SI promote social impact integration at all levels?

Source: McLoughlin et al. (2009).

Analysis and results

The analysis of disclosure of social impact in agrifood initiatives is structured in tables (Tables 2.5 to 2.8). These tables include a brief description (promoter, origin, age, products, channels, volunteers and social media) of the agrifood initiative or the social enterprise, and then, only those disclosed items from all the items adapted from the SIMPLE methodology. After that, a brief descriptive analysis is provided in relation to the social impact reporting.

Huertos de Soria (see Table 2.5) sells certified organic fruits and vegetables with the aim of revitalizing unused land, avoiding depopulation and promoting employment in groups of social exclusion. Although they disclose several items in the "Company" section of its website, such as mission, objective and

Table 2.5 Profile and disclosure of social impact in the social initiative *Huertos de Soria* (Spain)

	Huertos de Soria *Castilla y León (Spain)* *www.huertosdesoria.org*
What do they do?	It is a project of social economy in collaboration with the NGO Cives Mundi
Promoter	Collective (NGO Cives Mundi)
When?	Since November 2012
What do they offer?	Fruit, vegetables, oil, cereals, dairy products, chocolates and others Produce is certified as organic agriculture
How do they market?	There are six types of channels: consumer groups, stores, online store, by phone, by email, other POS.
Do they have volunteers?	Not disclosed
Social media	Twitter: @huertosdesoria Vimeo: https://vimeo.com/huertosdesoria Facebook: www.facebook.com/huertosdesoria

Disclosure of social impact

Items disclosed (see Table 2.4)	*Description*
I.1.1. Does the Social Initiative (SI) disclose its mission/objective?	Their mission is to help collectives at risk of social exclusion: disabled people, long-term unemployed and battered women. The objective is twofold: create jobs for people at risk of social exclusion and foster organic agriculture as a way to recover unused land and help avoid depopulation in rural areas.
I.1.2. Does the SI identify the major stakeholders?	Those social sectors with more difficulties to find a job Farmers' network
I.1.5. Does the SI disclose its transforming potential?	*Huertos de Soria* is committed to its immediate environment, helping to create wealth and settle the population

Source: Authors

commitments, the website is really an online store that offers no dissemination of information regarding the social impact of the activity.

Second agrifood initiative is called *Espigoladors*[1] (Table 2.6). Although they do not specify a mission, the website determines that *Espigoladors* is a non-profit organization that fights against food waste while empowering people at risk

Table 2.6 Profile and disclosure of social impact in the social initiative *Espigoladors* (Spain)

	Espigoladors *Cataluña (Spain)* *www.espigoladors.cat/es/*
What do they do?	It is non-profit organization that fights against food waste while empowering people at risk of social exclusion in a transformative, participatory, inclusive and sustainable manner.
Promoter	Jordi, Marina and Mireia (no information about them)
When?	NA
What do they offer?	"EsIm-perfect" is the first brand in Spain that produces and sells high quality food products from surplus or ugly fruit and vegetables.
How do they market?	Several POS in Spain.
Do they have volunteers?	Yes
Social media	Twitter: @espigoladors Facebook: www.facebook.com/espigoladors Instagram: esimperfect

Disclosure of social impact

Item (see Table 2.4)	*Description*
I.1.1. Does the Social Initiative (SI) disclose its mission/objective?	Fighting against food waste while empowering people at risk of social exclusion
I.1.2. Does the SI identify the major stakeholders?	Advisors "Dreamers" (supporting entities) Committed producers
I.1.5. Does the SI disclose its transforming potential?	Food waste reduction and people empowerment are achieved in a transformative, participatory, inclusive and sustainable manner. They promote dignity of people and the generation of labour and social opportunities from a transformative perspective.
I.2.2. Does the SI disclose its activities?	Activities with producers, awareness campaigns, "EsIm-perfect" brand.
I.5.1. Does the SI promote social impact integration at all levels?	They enhance collaboration with producers, receiving entities, retailers and volunteers.

Source: Authors

of social exclusion in a transformative, participatory, inclusive and sustainable manner. In addition, they do not use the term stakeholders, but they state that 95 percent of collected food is distributed to social entities, which are close to the collection area. The other 5 percent of collected food is transformed into "*EsIm-perfect*" ("It is not perfect"), the first national brand that manufactures high quality products from imperfect and ugly food.

In addition, they call the "imperfect dream team" to the eight advisors (from reputed companies and institutions), the promoters and those who make the project real: producers and twenty-six collaborating companies.

In the section "What do we do?" of its webpage, the information is divided into activities focused on citizens and businesses; tailor-made workshops for children, youth, adults and businesses; and awareness campaigns, cooking and reuse tips targeted to establishments and companies.

Although the social enterprise *Espigoladors* does not quantify neither report any social impact, it promotes the social impact in each of the activities by appealing to the different groups: "If you want to be a producer/receiving entity/volunteer/retailers, fill in this form".

The third initiative is called *Rubies in the Rubble* (see Table 2.7).

The website of Rubies in the Rubble is very colourful, including direct and visual information. First site includes a video presenting the company, with informative headlines that give an idea of the reason of this company ("A third of food is wasted", "In the UK, 20–40% of crops never reach the shelves"). This information is reinforced with links throughout the website. Although they don't disclose stakeholders, the "Who we are" section of the website include "Our Story", "Team", "Press" and "Contact us". There is also a subscription available to receive the latest news, recipes and offers of the company.

Disclosure of impact is made through a dynamic infographic showing the number of fruits and vegetables, tonnes of CO_2 and miles saved with the purchase of Rubies in the Rubble's products. It does not use any of the methodologies discussed earlier, but at least the website reflects the impact that has the purchase of their products. Then, the buyers feel that by acquiring them, they are collaborating with the improvement of the environment and society.

The fourth initiative is called *DC Central Kitchen* (Table 2.8). DC Central Kitchen represents a role for disclosure and reporting in the area of agrifood entrepreneurial initiatives. It was founded in 1989 by Robert Egger, who pioneered a new model aimed at liberating people from the conditions of poverty. DC Central Kitchen has five social ventures: Culinary Job Training, Community Meals, Healthy School Food, Healthy Corners, and The Campus Kitchens Project. In addition to the report, each site of the social ventures offers data about impact through visual information.

The impact presented throughout the website is also included and developed in a report. This report (online and print version) is targeted to investors ("Thank you for choosing to invest in DC Central Kitchen"), and the objective is to show how investor's support is making their community a healthier, more equitable place for us all. Information about impact is complemented with stories of protagonists in the social venture. This technique enhances credibility and trust in the information provided.

Table 2.7 Profile and disclosure of social impact in the social initiative *Rubies in the Rubble* (UK)

	Rubies in the Rubble *London (UK)* *https://rubiesintherubble.com/*
What do they do?	They produce jars of sauces (relish, ketchup and mayo) and work directly with UK farmers, obtaining fresh fruit and veg from their surplus produce.
Promoter	Jenny Dawson
When?	2010
What do they offer?	Relish, jams, chutneys and ketchup
How do they market?	Online shop, Waitrose, Ocado, Selfridges, Fortnum & Mason, Cook, Lakeland, Harrods, Whole Foods
Do they have volunteers?	NA
Social media	

Disclosure of social impact

Item (see Table 2.4)	Description
I.1.1. Does the Social Initiative (SI) disclose its mission/objective?	The scale of the problem of food waste got Jenny thinking about what could be done with all this surplus produce. Surely there was a way of creating a delicious, first-class product using excess produce? We are on mission to encourage people to waste less, treasure their resources and live more sustainably. We want to save the planet one jar at a time by providing a delicious and practical solution to food waste.
I.1.5. Does the SI disclose its transforming potential?	The website states: "Ask any of our customers, and they'll tell you that our range of relishes are too good to refuse".
I.4.1. How does the SI report impact?	The website reports (March, 2018): "To date you have helped us save 4,344,479 fruits & vegetables, 202 tonnes of CO_2, and the equivalent of 236,393 miles driven".

Source: Authors

In spite of not using any of the methodologies presented earlier, they focus on the economic returns for their community, explaining how much they saved (not only money, but also criminal records). They combine the approach of information based on outputs and information based on impacts (Epstein and Yuthas, 2014).

Discussion and conclusion

After a brief review of the methodologies of social impact measurement and reporting, this chapter analysed the level of disclosure of various social initiatives that fight against food waste in the agrifood field. This field provides diverse

Table 2.8 Profile and disclosure of social impact in the social initiative *DC Central Kitchen* (USA)

	D.C. Central Kitchen *USA* *https://dccentralkitchen.org/*
What do they do? Promoter When? What do they offer?	They combat hunger and create opportunities through culinary training Robert Egger 1989 It is a community kitchen. They prepare 3 million meals for homeless shelters, schools, and non-profits each year.
How do they market?	They have several ventures to create opportunities for meaningful careers, expand access to healthy food, and test innovative solutions to systemic failures.
Do they have volunteers? Social media	There is a Volunteer Page to find information about and to register for volunteer opportunities. Twitter: @dcck Vimeo: https://vimeo.com/dcck Flickr: www.flickr.com/photos/dccentralkitchen/albums

Disclosure of social impact

Item (see Table 2.4)	*Description*
I.1.1. Does the Social Initiative (SI) disclose its mission/objective?	Our mission: to use food as a tool to strengthen bodies, empower minds, and build communities. Our model: DC Central Kitchen develops and operates social ventures targeting the cycle of hunger and poverty. Our values: We believe that hunger is a symptom of the deeper problem of poverty, and that food is our chosen tool for changing individual lives while addressing systemic failures. We believe in the transformative power of a job, and that everyone deserves the chance to share in the dignity of work while contributing to our community. We believe in building a more equitable food system that ensures access to healthy, dignified food and economic opportunity for all. We believe that waste is wrong, be it the waste of nutritious food, productive minds, or charitable dollars spent on unsustainable, redundant, and ineffective efforts.

(Continued)

Table 2.8 (Continued)

Disclosure of social impact

Item (see Table 2.4)	Description
I.1.2. Does the SI identify the major stakeholders?	They identify their partners and their industrial partners (79). The report includes information about contributors.
I.1.4. Does the SI disclose something about governance?	The report includes information about the board of directors.
I.1.5. Does the SI disclose its transforming potential?	We're fighting hunger differently by training jobless adults for culinary careers and then hiring dozens of our own graduates to prepare the 3 million meals we provide for homeless shelters, schools, and non-profits each year. Our venture also prevents the waste of millions of pounds of nutritious food, expands access to healthy, local options in urban food deserts, and scales our model nationally through strategic partnerships with colleges and universities.
I.2.2. Does the SI disclose its activities?	Website includes social ventures: Culinary Job Training, Community Meals, Healthy School Food, Healthy Corners, and The Campus Kitchens Project
I.2.3. Does the SI disclose its outputs/outcomes?	Neither the website nor the report divide the results by outputs or by outcomes, but they specify the impact in the last year of the several social ventures. • Culinary Job Training. Their impact last year: "88% of job placement rate among our graduates", "50% of last year's grads secured a wage increase within 12 months". • Community meals. Their impact last year: "1.8 million meals prepared for partner non-profits across the city"; "680,987 pounds of food recovered from grocery stores, farms, and other sources to prepare our meals"; "Nearly $3 million saved by non-profits who no longer need to prepare meals for their clients". • Healthy School Food. Their impact last year: "3,600 students chose our fresh, locally-sources, scratch-cooked meals"; "1,000,000 healthy school meals served to low-income students"; "locally sourced at least 50% of every plate". • Healthy corners. Their impact last year: "207,283 units of healthy snacks sold in DC's food desert"; "74 corner stores participated in Healthy Corners"; "100% participating stores reported an increase in profits". • The Campus Kitchens Project. Their impact last year: "378,423 nutritious meals delivered to clients"; "32,018 student volunteers prepared meals for communities across the country"; "991,872 pounds of food recovered".

I.3.1. Does the SI disclose evaluation of impact dimensions (ESG, financial)?	They don't disclose the evaluation of impact dimensions, but they provide a financial report: consolidated statements of activities and consolidate statements of financial position.
I.4.1. How does the SI report impact?	With the sentence: "See how we're making change. DC Central Kitchen presents our latest annual report, with highlights and success stories from the year". They also report impact all along the website ("We transform 3,000 pounds of donated and recovered food into 5,000 healthy meals"; "Last year, we saved our partners $3.7 million in food costs").
I.5.1. Does the SI promote social impact integration at all levels?	Absolutely. The engage volunteers ("Be a hungerfighter") and partners ("Donate food", "Receive or meals", "Hire us").

Source: Authors

transformative initiatives, not only due to its nature of food redistributors but also due to its capacity of social transformation.

The first conclusion that can be drawn from the study is that formal disclosure of social impact is insufficient, probably due to the consideration of additional burden that social impact measurement has traditionally had. The expertise of the authors of this chapter reflects that most of them begin as small initiatives that are constituted in legal entities; after a time, therefore, disclosing information and being accountable constitutes a challenge for them. In addition, they are constituted as hybrid organizations, in which economic goals converge for social and environmental purposes. This forces them to look for new formulas of efficient accountability, considering the nature of social information (more heterogeneous, not standardized, depending on the activity developed by the organization, with a more diverse audience . . .) and the difficulties when measuring social impact. They need to learn that social impact measurement complements their strategy "based on personal contacts and networking that aims at getting the attention of resource holders" (Arvidson and Lyon, 2014, p. 880).

In this sense, new formulas of accountability cover not only the methodologies of measuring and reporting social impact, but also the way to show it. Although the sample of initiatives follow no previous methodology of social impact measurement, when they disclose data about impact, the do not use a traditional report. For what purpose? They are simply more engaged to stakeholders (volunteers, donors, investors. . .) and develop more effective initiatives to disclose social information: visual, spoken, written formats (Knowhow Nonprofits, 2018). They use storytelling, videos, info graphics, dynamic info graphics, pictures . . . and these allow them to connect to the receivers of information and increase their trust and gain credibility. These new ways of communication also represent new ways of doing things differently, which represent its transformational and adaptive character (Schoar, 2010). In short, companies should use those forms of communication they consider most appropriate to reach their social impact to stakeholders more efficiently.

However, the way information is wrapped is not all. The initiative in the sample that can be said to be the most accountable, DC Central Kitchen, is the only one that combines a results-oriented information and an impact-oriented information in the sense exposed by Epstein and Yuthas (2014). Changing this concept will help assess the transformative capacity of these initiatives and promote change in society. We take the example of DC Central Kitchen to reflect that the analysis of this type of initiative serves to find excellence, and some of them can act as benchmarks to other social enterprises, in order to inspire both the nature of the new venture and also the level of accountability.

Finally, we assume that the limited number of examples of agrifood initiatives constitutes a clear limitation in the study. However, it has allowed us to reflect the lack of information and the wide field of improvement that these social initiatives have in terms of accountability and dissemination of social impact, taking into account that information available can attract more resources that increase even more its transforming capacity.

Note

http://balance.ecogood.org/matrix-4-1-en/ecg-matrix-en.pdf.

1 *Espigoladors* is a Catalan word that could be translated as gleaner.

References

Abu-Saifan, S. (2012). Social entrepreneurship: Definition and boundaries. *Technology Innovation Management Review*, 2(2), 22–27.

Alvord, S.H., Brown, L.D., and Letts, C.W. (2004). Social entrepreneurship and societal transformation. An exploratory study. *The Journal of Applied Behavioural Science*, 40(3), 260–282.

Arvidson, M., and Lyon, F. (2014). Social impact measurement and non-profit organisations: Compliance, resistance, and promotion. *VOLUNTAS: International Journal of Voluntary and Nonprofit Organizations*, 25(4), 869–886.

Azqueta, D., and Montoya, A. (2017). The social benefits of water and sanitation projects in Northern Colombia: Cost – Benefit analysis, the water poverty index and beyond. *Development Policy Review*, 35, 118–139.

Barraket, J., and Yousefpour, N. (2013). Evaluation and social impact measurement amongst small to medium social enterprises: Process, purpose and value. *Australian Journal of Public Administration*, 72(4), 447–458.

Blended Value. (2018). Website. Retrieved from: www.blendedvalue.org/framework/ [Accessed March 2018].

Burdge, R. (2004). *The concepts, process and methods of SIA.* Middleton, WI: The Social Ecology Press.

Céspedes, H. (2009). El emprendimiento social y su sustentabilidad. *HC Global Group*, 2–12.

Ecogood. (2018). Website of the economy for the common good. Retrieved from: www.ecogood.org/en/common-good-balance-sheet/common-good-matrix/ [Accessed March 2018].

The Economist. (2009). Triple bottom line. It consists of three Ps: profit, people and planet. November, 17. Retrieved from: www.economist.com/node/14301663.

Epstein, M.J., and Yuthas, K. (2014). *Measuring and Improving Social Impacts: A Guide for Nonprofits, Companies and Impact Investors.* Berrett-Koehler Publishers.

Emerson, J. (2003). The blended value proposition: Integrating social and financial returns. *California Management Review*, 45(4), 35–51.

Food and Agricultural Organization. (2018). Website. Retrieved from: www.fao.org/platform-food-loss-waste/food-loss/food-loss-measurement/en/.

Gibbon, J., and Dey, C. (2011). Developments in social impact measurement in the third sector: Scaling up or dumbing own? *Social and Environmental Accountability Journal*, 31(1), 63–72.

Ghisellini, P., Cialani, C., and Ulgiati, S. (2016). A review on circular economy: The expected transition to a balanced interplay of environmental and economic systems. *Journal of Cleaner Production*, 114, 11–32.

Inspiring Impact. (2018). Website. Retrieved from: https://inspiringimpact.org/about-us/ [Accessed March 2018].

Kaplan, R.S., and Norton, D.P. (1992). The balanced scorecard – Measures that drive performance. *Harvard Business Review*, January–February, 71–79.

Life Cycle Initiative. (2018). Website. Retrieved from: www.lifecycleinitiative. org/starting-life-cycle-thinking/life-cycle-approaches/social-lca/ [Accessed March 2018].

Lyon, F., and Arvidson, M. (2011). Social impact measurement as an entrepreneurial process. Briefing Paper 66. TSRC Informing civil society.

Maas, K., and Liket, K. (2011). Social impact measurement: Classification of methods. Environmental management accounting and supply chain management (Eco-efficiency in industry and science book series – ECOE, volume 27), 171–202.

McLoughlin, J., Kaminski, J., Sodagar, B., Khan, S., Harris, R., Arnaudo, G., and Mc Brearty, S. (2009). A strategic approach to social impact measurement of social enterprises: The SIMPLE methodology. *Social Enterprise Journal*, 5(2), 154–178.

Miller, R.A., and Collier, E.W. (2010). Redefining entrepreneurship: A virtues and values perspective. *Journal of Leadership, Accountability and Ethics*, 8(2), 80.

Nargundkar, R. (2003). *Marketing Research: Text and Cases* (2nd edition). Tata McGraw Hill.

Nicholls, J., Lawlor, E., Neitzert, E., and Goodspeed, J. (2008). *A Guide to Social Return on Investment*. London: Cabinet Office, Office of the Third Sector.

Nicholls, A. (2009). We do good thinks, don't we?: 'Blended Value Accounting' in social entrepreneurship. *Accounting, Organizations and Society*, 34(6–7), 755–769.

Pomerantz, M. (2003). The business of social entrepreneurship in a "down economy". *Business*, 25(3), 25–30.

Retolaza, J.L., San-Jose, L., and Ruiz-Roqueñi, M. (2015). Process model analysis and calculation: Spoly. In: *Social Accounting for Sustainability*. Springer Briefs in Business. Springer: Cham.

Schoar, A. (2010). The divide between subsistence and transformational entrepreneurship. *Innovation Policy and the Economy*, 10, 57–81.

Social Accounting Network. (SAN). Website. Retrieved from: www.socialaudit network.org.uk/getting-started/what-is-social-accounting-and-audit/ [Accessed March 2018].

Soul Record. (2018). Website. Retrieved from: http://soulrecord.org/about-soul-record%C2%AE [Accessed March 2018].

United Nations. (2018). Website. Retrieved from: www.un.org/sustainabledevelop ment/sustainable-development-goals/ [Accessed March 2018].

United Nations Environment Programme. (2009). Guidelines for social life cycle assessment of products. Retrieved from: www.lifecycleinitiative.org/wp-content/ uploads/2012/12/2009%20-%20Guidelines%20for%20sLCA%20-%20EN.pdf.

3 Sustainable transformational entrepreneurship at Arouca UNESCO geopark, Portugal

Vanessa Ratten, Antonio Duarte, Carla Susana Marques and Vitor Braga

Introduction

Geoparks are characterized as parks that have a geological heritage with regional importance and they play an important role in developing and popularizing science (Ruban, 2016). There is a curiosity about the past conditions of an area, which is why geoparks are a tourist attraction. The importance of geoparks is evident in network activities within a geographic region around the conservation of geology that has an important cultural element. Increasingly, geoparks are seen as sustainable business models that utilize local knowledge for business activities.

Farsani et al. (2014, p. 1) states that geoparks have "values associated with education, science, culture and socio-economic development". These values are evident in the educational and sustainability collaboration geoparks have with people through tourism, schools and education. This study takes a broad definition of geoparks by defining them as territories that have rare geological attractions. The role of sustainable entrepreneurship in geoparks has not previously been considered in the literature, which is the aim of this chapter.

The UNESCO global geopark network provides a way to attract tourists to geological phenomena (Ruban, 2016). The goal of UNESCO global geoparks is to engage with communities in cultural and sustainable development (Zouros, 2017). UNESCO global geoparks are classified as unified geographical areas that have geological importance and are managed with educational objectives. This ensures that the geoparks are preserved through sustainable development but by combining education with conservative initiatives. A core objective of UNESCO global geoparks is education through involving the local community and region in knowledge dissemination. There are 127 recognized UNESCO global geoparks worldwide that are part of a network of educational exchange. The benefit of having a UNESCO certification on geoparks is that cooperation and knowledge can be shared through management education policies. There are four geoparks in Portugal that are part of the European geoparks network: Arouca, Azores, Naturtejo and Terras de Caveliros. This study focuses on the Arouca UNESCO geopark.

Dowling and Newsome (2006a, p. 253) states "through the international respect and reach of UNESCO, geoparks have already begun to make their mark on communities and regions". The branding of geoparks as UNESCO has heightened awareness of the importance of geoparks to the cultural heritage of an area. Each geopark as its own story that is linked to the culture and history of the area. In addition, geoparks are a way for governments to legitimize businesses in conjunction with the principles of sustainability.

There is little academic interest about geotourism due to it being a relatively recent research area (Hurtado et al., 2014). This chapter illuminates the link between geotourism and sustainable entrepreneurship as evidenced in the Arouca geopark. Sustainable entrepreneurship involves interaction with a community or region in order to derive positive impacts. Many decisions in a geopark are based on social implications that influence tourism in an area. This chapter argues that a consideration of sustainable entrepreneurship is useful to attracting more national and international attention on geoparks. Due to the impact tourism has on communities, sustainable entrepreneurship can be seen as an appropriate way to ensure the social and business elements of geoparks are realized. This means producing a new way of understanding the sustainable character of geoparks in preservation but building related business endeavours.

The aim of this chapter is to investigate the sustainability ecosystem around a geopark to determine how industry and government interact to create entrepreneurial opportunities. Thus, the study has the major purpose of determining how geoparks utilize sustainability to create entrepreneurial ecosystems. This is achieved by reviewing the practical significance of geoparks in regional economies and their growing global importance.

Literature review

Geoparks

European geoparks are an organization designed to contribute to formal and informal knowledge about geological heritage through education. The goal of European geoparks is to share knowledge about the culture and geological significance of geoparks. This ensures that knowledge is disseminated to a wide audience and can serve as a form of outdoor laboratory. The educational focus of European geoparks is to ensure cultural, economic and social development of geoparks through collaboration with industry and educational providers. A major way educational programmes are conducted are through geotourists who visit geoparks to learn about the geological significance of a region. This enables knowledge transfer through experiential participation in the geopark and ensures learning through experiencing the geology and historical development of a geopark.

Farsani et al. (2014) suggests that geopark networks help exchange best practices, experiences and ideas through education. Thus, geoparks contribute to the sustainable development of an area through geotourism. This involves geoparks in cooperation with local communities sharing information about educational programmes. Pralong (2006, p. 21) states geoparks incorporate "the essential components of natural landscapes, which are rocks (e.g. stones, minerals, fossils etc) and forms (e.g. streams, glaciers, caves etc) of the Earth's surface". These natural landscapes mean that more communities are appreciating geoparks for their contribution to the economic and social life of an area. This is reflected in the contribution of a geopark to the cultural protection of an area.

Ruban (2016, p. 204) states "geoparks are created for tourist-oriented promotion of geological knowledge via demonstration of unique and/or peculiar geological features". Therefore, the main function of geoparks is to connect people with the culture and nature of an area in conjunction with educational purposes. There is an emphasis on time and history in tourism, which is evident in geoparks. Geologic time is the focus of geoparks as they link past events to current educational programmes. Hence, geoparks enable an easy way to learn about geologic time due to the existence of fossils and rocks that can be seen via infrastructure such as roads and buildings (Ruban, 2016).

Geotourism

Geotourism involves geosites (geological heritage places), objects typically from museums and other geological features that are utilized for the purpose of recreation. More tourists are interested in education as part of their experience in conjunction with the natural environment. Geotourists seek experiences that are linked to the cultural and historical conditions of a region. Pralong (2006, p. 20) defines geotourism as a "multi-interest kind of tourism exploiting natural sites and landscapes containing interesting earth science features in a didactic and entertaining way". Buckley (2003) suggests that geotourism involves ecotourism that has a social, environmental and economic component. The goal of geotourism is to transfer knowledge and information about geological landscapes to people.

Hurtado et al. (2014, p. 613) states "geotourism is a relatively newly defined subsector of natural area tourism". Geotourism occurs when people visit a region due to its distinct geological character (Farsani et al., 2014). This occurs when people gain knowledge about geological sites within a geographic area that provides education about past events. Newsome and Dowling (2006b) suggest that there is a hierarchy of features in geotourism from most important being the landscape, landforms and rock types to the least important including sediments, rocks and crystals.

The main emphasis in geotourism is on the process and sites that provide direct knowledge about geological history within an area. This is important as more people are interested in understanding earth sciences through learning about geology and the landscape (Dowling and Newsome, 2006b). The natural environment is a way to appreciate the geological heritage of an area. Dowling and Newsome (2006a, p. 248) state "we can broadly categorize rocks into three main types of sedimentary, metamorphic and ignesous, and landforms into the four main types of mountains, plateau, hills and plains". Most geoparks are located in rural areas that require the interaction with educational institutions in preserving the cultural heritage. This is evident in the socio-cultural learning that occurs when people visit a geopark because of its natural attractions.

Newsome et al. (2012, p. 19) states "geotourism is often referred to as a form of nature-based tourism that focuses primarily on the geosystem". Thus, geotourism occurs when people visit geosites and visitor centres. More countries are realizing the importance of protecting their geodiversity through the management of geoparks. To function effectively geotourism needs to be integrated into a region through collaboration with educational institutions.

Hurtado et al. (2014) utilizes a geologically focused approach by focusing on the abiotic features, biotic features and cultural characteristics of geotourism. The abiotic features involve the geology of an area in terms of the land and rocks. The biotic features are about the fauna and flora in an area that forms part of the animal and plant life. The cultural characteristics are based on human's connection to the past and present in an area. Most studies of geotourism focus on the geomorphological features of an area, with fossils and landforms being the main areas of interest. Thus, the study of earth sciences is at the core of geotourism.

Bosak et al. (2010, p. 162) states "the term geotourism has two different definitions that refer to the 'geo' component from either a geological or geographical perspective". Geotourism is part of sustainable tourism due to the focus on the environment and preserving an area. Therefore, importance is place on the aesthetics of an area in terms of its culture and natural characteristics. Geotourists visit a place due to its environment, heritage and link with a previous way of life. There is an emphasis on geotourism in bringing about a positive impact to a community through storytelling and education.

Sustainable entrepreneurship

The underlying issue of sustainability is the future survival of the natural environment including land, biology and humans living together in a mutually respectful way. Buckley (2003, p. 79) states "sustainability is fundamentally about human interactions with the natural environment". Human society has changed the natural environment through building and occupation. This has led to there being a trend amongst sustainable entrepreneurs to preserve the natural environment whilst progressing society in an economic way. Sustainable entrepreneurship is conceptualized as "a variation of the discovery, creation and exploitation of economic opportunities to create goods and services toward a more sustainable society" (Poldner et al., 2015, p. 2). The process of sustainable entrepreneurship involves exploiting opportunities that provide environmental gains for society (Shepherd and Patzelt, 2011). This includes discovering ways to create value from creating social ventures in conjunction with the environment. This helps reduce degradation in the natural environment by finding innovative business models (Capaldo et al., 2016).

Sustainable entrepreneurs try to utilize the natural environment by working with institutional structures to create business opportunities (Dean and McMillen, 2007). Kirkwood and Walton (2010) suggest sustainable entrepreneurs are motivated by five key reasons: green values, passion, earning a living, market gaps and being their own boss. Therefore, the aim of sustainable entrepreneurship is to bring positive change to the natural environment. This means the key difference between sustainable entrepreneurs and other types of entrepreneurs is their interest in the environment and social issues rather than just financial gain. Part of sustainable entrepreneurship involves ethical behaviour in ecological aspects of the natural environment. Thus, sustainable entrepreneurs have a desire to preserve the present ecological environment whilst protecting the past. They do this by creating value through sustainability initiatives that focus on knowledge about the environment. Increasingly, more people are interested in sustainable entrepreneurship as it balances economic initiatives with environmental and social value creation.

Fischer et al. (2018, p. 408) defines sustainable entrepreneurs as "entrepreneurs who launch sustainable products, services and processes as possible key agents for a transition towards a more tenable future". There is more interest in protecting the environment for future generations, which has influenced more focus on sustainability in business research (Yoon, 2017). Sustainable entrepreneurship offers a way of engaging in prosocial behaviour about ecology through a business context.

Case study

The area including Arouca geopark is more than 600 million years old and is situated on the river Paiva. At Arouca geopark there are 41 sites of geological heritage that tell the story of life in the natural environment. The mountains of the Serra da Freita are closeby and Arouca is located in the north of Portugal between Aveiro and Porto. Arouca focuses on geotourism through educating people about the past and present. Geotourism involves the geology and geographical character of an area. The geological heritage at Arouca includes more than 200 sites of archaeological interest. This includes the remains of gold mines by the Romans.

Arouca geopark is located in northern Portugal approximately one hour drive from Porto, which is a world heritage city. There are 41 geosites in Arouca geopark with the most famous being the birthing stones and the giant trilobites. The goal of Arouca geopark is to preserve the geological environment through conservation, education and tourism. Arouca geopark was recognized in 2009 as a UNESCO listed geopark, which has further fuelled tourism and regional interest in this geological significant area. In a study on network indicators for European geoparks, network members Farsani et al. (2014) found that all geoparks including Arouca participate in educational activities such as conferences, writing books chapters and tourism activities.

Methods

A case study approach was utilized to understand the role of sustainable entrepreneurship in geoparks. Whilst sustainable entrepreneurship has been considered in other fields, we were not aware of any research in geoparks. Utilizing the approach suggested by Yin (2009) existing theory was utilized as a way to understand the potential implications of the study. In this study, the theory of sustainable entrepreneurship and geoparks was utilized. The research context was Arouca geopark, which has a range of sustainable entrepreneurship programmes. Arouca geopark provided a rich research context to gain an in-depth understanding of the impact of social entrepreneurship. A purposive sampling method was utilized as it provided a way to understand the contextual elements of the case study (Pratt, 2009). We studied three different elements of the geopark: business, education and community. To collect the data archival documents including websites and government papers were utilized in addition to a site visit.

The information collected was then characterized in terms of type of sustainable entrepreneurship. For example, industry association data from the UNESCO Global Geopark network was utilized. Then policy information about the role of Arouca geopark and other geoparks in social applications was utilized. This helped assess how government policy impacted the development of sustainable entrepreneurship at the geopark.

To analyse the data, information was collected then analysed under themes that emerged in conjunction with the literature review. The data analysis approach suggested by Miles and Huberman (1994) to explore patterns using theoretical concepts was utilized. This involved an exploratory approach that helped build a sense of understanding of sustainable entrepreneurship. This enriched our initial literature review and analysis of how sustainable entrepreneurship worked in a geopark setting.

Findings

It is becoming more important to consider the conservation of landscapes through geoparks. An important biodiversity ecosystem exists in geoparks that contributes to local communities. Geoparks are considered an asset in their communities because of their link to culture and sustainable entrepreneurship. However, the Charter of the Global Geoparks Network has restrictions on the kind of business growth. This is due to the emphasis on sustainable economic development in stimulating tourism. In order to stay classified as a UNESCO geopark there needs to be the guarantee of environmental protection and sustainable tourism. This means that the area of a geopark needs to be managed in a way that considers nature but also business opportunity. The European Charter for Sustainable Tourism was established to promote strategies that emphasizes sustainability in their areas. Arouca geopark practices sustainability by cooperating with other stakeholders in their community. This includes working with local schools and universities by providing sustainability education. This helps to inform people about the importance of business working with the ecology and biodiversity existing in the geopark. In this way, the geopark serves as an entrepreneurial ecosystem by linking stakeholders in the community to the development of new ideas.

Arouca geopark has established its own brand image that products and services can include to indicate their association with the park. This is called the Arouca Geopark Association whose objective is to develop associated businesses in the Arouca region in conjunction with the geopark. An example of a business developed in association with the Arouca geopark is Pinguca, a Portuguese brand of handmade alcoholic drinks. The company utilizes the homemade brandy-based beverages from a family recipe. The company was created in 2013 and constructed a new distillery next to the current owner's grandfather's original wine cellar. Part of the distillery process involves using an alembic (cap of the still) made of brass and copper for bottling of the beverages. The company has received an award the "National Rural Creative Prize" for its traditional product with a cultural link to the Arouca area.

The analysis from Arouca geopark suggests the concept of geotourism acts as a form of sustainable entrepreneurship when it is linked to business activity. The business related to geoparks is fluid, dynamic and changing based on societal needs. Geotourists often draw on their own experiences to start businesses with a social or community element. The birthing stones at Castanheira village are one of the main geotourism attractions. Pedras par deiras (the birthing stones) is the name given by the inhabitants at Castanheira for the stones that are reproduced out of other stones.

Geoparks serve as a way to learn about the legacy of previous shifts in the earth as well as previous animal and plant life. This means that geoparks are places to see how the landscape has evolved. Newsome and Dowling (2006a) propose that geotourism involves attractions, accommodation, activities, interpretation, management and tours. The attractions can be categorized as macro, meso and microscale. At Arouca the macro-scale attraction is the territorial area of landmass whilst the mesoscale involves the birthing rocks and the microscale are the trilobites. Accommodation at Arouca is focused at the town centre but there is a geolodge being built at Castanheira near the birthing stones. The activities at Arouca include the interaction visitor centre and library. There are also interpretation via trails and brochures about geodiversity in Arouca geopark. The management of Arouca geopark has an association that brands and markets businesses in the area. This helps to manage visitors by also engaging in geoconservation. The tours involve self-directed drives around the Arouca geopark area and organized tours.

Managerial implications

This chapter focuses on social entrepreneurship in Arouca geopark. The main objectives of the chapter are to link the geotourism and sustainable entrepreneurship literature. This chapter has contributed to the geotourism literature by suggesting that sustainable entrepreneurship is a theoretical framework to understand its significance and impact in the global economy. There is still much to learn about how to incorporate sustainable entrepreneurship in geoparks. There are three main practical outcomes from this study. First, geoparks should emphasize the business ventures that have a sustainability component in their activities. Second, geoparks need to market themselves as sustainable entities that are tourism destinations but also linked to the business activities in a region. Third, there needs to be more emphasis on sustainable entrepreneurship to education and government authorities.

Future research suggestions

This chapter has taken a transformational view to the role of entrepreneurship in geoparks. As most previous research on geoparks focuses on the tourism and heritage perspective, this chapter adds to the existing literature by taking an entrepreneurship perspective. More research is needed though on how geoparks transform regions through sustainable and social entrepreneurship initiatives. As geoparks require the cooperation of multiple stakeholders more research is required on how they do this through entrepreneurial policies. An interesting research avenue is the use of smart specialization strategies that link geoparks like Arouca to broader government initiatives from regional authorities such as the Porto and Portugal tourism entities. This would help to further understand how geoparks can utilize geology and educational programmes to transform regions.

This chapter has focused on Arouca geopark but additional research is needed on further understanding from a longitudinal perspective the transformations that have occurred in the region. This could include how Arouca geopark becoming a UNESCO member further transformed the area. Whilst much has been written about the tourism benefits of geoparks there needs to be more international comparative case studies on successful transformational strategies. In addition, comparing micro/macro/meso level transformational strategies that are integral to the role geoparks play in society is required.

Future potential research questions include: How has geotourism transformed regions into globally competitive entities? What is the role of geoconservation in the transformation of a region? What kind of transformational entrepreneurial strategies are geoparks utilizing? And what is the role of UNESCO in transforming geoparks? To answer these questions requires further work on the power of transformational entrepreneurship in society. Hopefully this chapter has paved the way for more research to focus on the role of transformational entrepreneurship in geoparks.

Policy implications

Geoparks are an integral part of communities and play a role in fostering entrepreneurial ecosystems. More policies need to take an entrepreneurial view in terms of how they engage with geoparks. To do this, policy should focus on the transformational elements of entrepreneurship. At the local level, geoparks like Arouca play an important role in developing linkages with businesses. This is particularly important in fostering artisan entrepreneurship and handicrafts that are linked to the heritage of a region. Thus, policies about small business and particularly family business need to be linked to geopark strategies. At the regional level, policy initiatives need to see how geoparks fit into the broader economic and social goals. This is important in developing entrepreneurial ecosystems. At the country and international level there needs to be more awareness of the entrepreneurship happening at geoparks. A more collaborative approach between governments is required in order to maximize the use of resources.

Conclusion

This study contributes to the growing literature on geoparks and geotourism by linking it to sustainable entrepreneurship. The findings shed light on how geoparks can utilize sustainability entrepreneurs to link the geodiversity with business opportunity. The challenge for sustainable tourism is how to balance resource constraints whilst protecting the natural environment. The findings of this study show that collaboration between geopark stakeholders particularly in conjunction with the Arouca Geopark Association can resolve business problems. Thus, our approach highlights the importance of utilizing sustainable entrepreneurship in geoparks. Our findings contribute to the geopark literature by providing insights into entrepreneurial activities in the region. We hope that this study encourages other geoparks to focus on sustainable entrepreneurship in the future.

References

Bosak, K., Boley, B., and Zaret, K. (2010). Deconstructing the 'crown of the continent': Power, politics and the process of creating national geographics geotourism map guides. *Tourism Geographies*, 12(3), 460–480.

Buckley, R. (2003). Environmental inputs and outputs in ecotourism: Geotourism with a positive triple bottom line. *Journal of Ecotourism*, 2(1), 76–82.

Capaldo, G., Costantino, N., Pellegrino, R., and Rippa, P. (2016). Factors affecting the diffusion and success of collaborative interactions between university and industry. *Journal of Science and Technology Policy Management*, 7(3), 273–288.

Dean, T.J., and McMillen, J.S. (2007). Toward a theory of sustainable entrepreneurship: Reducing environmental degradation through entrepreneurial action. *Journal of Business Venturing*, 22(1), 50–76.

Dowling, R., and Newsome, D. (eds.) (2006a). *Geotourism, Sustainability, Impacts and Management*. Oxford: Elsevier, Butterworth Heinemann.

Dowling, R., and Newsome, D. (2006b). Geotourism's issues and challenges. In R. Dowling and D. Newsome (eds.), *Geotourism*, Oxford: Elsevier, Butterworth Heinemann.

Farsani, N.T., Coelho, C.O.A., and Costa, C.M.M. (2014). Analysis of network activities in geoparks as geotourism destinations. *International Journal of Tourism Research*, 16, 1–10.

Fischer, D., Mauer, R., and Brettel, M. (2018). Regulatory focus theory and sustainable entrepreneurship. *International Journal of Entrepreneurial Behavior & Research*, Online First.

Hurtado, H., Dowling, R., and Sanders, D. (2014). An exploratory study to develop a geotourism typology model. *International Journal of Tourism Research*, 16, 608–613.

Kirkwood, J., and Walton, S. (2010). What motivates ecopreneurs to start businesses? *International Journal of Entrepreneurial Behavior & Research*, 16(3), 204–228.

Miles, M.B., and Huberman, A.M. (1994). *Qualitative Data Analysis- An Expanded Sourcebook*. Thousand Oaks, CA: Sage Publications.

Newsome, D., and Dowling, R. (2006). The scope and nature of geotourism. In R. Dowling and D. Newsome (eds.), *Geotourism*. Oxford: Elsevier, Butterworth Heinemann.

Newsome, D., Dowling, R., and Leung, Y-F. (2012). The nature and management of geotourism: A case study of two established iconic geotourism destinations. *Tourism Management Perspectives*, 2–3, 19–27.

Poldner, K., Shrivastava, P., and Branzei, O. (2015). Embodied multi-discursivity: An aesthetic process approach to sustainable entrepreneurship. *Business & Society*, 1–39.

Pralong, J.P. (2006). Geotourism: A new form of tourism utilizing natural landscapes and based on imagination and emotion. *Tourism Review*, 61(3), 20–25.

Pratt, M.G. (2009). For the lack of a boilerplate: Tips on writing up (and reviewing) qualitative research. *Academy of Management Journal*, 52(5), 856–862.

RRuban, D.A. (2016). Representation of geological time in the global geopark network: A web-page study. *Tourism Management Perspectives*, 20, 204–208.

Shepherd, D.A., and Patzelt, H. (2011). The new field of sustainable entrepreneurship: Studying entrepreneurial action linking "what is to be sustained" with "what is to be developed". *Entrepreneurship Theory and Practice*, 35(1), 137–163.

Yin, R.K. (2009). *Case Study Research: Design and Methods* (4th edition). Thousand Oaks, CA: Sage Publications.

Yoon, D. (2017). The regional-innovation cluster policy for R&D efficiency and the creative economy: With focus on Daedeok Innopolis. *Journal of Science and Technology Policy Management*, 8(2), 206–226.

Zouros, N. (ed.) (2017). Geoparks as sustainable tourism destinations. *European Geoparks Network Magazine*, 14, 1–63.

4 Development of transformational social entrepreneurship through innovation determinants in the handicraft industry of the Wayuu community in Colombia

*Stephanie Juliette Moreno Hernández,
Jessica Rubiano Moreno and Carlos
López Hernández*

Introduction

There are many studies about the handicraft industry and its impact in communities. Some of them are devoted to studying the participation of an indigenous community in the labour market (Martinez, 2006). Others do it from the perspective of financial support of security loans and utilization of loans for productive activities (Qureshi, 1990). Some others were devoted to contributing to job creation and reduction of poverty and unemployment from the entrepreneurial outlook of women (Dzisi, 2008). For a handicraft company to be innovative, it must be capable to make its entrepreneurs produce unique items and reach the corresponding market to become competitive (Gupta and Mukherjee, 2006; Girón et al., 2007; Hipp and Grupp, 2005). The community where there is a competitive handicraft industry benefits from this. There are some cases that have been studied such as the one of the indigenous palm candy in India (Sanu et al., 2010) and an entrepreneurial case from India (Sharma et al., 2012); in Portugal (Carrizo Moreira and Leitao Martins, 2009); in the Maltese islands (Marwick, 2001); in Scotland (McAuley, 1999); in Fiji and Tonga (Naidu et al., 2014); Canada; New Zealand and UK (Randall, 2005).

The handicraft industry is influenced by internal factors such as the ones mentioned before and by other external factors. Some external factors are, for instance a wider distribution and alternative business strategies to increase their market share (Randall, 2005). A second factor is social and economic where the standard of living should be improved (Naidu et al., 2014). The third factor is the involvement of government agencies to be able to transfer the business to the next generation (Naipinit et al., 2016).

The handicraft industry's growth potential of the Wayuu community is very big. However, this potential has not been able to be developed due to different internal and external factors. In this research work, it is intended to determine if the Wayuu community entrepreneurs have the growth potential to develop an industry of innovative handicraft. In the following sections, a literature review is presented; it corresponds to the topic of handicraft innovation and entrepreneurship. Afterwards, the methodology and main findings are described. Finally, the discussion of this research is presented along with some conclusions.

Literature review

The literature review is presented in two parts. In the first one, there are the most relevant research works of social entrepreneurship, especially of social innovation in the handicraft industry. In the second part, we explain the determining factors of innovation for successful entrepreneurial companies to be developed.

For some people, social innovation means having public policies that allow some kind of positive impact in more than one population group at local, intermediate or national levels (CEPAL, 2015). For others, this type of innovation and entrepreneurship allows confidence to be developed in communities so that they become aware of their abilities. In addition, they may develop them if they help to identify the need, pose an idea and develop it because they are the ones who will be benefitted by the implementation of the mechanisms that look for the improvement of life quality or the problems that the community has (ANSPE, 2016). Finally, there are some studies that claim that boosting social innovation through the creation of companies that comply with the three pillars of corporate social responsibility (society, environment and economy) (Alonso et al., 2015) is what will generate greater benefits for these communities.

This research work focuses on this last proposal for the development of innovative companies in the craft sector of the Wayuu community whose premise is that the social contribution be beneficial for its inhabitants. In addition, this is intended to be not a temporary solution, but a permanent source of economic income that allows growth.

A way of seeing entrepreneurship is as a networking that reflects in a greater social capital or as a societal phenomenon which may boost and develop people in their life context (Johannisson and Olaison, 2007). These entrepreneurs face different problems and challenges which are typical of community enterprises (Naipinit et al., 2016). These community enterprises need to develop as entrepreneurs (Summatavet and Raudsaar, 2015). This phenomenon is known as social entrepreneurship. Randall (2005) concludes that when performing a change, both social and political, where the result is fair trade results in competitive advantage.

A handmade product is one which does not follow an industrialized process, which is produced in a geographic region and with a defined culture (Grisales, 2015).

The social entrepreneur may be defined as someone who develops him or herself. Johannisson and Olaison (2007) define "emergency entrepreneurship" as spontaneous.

Some authors have studied success factors for the handicraft industry to be developed. The first one was McAuley (1999) who relied on the case of Scottish handicrafts. The factors that he considered are related to the product, such as design; secondly, personal and psychological factors such as education and training; thirdly, the cognitive industry such as the customer focus and the access to the know-how; finally, the one of the industry as the global market.

Sakolnakorn and Sungkharat (2014) studied eight factors related to the problems of community enterprise. These factors are lack of accounting and finance systems, lack of marketing management, a labour comprised primarily of older people, government support in terms of training and knowledge, production issues caused by old machinery, high labour cost/wages, product design and package design that are not attractive and finally, lack of technological skill and knowledge (Sakolnakorn and Sungkharat, 2014). On the other hand, Naidu et al. (2014) made a study where they make a list of determining factors of the handicraft industry. The three studies have various important coincidences. This research study is based on this last study due to the similarities that their study and the handicraft industry of the Wayuu community possess (Naidu et al., 2014).

Naidu et al. (2014) made a study which presents the determining factors of handicraft innovation. It is based on the study of tourist companies because there are few studies related to the handicraft industry and because the tourism industry encompasses the handicraft industry (Novelli, Schmitz, and Spencer, 2003). These eight key factors are, namely, value adding, design uniqueness, new product development, cultural uniqueness, advanced technology, experience of owner, ability of owner to adapt to trends and market quality of raw materials (Naidu et al., 2014).

Next, each of them is defined:

1 Value adding of products: Waits (2000) and Nyseen et al. (2003) defined this concept as an incremental improvement in products.
2 Design uniqueness: Allows companies and especially those related to handicraft to have their products reach a market position (Gooroochurn and Sugiyarto, 2005) and differentiate its product from competitors (Dhingra, V. and Dhingra, 2012).
3 New product development: Refers to the process starting with designing and ending with launching into the market (Pujari et al., 2003). Qureshi (1990) and Bossen (2000) mention how the use of technological innovations can rejuvenate the traditional crafts.
4 Cultural uniqueness: A quality handicraft captures a unique cultural aspect (Marwick, 2001).
5 Using advanced technology: Defined as how to manufacture unique handicrafts by using advanced technology (Trivedi, et al., 2006).
6 Experience of owner: Means whether entrepreneurs possess the know-how to design new handicrafts (Rutashobya and Jaensson, J., 2004).
7 Ability of owner to adapt to market trends: Artisans need support from specialist networks to adapt to market trends and be able to test the ideas and

products in the community directly (Summatavet and Raudsaar, 2015), and to satisfy consumer needs and wants (Taylor and Owusu, 2012).

8 Quality of raw materials: Without enough raw quality materials (Kamal and Vinnie, 2007) the handicraft industry may not be developed.

Research methodology

The research considers a non-experimental design of descriptive transverse type; the study regards a mixed descriptive qualitative and quantitative research (Hernández et al., 1991) divided in three phases, the first one consisted in survey application with nominal measurement questions (Montero, I. and León, 2002) which allow us to identify the problems. Then, the second phase takes place with the application of instruments to the actors of the chain value of the Wayuu handicrafts. Its last phase is the analysis of the commercial process to compare it with the proposal of Naidu, Chand and Southgate, to propose improvements to the initial diagnosis of the Wayuu community.

In this research, face-to-face interviews with: (a) suppliers, (b) artisans of the Wayuu community, (c) traders were performed, and (d) surveys to potential clients were carried out (Guerra, 2002). All of them are directly related to the industry of Wayuu handicraft. The suppliers were traders from the municipality of Manaure. The artisans interviewed were from the villages of Epieyu and San Martin de Poloi, which are part of the Wayuu Association of Traditional Indigenous Authorities: Shipia Wayuu. Traders were interviewed in the streets of Riohacha and in stores at malls in Bogota.

The potential clients interviewed had clear characteristics in their profiles, such as the fact that they had an affinity to travel and to know other cultures; that they had an average or a high acquisitive power; that they had a university level of education; and that they were between 18 and 25 years of age. All of them living in Bogota. A total of 350 surveys were made; where 119 of the interviewed knew the Wayuu handicrafts and 101 knew where to find a store in the City of Bogota that sold these products with a known brand; with some type of tag, or with no tag at all.

Following, some of the findings of the performed field research are shown, and the eight determining factors for handicraft innovation are contrasted.

Research finding

In this section, first, the description of the industry of the Wayuu community's handicrafts is shown. Second, some of the most important characteristics regarding this industry and that came up in the field research work are presented. Finally, the analysis of the eight determinants of innovation in the handicraft industry, which were posed in the section of Literature Review, is presented.

The handicraft sector represents 15 percent of employment of the manufacturing industry according to the Ministry de Comercio, and Artesanias (2009), where 60 percent are women and 40 percent are men. The Wayuu indigenous community represents almost 69 percent of the total indigenous population of

Colombia, and it is located mainly in the high and low regions of la Guajira. One of its most important industries is handicrafts (Arango, 2004). However, the measurement of this industry is not exact because it does not have a differentiated nomenclature (NULL, 2005). The production of handicrafts is distributed in 57 percent textile, 13.5 percent wood and the rest is divided in ceramic and pottery, leather goods and jewellery. Most of the commercialization of Colombian handicrafts is done within their national territory and only 1.3 percent is exported (Ministerio de Comercio and Artesanías, 2009).

The handicrafts industry at the Wayuu community has some significant characteristics. Firstly, the Wayuu community depends a lot on handicrafts economically. Unfortunately, most business people – 70 percent according to the Ministerio de Comercio y Artesanías (2009) – are incapable of covering their basic needs. Secondly, Wayuu women have a preponderant role in this industry (Guzmán and García, 2010) (Artesanías de Colombia, 2010) similar to other cases in the world such as Africa (Dzisi, 2008). Thirdly, even though various national laws such as the Political Constitution of 1991; the General Law of Tourism and the Sectoral Plan of Tourism; the General Law of Culture and the Ten Year Cultural Plan 2001–1010; and some international ones such as the Law of the Artisan of 1984 (UNESCO, 1984) among many others protect and prioritize the handicraft sector, the industry of Wayuu handicrafts is very poorly developed (Artesanías de Colombia, 2010). This happens also in other countries where more government support is needed and policymakers should be urged to readjust economic policies that increase level of innovation in the handicraft industry. A fourth characteristic is the intervention of foreign agents in the chain of value who are those that benefit the most (Artes, 2013).

The field research showed the necessary information to determine how many of the determinants of innovation in the handicraft industry (Naidu et al., 2014) are present in the Wayuu community, and how many of them need to be developed. In Table 4.1 it is shown that most determinants are needed in order for the industry to be competitive.

Table 4.1 Determinants of innovation in the handicraft industry in the Wayuu community

Determinants of innovation	Current state
1. Value adding of products	+++
2. Design uniqueness	++
3. New product development	–
4. Cultural uniqueness	+++
5. Using advanced technology	–
6. Experience of owner	–
7. Ability of owner to adapt to market trends	–
8. Quality of raw materials	–

Source: Prepared by the authors.

In Table 4.1, it is observed that the determinants of innovation that the industry of Wayuu handicrafts has developed are focused in the value adding of products in design uniqueness and cultural uniqueness. It is also shown that the rest of the determinants of innovation need to be developed. Following, the findings regarding each one of them are described and the reason for its classification is explained.

The research resulted in the value adding of the Wayuu handicrafts being perceived by the local market. However, this was not the case of international markets where the perception of added value is almost non-existent and there is a great commercial opportunity. The *design uniqueness* is evident because the designs contained in the handicrafts have many features of the Wayuu culture, which gives them a differentiating element to their image. It was found that colours and geometrical figures are the identity of the Wayuu culture and it expresses life histories, dreams and representations of their gods that when known, the value of these handicrafts increases.

The *cultural uniqueness* is a distinctive factor of the Wayuu handicrafts and it intends to keep on caring for its identity and industrial property. Collective brands have not yet been registered in the market and the designation of origin is indicated in few products. The marketers simply change these tags for some of their stores and this makes it look like these products were produced in the place of their commercialization. For example, it might be that a store purchases Wayuu belts and they are placed in the bags they use to sell, so that makes people believe that their production is a strategic alliance between them.

The *new product development* has various areas of opportunity. In the fieldwork, it was observed that the price of the Wayuu handicrafts does not reflect the time that artisans devote to their creation. Wayuu craft production is labor intensive. A "chinchorro" (hammock) can take 60 to 90 days to be made, a hat 30 days, "waireñas" (sandals) 8 days, and a backpack from 5 to 8 days.

From the perspective of *using advanced technology* it was found that in order to maintain the quality of production, this must continue to be manually processed avoiding any use of industrial machinery. It was found that some artisans use machinery (looms) which reduces the time of production, but they remove originality and quality to the product, since for this they use thinner threads. However, there is an area of opportunity for technology to be used in other stages of the value chain process, such as design or commercialization of products, even regarding transportation since it is frequently done by motorcycle.

The *experience of owner* has some deficiencies because even though artisans have knowledge of the productive process, they do not have knowledge of entrepreneurship, which limits their industrial growth and development. In the field research work it was identified, for instance, that the time that women (most of them) devote to the production of handicrafts is the time they have left after finishing their house chores, which diminishes productivity.

Regarding *ability of owner to adapt to market trends* it is evident that it is non-existent and that it is possible to identify many areas of improvement to be able to adapt the handicraft designs to what the international market (mainly) requires, caring for their cultural identity. Artisans can be more innovative if they are able to adapt to the market trend changes (Naidu et al., 2014) and thus stop depending on foreign agents for commercialization and distribution.

Finally, regarding *raw materials,* there is an opportunity to develop new suppliers that provide quality materials and do not affect the production process. An important finding is that the supply of the raw materials is inefficient because they do not have direct access to these products in their places of origin and they have to travel to be able to acquire new products or continue with their production; thus interrupting their productivity.

Discussion

Innovation in the handicraft industry in the Wayuu community is indispensable to achieve the growth of its economy. Social entrepreneurship is a solution that may develop the potential of Wayuu artisans that will turn them into business people capable of innovating in the industry. This development may be achieved if the determinants of innovation in the handicraft industry are implemented in the case of the Wayuu community.

In this research work, it was demonstrated that Wayuu handicrafts are products with high value adding but that they must be commercialized in international markets. In addition, it was found that the design uniqueness is present in these handicrafts and that the cultural uniqueness has been kept. However, it is considered necessary that a brand that represents all the Wayuu community be created, so that products tagged with this image have the same quality and identity. This brand may be Shipia Wayuu and it may strengthen the presence of these products in the market. In addition, while being an umbrella brand, it should allow some artisans to reflect their very personal brand and design.

Some determiners of innovation that required a strong development were found as well. The first and most urgent was the experience of the owner, which for the case of the Wayuu community needs to have advisers or training that provides the know-how necessary to design and produce new models of handicrafts. The only way for an artisan to stop seeing himself or herself as one is that he or she starts seeing himself or herself as a business person and entrepreneur; it is the change of mindset (McAuley, 1999).

It can be concluded that modifying the Wayuu artisans' development will result in an easier development of the second determinant of innovation, which is the ability of an owner to adapt to market trends. This means that not only will they be capable of recognizing what national and international handicraft markets seek, but also they will be able to adapt in other stages of their value chain such as distribution and commercialization.

In third place, the development of new products can be achieved if they succeed in implementing the previously described determinant. This determinant is different from the experience of an owner in that the Wayuu artisans could create new different handicrafts to the hammocks, hats, dresses, sandals and belts they already produce as they may find new crafting products in which they might apply their technique. In this way, they can reach new markets or at least this will allow them to broaden their portfolio of products.

In fourth place, it is proposed to introduce advanced technology in some stages of the value chain; mainly in the design and commercialization by taking advantage of electronic commerce and the promotion through social networks as well as the use of technologies for distribution logistics. Finally, it is necessary to develop a supply network that delivers quality raw materials, but this determinant will not have a great impact if the other previously mentioned factors are not improved.

It was also found that it is important to prioritize entering and commercializing Wayuu handicraft products in the exporting market where the price that clients pay is much higher. Strengthening exportations of handicrafts focusing on the client, innovation and brand initiatives and commercialization (Sharma et al., 2012) where the role of the government is protecting and facilitating so that the exportations of handicrafts can be improved, local companies can be strengthened and local production can be certified of origin (Naidu et al., 2014).

It was also detected that it is indispensable to develop a process of data collection of all the value chain to develop a market intelligence that allows for strategic decision making of a longer term.

Conclusions

There are great economic and social needs in the Wayuu community; at the same time, it is a very rich community regarding its culture. A solution to the current situation in this community is to develop the entrepreneurial capacity of its inhabitants and make them self-sufficient. Empowering Wayuu artisans aims to turn them into social entrepreneurs. Innovation in handicraft products is indispensable to develop an industry that grows and is profitable. To accomplish this, the Wayuu community must perform various actions that have been mentioned in this chapter and are determinant to be able to reach this goal.

The growth potential in the handicraft industry in this Wayuu community is possible, but they need to work, especially with artisans and make them grow as business people. This research work focused on developing a development and growth strategy of entrepreneurship and social innovation of the Wayuu handicraft community. However, the plans required to implement the different proposals suggested are not explained in detail. It is recommended that authorities participate in an active way in providing the foundation of development and brand ownership protection. It is recommended to develop other interdisciplinary works with study areas such as fashion design or international marketing to boost the findings of this research work.

Note

The use of drones has been developed lately and many industries use them with the same purpose, which is to improve the delivery time and improve the cost of doing it.

References

Alonso, D., Gonzalez, N., and Nieto, M. (2015). *La innovación social como motor de creación de empresas*. España: Universia Business Review.

ANSPE. (2016, 8 de 1 de). *Agencia Nacional para la Superación de la Pobreza Extrema*. Obtenido de anspe: www.anspe.gov.co/es/programa/que-es-el-centro-innovacion-social/proyectos-de-innovacion-social.

Arango, R. (2004). *Los pueblos indígenas de Colombia en el umbral del Nuevo Milenio*. Bogotá: DNP.

Artes, C.N. (2013, 1 de Abril de). *Cultura*. Obtenido de Cultura.gob.cl: www.cultura.gob.cl/wp-content/uploads/2013/06/estudio-caracterizacion-canales-comercializacion-artesania.pdf.

Artesanías de Colombia. (2010). *Protegiendo Nuestra Identidad: Proyecto sensibilizacion en derechos de propiedad intelectual asociatividad a industrias creativas artesanales*. Bogotá: Ministerio de Comercio, Industria y Turismo.

Bossen, C. (2000). Festival mania, tourism and nation building in Fiji: The case of the hibiscus festival. *The Contemporary Pacific, 1956–1970*, 12(1), 97–116.

Carrizo Moreira, A., and Leitao Martins, S. (2009). CRER: An integrated methodology for the incubation of business ideas in rural communities in Portugal. *Journal of Enterprising Communities: People and Places in the Global Economy*, 3(2), 170–192. doi:10.1108/17506200910960860.

CEPAL. (2015). *Comisión Económica para América Latina y el Caribe*. Obtenido de cepal: www.cepal.org/es.

Dhingra, V., and Dhingra, M. (2012). Factors affecting quality of work life of handicraft workers: A study of handicraft units in and around Moradabad. *New York Science Journal*, 5(10), 105–113.

Dzisi, S. (2008). Entrepreneurial activities of indigenous African woman: A case of Ghana. *Journal of Enterprising Communities: People and Places in the Global Economy*, 2(3), 254–264. doi:10.1108.

Girón, J., Hernández, M., and Castañeda, J. (2007). Strategy and factors for success: The Mexican handicraft sector. *Performance Improvement*, 11(1), 25–43.

Gooroochurn, N., and Sugiyarto, G. (2005). Competitiveness indicators in the travel and tourism industry. *Tourism Economies*, 11(1), 25–43.

Grisales, A. (2015). *Artesanía, arte y diseño. Una indignación folosófica acerca de la vida cotidiana y el saber práctico*. Manizales: Universidad de Caldas.

Guerra, G. (2002). *Cadena de Valor*. Obtenido de Cadena de Valor: https://books.google.com.co/books?id=XPLV3n3UY50C&pg=PA102&dq=cadena+de+valor&hl=es-419&sa=X&ei=Mp2OVISUKIHasASMs4D4Aw&ved=0CBoQ6AEwAA#v=onepage&q=cadena%20de%20valor.

Gupta, R., and Mukherjee, I. (2006). *Scope of Cottage and Small Scale Industry in West Bengal in early 2000*. ICFAI University Press. Available at SSRN: https://ssrn.com/abstract=888501 or http://dx.doi.org/10.2139/ssrn.888501

Guzmán, A., and García, F. (2010). *Diseño, Artesanía e Identidad: Experiencias académicas locales de Diseño Artesanal en Colombia y el Salvador*. Popayán: Popayán Ediciones Axis Mundi Institución Universitaria Colegio Mayor del Cauca.

Hernández, R., Fernández, C., and Baptista, P. (1991). *Metodología de la Investigación*. México: McGraw-Hill.

Hipp, C., and Grupp, H. (2005). Innovation in the service sector: The demand for service specific innovation measurement concepts and typologies. *Research Policy*, 34(4), 517–535.

Johannisson, B., and Olaison, L. (2007, March de). The moment of truth – Reconstructing entrepreneurship and social capital in the eye of the storm. *Review of Social Economy*, 65(1), 55–78.

Kamal, M., and Vinnie, J. (2007). Exploring consumer attitude and behavior towards green practices in the loding industry in India. *Research Policy*, 19(5), 364–377.

Martinez, M. (2006). A living exhibition: Labor, desire, and the marketing of American Indian art crafts in Santa Fe. *Traditional Dwellings and Settlements Review*, 18(1), 33–34.

Marwick, M. (2001). Tourism and the development of handicraft production in the Maltese islands. *Tourism Geographies*, 3(1), 29–51.

McAuley, A. (1999). Entrepreneurial instant exporters in the Scottish arts and crafts sector. *Journal of International Marketing*, 7(4), 67–82.

Ministerio de Comercio, I.y., and Artesanías, d.C. (2009). *Política de Turismo y Artesanías: Iniciativas conjuntas para el impulso y la promoción del patrimonio artesanal y el turismo colombiano*. Bogotá: MINISTERIO DE COMERCIO, INDUSTRIA Y TURISMO.

Montero, I., and León, O. (2002). Clasificación y descripción de las metodologías de investigación en psicología. *International Journal of Clinical and Health Psychology*, 503–508.

Naidu, S., Chand, A., and Southgate, P. (2014). Determinants of innovation in the handicraft industry of Fiji and Tonga: An empirical analysis from a tourism perspective. *Journal of Enterprising Communities: People and Places in the Global Economy*, 8(4), 318–330. Obtenido de: http://doi.org/10.1108/JEC-11-2013-0033.

Naipinit, A., Na Sakolnakorn, T., and Kroeksakul, P. (2016). Strategic management of community enterprises in the upper northeast region of Thailand. *Journal of Enterprising Communities: People and Places in the Global Economy*, 10(4), 346–362. doi:10.1108/JEC-06–2015–0032.

Novelli, M., Schmitz, B., and Spencer, T. (2003). Networks, clusters and innovation in tourism: A UK experience. *Tourism Management*, 27(6), 1141–1152.

NULL, V. (2005, 16 de Marzo de). CON CADENAS PRODUCTIVAS, EL SECTOR ARTESANAL AFRONTARÁ EL LIBRE COMERCIO. *CON CADENAS PRODUCTIVAS, EL SECTOR ARTESANAL AFRONTARÁ EL LIBRE COMERCIO: Del espacio que gane la artesanía nacional en el Tratado de Libre Comercio depende en buena parte que los artesanos puedan tener productos con identidad, innovadores, y competitivos*, págs. www.eltiempo.com/archivo/documento/ MAM-1683345.

Nyseen, H., Methlie, L., and Pedersen, P. (2003). Tourism websites and value added services: The gap between customer preferences and websites offerings. *Information Technology and Tourism*, 5(3), 165–174.

Ojeda, E., and Rodríguez, A. (2015). La Innovación en los emprendimientos sociales: Una tipología. *Debates IESA*, 26–30.

Pujari, D., Wright, G., and Peattie, K. (2003). Green and competitive: Influences on environmental new product development performance. *Journal of Business Research*, 56(8), 657–671.

Qureshi, M. (1990, March de). Social link pages of artisans with technology: Upgradation of village pottery craft. *Economic and Political Weekly*, 25(13), 683–688.

Randall, D. (2005, January de). An exploration of opportunities for the growth of the fair trade market: Three cases of craft organisations. *Journal of Business Ethics*, 56(1), 55–67.

Rogerson, C., and Sithole, P. (2001). Rural handicraft production in Mpumalanga, South Africa: Organisation, problems and support needs. *South African Geographical Journal*, 83(2), 149–158.

Rutashobya, L., and Jaensson, J. (2004). Small firms' internationalization for development in Tanzania: Exploring the network phenomenon. *International Journal of Social Economics*, 31(1), 159–172.

Sakolnakorn, T., and Sungkharat, U. (2014). Development guidelines for small and micro community enterprises in Songkhla Lake Basin. *Journal of Humanities and Social Sciences*, 10(1), 97–122.

Sanu, V., Kumar, A., and Newport, J. (2010). Green and fair trade of indigenous palm candy. *Journal of Enterprising Communities: People and Places in the Global Economy*, 4(2), 142–147. doi:10.1108/17506201011048040.

Sharma, A., Dey, A., and Karwa, P. (2012). Buyer-seller relationship – Challenges in export marketing for the handicrafts and handlooms export corporation (HHEC). *Emerald Emerging Markets Case Studies*, 2(1), 1–11.

Summatavet, K., and Raudsaar, M. (2015). Cultural heritage and entrepreneurship – Inspiration for novel ventures creation. *Journal of Enterprising Communities: People and Places*, 9(1), 31–44. doi:10.1108/JEC-03-2013-0010.

Taylor, T., and Owusu, E. (2012). Factors adopting internet and e-commerce adoption among small and medium sized enterprise non-traditional exporters: Case studies of Ghanaian handicraft exporters. *European Journal of Business and Management*, 4(13), 25–37.

Trivedi, T., Tiwari, A., Chatterjee, A., Pathak, V., Dhande, S., and Chauhan, D. (2006). Application of CAD, rapid prototyping and reverse engineering in handicrafts sector: A success story. *9th International Conference on Engineering*. http://citeseerx.ist.psu.edu/viewdoc/download?doi=10.1.1.607.4881&rep=rep1&type=pdf

UNESCO. (1984, 19 de Noviembre de). *Ley 36 de 1984: Reglamento de la profesión de artesano Junta Nacional de Artesania*. Obtenido de Ley 36 de 19 de noviembre de 1984: www.unesco.org/culture/natlaws/media/pdf/colombia/colombia_ley_36_19_11_1984_spa_orof.pdf.

Waits, M. (2000). The value added of the industry cluster approach to economic analysis, strategy development and service delivery. *Economic Development Quarterly*, 14(1), 35–50.

5 Innovation in informal ethnic entrepreneurship – a result of the opening of the EU's borders?

Alexandra David and Judith Terstriep

Introduction

For many years Europe did not consider itself as a continent of immigration, but rather of emigration. Europe's history, however, shows the opposite. Intra-European migration flows and immigrants from overseas have shaped Europe's societal and economic development since the beginning of industrialization. Consequently, businesses run by ethnic minorities are not a new phenomenon in Europe (Yildiz, 2017; Volery, 2017). While the debate in the UK and the Netherlands has been ongoing for the last two decades (cf. Clark and Drinkwater, 2000; Kloosterman and Rath, 2003), in other Western European countries such as Germany the topic only slowly entered the political, economic and research agenda (Yildiz, 2017; Bertelsmann Stiftung et al., 2016).

More recently, ethnic entrepreneurship in Europe has undergone a transition and a revival caused by two main factors. First, it has been reformed by the increase in new ethnic populations in Western European societies in the last two to three years (Oltmer, 2017; Ther, 2017; Volery, 2017). Second, it has been reshaped by new transnational and cross-border frameworks and conditions facilitated by Europe's open borders (Nowicka, 2013; Pries, 2011; Kaczmarczyk, 2008).

The latest immigration flows to Europe from overseas in 2015–2016, which became popularly known as the European *refugee crisis*, and the increasing intra-European movement of people have their bearing on the continent (Krastev, 2017; Ther, 2017). Especially Germany, as one of the most popular host countries for immigrants in Western Europe, was the focus of the newest immigration flows (Aiyar et al., 2016). In 2017, 650,670 refugees applied for asylum in one of the EU member states, and Germany accounting for 30% (198,255) was ranked first among the top eight countries in terms of numbers of "first-time asylum applications" (Eurostat, 2018). However, the number of EU immigrants entering Germany exceeded the number of refugees. In 2016 alone, 171,380 Romanians, 123,134 Poles, 66,790 Bulgarians, 51,163 Croatians and 42,698 Italians held the first three ranks, along with citizens from Hungary, Greece, Spain and other countries (BAMF, 2017).

Under certain conditions, these developments can create a breeding ground for the further materialization of *informal ethnic entrepreneurship*. First, fast labour market integration of the target groups is less successful (David and Coenen, 2017; Knuth, 2016) and barriers to running a business in the formal sector are insuperable for ethnic groups. Second, the ethnic customer base broadens and the free movement of people, goods, capital and ideas creates new yields and new growth opportunities.

The main objective of this chapter is to present innovative types of informal ethnic entrepreneurship. Often, literature on informal ethnic entrepreneurship (OECD, 2015) argues that informal ethnic entrepreneurs (comparable to ethnic entrepreneurs) are less innovative and stick to proven community needs, approaches and concepts. Applying an *informal ethnic business model canvas* to the case of a Polish informal ethnic entrepreneur in Germany, uncovering his informal ethnic cross-border business, this chapter sheds light on the motives, incentives and barriers of such an endeavour and its changes over time. Particular attention is given to transnational flows of knowledge, goods and ideas as well as network building since the EU opening of borders between Germany and Poland. In doing so, we argue that the opening of EU borders leads to innovative entrepreneurial activities, including informal ethnic businesses. Based on our results, initial ideas for facilitating transition processes from informal to formal ethnic entrepreneurship are presented.

Understanding (informal) ethnic entrepreneurship

Theoretical framework

There is a large body of literature describing migrant entrepreneurial activities and businesses run/owned by immigrants or individuals with different ethnic roots in the receiving, host or arrival countries (i.e. Yildiz, 2017; David, 2017; Volery, 2017; Pekkala Kerr and Kerr, 2016; Kloosterman and Rath, 2003). The most popular terms used in this context are (1) *immigrant economy/business/ entrepreneurship* and (2) *ethnic economy/business/entrepreneurship*. Nonetheless, there is no standard definition and the terms are used inconsistently depending on the background.

Referring to Haberfellner (2011) as well as Kloosterman and Rath (2003), the term *immigrant* is defined by the *process of migration, or the movement process itself*. Staying with their understanding, the term immigrant describes individuals with a first-hand experience of movement from one country to another, including their descendants (often also termed the second generation of immigrants in Western Europe; Yildiz, 2017). The term immigrant does not distinguish the motives or the conditions of a migration process, nor does it refer to a specific ethnic background. Generally, the term immigrant subsumes all incoming or once immigrated ethnic groups. *Ethnic*, on the contrary, is a set of connections, contacts and communication patterns between individuals with the same national background and/or the same migration experience (Yildiz, 2017; Haberfellner, 2011). More precisely, to be part of an ethnic group means having a common origin and sharing important segments of a common culture (Volery, 2007). In turn, the term immigrant excludes the cultural dimension in the first instance. It concentrates on the immigrated individuals over the past few decades, but disregards generations of ethnic ancestors who lived for centuries in a specific host country and created settings based on ethnicity.

In line with the terms immigrant and ethnic, Smelser and Swedberg (2010) define *ethnic economy* as consisting of the self-employed employers, their co-ethnic employees, and their unpaid family workers. Drawing on such understanding, Heberfellner (2011) sets limits on the definition and argues that consequently relatives of an ethnic group who work in other parts of the economy are no longer part of an ethnic economy. She also distinguishes between *immigrant* and *ethnic business*. According to her understanding, *immigrant business*, based on the aforementioned idea that immigrant refers to the migration process – the movement itself – includes the first and second generation of immigrants or people with a migration background (Yildiz, 2017) who run their own businesses. *Ethnic business* is not necessary linked to the connotation of the process of migration. It simply describes an economy and related businesses that are led and mainly owned by individuals of specific ethnic groups with the main idea of serving other members of the same ethnic group. In contrast, not every business that is founded by an immigrant is ethnic. Ethnic businesses are businesses specialized on the needs and concerns of a specific community. They provide an ethnic community with goods and services that are usually not available on the market of the host countries and can only [mainly] be fulfilled by co-ethnics. Often these goods and services refer to the food industry, traditional and culture-specific clothes as well as religious utensils. Volery (2007, p. 34) states that "[t]he greater the cultural differences between the ethnic group and the host country, the greater the need for ethnic goods and the bigger the potential niche market".

Yildiz (2017) points out that the concept of ethnic businesses/entrepreneurship and informal business/entrepreneurship overlap in literature and practice. Volery (2017) specifies that often, in order to keep a competitive market position, ethnic entrepreneurs become informal. Also, when the chances of legal labour market entrance are perceived weak, individuals of a specific ethnic community start informal entrepreneurial activities within their community, hoping to find support and security among peers. Their informal practices cover tax-related issues, labour (market) regulations and wages. Schmidt (2000) expands this list with elements of illegal employment, employment of family members or friends and ethnic network members, irregular payments and below-average wages. In reality, all these practices can be found. Nonetheless, some experts (OECD, 2015) argue that informal ethnic entrepreneurship often balances out the labour markets, is innovative under certain conditions, and has a chance of becoming formal when political frameworks and regulations change. Such reasoning is also part of the ongoing debate on social entrepreneurship (cf. Kleverbeck et al., 2017).

According to ethnic entrepreneurship, Yildiz (2017) identifies the following characteristics which likewise apply to informal ethnic entrepreneurship. (1) The entrepreneurs identify with their own ethnic group; (2) family members or further groups of the ethnic community are involved in the daily entrepreneurial activities; (3) the main customer base consists of members of the ethnic community; (4) as co-workers, suppliers and employees mainly members of the ethnic community are taken into consideration; (5) a horizontal and vertical networking of companies of the same kind and between upstream and downstream production steps can be observed. These characteristics are based on a common cultural background, ethnicity and social capital (Bourdieu, 1983).

The interactive model (Waldinger et al., 1990) supports the hypothesis, suggesting that the success of ethnic entrepreneurship depends on complex interactions and interlinkages between opportunity structures and group resources. All together, these ingredients create a protected space and a shelter for ethnic entrepreneurs and their co-ethnic workers, family and friends. In some cases, this protected space becomes a parallel informal labour market, with its own regulations that are fully endorsed by all participants. The parallel informal labour market is defined by so-called gentlemen's agreements among the members. Even if these agreements seem and are informal in comparison to the regulated formal labour market, for the involved participants this is often a unique opportunity to earn their own salary and to survive away from home. A huge factor here seems also to be disappointment about the "appropriate" dealing with incomers, ethnic differences and intercultural tensions between groups of individuals in the host countries.

Formation of (informal) ethnic entrepreneurship

Already at the beginning of the 19th century research on immigrant and ethnic entrepreneurship was widespread (cf. Weber, 1930; Simmel, 1950). Referring to this body of work, ethnic business usually starts with an ethnic entrepreneur's idea to serve other ethnic members, in order to fulfil their needs (Volery, 2007; Greene and Owen, 2004). The incentive to start an ethnic business is usually involuntary, the result of having no escape route. In this vein, further authors argue (cf. David and Coenen, 2017; Fregetto, 2004) that most immigrants faced disadvantages such as a lack of human capital, lack of highly developed language skills, challenges with the recognition of qualifications and unequal education opportunities. These disadvantages inhibit their entry in the labour market with regular salaried jobs. Self-employment often seems the only way out. In addition, discrimination of ethnic groups as well as immigrants remains a huge issue (cf. Kaas and Manger, 2010), foremost in times of increasing migration flows. Cultural differences, which become clearer with the newest refugee inflows to Europe, split European citizens in their opinions and create uncertainty and anxiety leading to populism, which again is mirrored in the even greater problems of labour market integration of the target groups (David, 2017; Krastev, 2017).

Especially newcomers, such as members of the current refugee flows in Europe, face strong barriers to the labour market and to formal entrepreneurship. Access to (permanent) work for refugees remains a key stumbling block, with unemployment, including youth unemployment, almost three times as high as among the native Western European populations (Huijnk and Andriessen, 2016; Terstriep et al., 2015). For many immigrants, self-employment seems a good way to enter the labour market faster (David, 2017; David and Coenen, 2017). However, they soon realize that starting their own business also involves tackling barriers. Prominent barriers are a lack of access to finance and regional knowledge bases, problems accessing open markets, which typically are occupied by local entrepreneurs, and the lack of established networks and social capital as supportive and protective mechanisms.

Against this background, Castells and Portes (1989) and Sassen (1996) regard the creation of informal ethnic entrepreneurship as often being necessity driven. Other literature (i.e. Maloney, 2004) claims that many individuals choose to work in informal sectors because this is worth more than regular employment possibilities. Recent literature (Williams, 2009) explores the way in which both factors of motivation can lead to the choice of informal types of work: the necessity motivation shifts to the opportunity motivation. This means that often individuals who enter informal entrepreneurship start with the necessity to earn money. As time progresses, they recognize more opportunities and stick with or even expand their businesses in informal ways.

With a closer look at Europe and especially at Germany, Yildiz (2017) and Volery (2017) argue that the boom in ethnic entrepreneurship started with deindustrialization. Here, several individuals of ethnic groups, who were even harder hit by the crisis of losing jobs than the German population, started an ethnic entrepreneurship. This mainly refers to the group of guest workers who were actively recruited for jobs related to the coal mining and steel sectors. After job cuts, these groups had to transform. Among them were many low-skilled workers who had no choice but to start their own businesses as an act born of necessity. In this vein, the materialization of informal ethnic entrepreneurship also grew. Nowadays, as is illustrated in the following, informal ethnic entrepreneurship or the attitude towards informal working conditions can be inherited by the next generations. A practice very similar to formal ways. Hereby, the next generation lives and believes a narrative created and reproduced over decades by their ancestors. In the case of Germany, these narratives are often based on the disappointment of individuals of specific ethnic groups about their high motivation to participate in the host societies and then being refused. Often this mix of anger, refusal and helplessness shifts moral borders from formal to informal actions. The motivation to prove one's skills and abilities and to overcome obstacles is a strong force and a rebellion against societal and economic disparities in the host countries.

Focusing on Germany

Ethnic and/or immigrant entrepreneurs in Germany

For a long time, neither ethnic nor immigrant entrepreneurship was on the German agenda. This might be one of the explanations for why there is no concrete data available that distinguishes these two groups of entrepreneurs by immigration and/or by ethnicity. Taking quantitative data on the immigrant or ethnic economy into account means dealing with data on entrepreneurs who are immigrants or the children of immigrants in the second or even third generation. In the existing data, immigrant is used as a synonym for ethnic and vice versa. Referring to migration and self-employment, it can be observed that to date approximately 750,000 self-employed persons in Germany, one-sixth of all self-employed entrepreneurs, are (im)migrants, with different backgrounds, different ethnicities and different migration processes (Yildiz, 2017). Thus, the importance of the group for the German economy and society is immense in terms of creating new employment possibilities, employment rates and the building of social, economic and financial capital.

Germany was and still is considered by various groups of immigrants as the most desirable destination country in Europe, because it is viewed as being among the more prosperous EU member states with a stable labour market, despite any crisis (Aiyar et al., 2016). Since industrialization Germany has mainly been associated with labour migration. Particularly prominent are Polish labour immigrants in Germany, who are pushed and pulled (Lee, 1966) by factors such as high wages and quality of life differences, labour market stability and the geographic proximity of the two countries.

But, beside the Polish ethnicity, there are numbers of further ethnic groups and types of immigrants living in Germany. Taking into account the time span after World War II, David and Coenen (2017) define five main immigrant groups in Germany: (1) *guest workers*; (2) *ethnic German resettlers*; (3) *EU-immigrants*; (4) *third countries immigrants*; and (5) *refugees*.

Starting in the 1950s, guest workers were actively acquired by Germany to perform so-called low-skilled work in the agricultural and the industrial sectors (i.e. coal mine and steel mill workers). In the first generation, this immigrant group was mainly dominated by a male workforce and late family reunions. Guest workers were acquired from Turkey, Greece, Italy or Spain, sometimes Morocco and Tunisia. The group of ethnic German resettlers is defined by migration inflows to Germany from mainly Eastern European countries since the 1950s, with a peak in the 1980s and 1990s. Ethnic German resettlers are ethnic Germans from the successor states of the former Soviet Union and from other Eastern European states such as Poland. By means of a special acceptance process they are entitled to live in Germany. Being recognized as ethnic German resettlers means that immigrants automatically receive German nationality. German ethnicity is key in the acceptance and certification procedure carried out by the Federal Office of Administration. The group of EU-immigrants became prominent in Germany with the opening of EU borders and the free movement of workers, giving EU-immigrants permission to reside in the receiving country with no time restrictions mainly for working reasons. Free movement of workers is a fundamental principle enshrined in Article 45 of the Treaty on the Functioning of the European Union and developed by EU secondary legislation and the case law of the Court of Justice. EU citizens are entitled to (1) look for a job in another EU country; (2) work there without needing a work permit; (3) reside there for that purpose and (4) stay there even after employment has finished; as well as (5) enjoy equal treatment with nationals in access to employment, working conditions and all other social and tax advantages. There is a predominance of people from South and East Europe (Poland, Romania, Spain and Italy) among today's EU-immigrants. As a further group, the third countries immigrants are characterized by labour migration in the higher education sectors and the status of the European *blue card*. The EU blue card is a residence permit for the purpose of gainful employment for non-EU citizens with an academic qualification and a certain minimum income. It facilitates mobility within the EU, excluding the member states Denmark, Ireland and the UK. Finally, refugees are immigrants characterized by an involuntary migration process, mainly caused by war or/and danger. In comparison to other immigrant groups, refugees are often marked by strong differences in culture, qualifications, work experience and religion in comparison to the receiving/host countries.

Each of these groups has its own characteristics. While the guest workers and the ethnic German resettlers often ended up employed in low-skilled sectors (i.e. steel and coal mine workers), the groups of the newcomer immigrants such as the EU-immigrants and the third countries immigrants are better educated and therefore are often termed highly skilled immigrants. While once the guest workers made up the biggest group of ethnic or immigrant entrepreneurs in Germany (Metzger, 2016), today the groups of EU-immigrants grow steadily (Yildiz, 2017). Among them are Polish people, who always have been very active in entrepreneurial activities in Europe, especially since cross-border entrepreneurship has been allowed and welcomed. Generally, regarding the distribution of self-employed persons in Germany with an immigration background by country of origin in 2016, the highest numbers of self-employed persons were from Poland (110,000) followed by Turks (94,000) (ifm, 2017). And also at the regional level, as the example of the city of Hamburg shows, from a total of 18,556 immigrant entrepreneurs, Poles ranked first with 5,775, followed by Turks with 2,042 as well as Bulgarian (1,714) and Romanian (1,502).

In the following, this chapter discusses how the open borders in the EU changed and to some extent innovated entrepreneurial activities in Europe, also regarding informal ethnic businesses.

Cross-border ethnic entrepreneurship

Transnational activities of entrepreneurs

In the early 2000s, when the European Union began to merge also in terms of shared territories by opening EU country borders, concepts based on transnational cross-border activities of migrants (cf. Wagner et al., 2013; Pries, 2001a,b,c, 2011) became popular. In the Anglo-Saxon and Anglo-American research context, it was Saxenian (2007, 2012) who unlocked the discussion on transnational migration networks using the example of Indian re-migrants (termed by the author as the New Argonauts), returning home from Silicon

Valley – full of experience and motivated to start their own businesses. The specific feature the author emphasizes in her studies is that the start-up activities of return migrants are based on cross-border or in this case transnational migration networks between the US and India. Transnational networks not only concentrate on two-way co-operation between parties, such as the domestic and the host regions, but also allow the actors to interconnect with ties in other regions/countries (David, 2015).

In the work of Saxenian (2007, 2012) and Pries (2001c), discussion on transnational migration networks and activities is strongly connected to highly skilled workers and migrant entrepreneurs who reach out to broad communities, based on their activity radius and international work experience. Studies by Ratten et al. (2017) on transnational entrepreneurs and the diaspora show how these target groups can innovate global societies by providing new products, services and processes. In the following section, we present how informal ethnic entrepreneurs are also interconnected transnationally and that cross-border activities and the opening of EU borders, as the European example shows, also brought new possibilities to informal ethnic businesses.

The use of further relations relying on second-hand contacts are called the "weak ties" of a network: the person I know personally knows another, whom I don't yet know personally, but I can trust him to co-operate, because of the involvement of an intermediary person, who is someone both I and he know (Granovetter, 1973). This principle can especially be used in an ethnic community, where trust-based connections, common ideas of helping each other and relying on common cultural roots are almost an unwritten law. In addition, Nowicka (2013) points out the fact that transnational connections are necessary for migrant self-positioning. They draw possibilities for the validation of cultural, social and economic capital in more than one country. In the previously described case of not being validated in the host country, transnational connections are a possible way to upgrade one's self-importance and entitlement. The human capital that was not recognized in the host country gains even more recognition in a transnational and cross-border context. Here, the (informal) ethnic entrepreneur all of the sudden becomes an important *middleman* (Volery, 2017).

Migration is often related to a [temporal] lowering of social position in the host country (Nowicka, 2013). Some of the immigrants manage gradually to improve their status. For those who do not, because of, for example, poor labour market entrance conditions, cross-border or transnational positioning is not solely a matter of financial protection but an identity-saving measure. In her work Nowicka (2013) presents cases of Polish migrants who position themselves in one single space, migrants who are positioned bi-locally and those who even overlap their social positioning. The latter do not switch between two local activities, but create a third space of interaction and entrepreneurial activities – located in-between and spreading wings to both sides of the borders or even internationally. This third space makes it possible for the target groups to take both sides of the coin into account and create benefits on both sides.

Occasions of cross-border entrepreneurship

There are many mechanisms influencing the development of a business. The past decades have exposed how international migration, knowledge, technological and financial flows can make regional businesses flourish or, on the contrary, break them down. Especially businesses and entrepreneurs in peripheral and non-core regions often struggle with growth and even survival (David, 2015). Smallbone et al. (2012) argue that cross-border entrepreneurship or entrepreneurial actions can provide opportunities for regional development as well as individual entrepreneurs. In the first instance, cross-border entrepreneurship relates to regions and countries bordering each other such as, for example, Germany and Poland. The term cross-border entrepreneurship does not exclude any kind of entrepreneurial activities. Such co-operations can range from formalized companies and even joint ventures to informal activities across the borders.

Cross-border entrepreneurial activities arose as a consequence of the opening of EU borders within the European Union. The extent to which the opportunities created by the enlargement of Europe can play out for an entrepreneur depends on several factors such as his/her economic environment; knowledge base and experience background; resources available; knowledge of international markets; and historical, social and cultural factors. The latter factors can help the entrepreneur starting a cross-border or transnational business to operate in changing business environments and use cross-border co-operation to innovate and grow (Smallbone et al., 2012; Schmiz, 2011). Positive effects of cross-border businesses are entering new or additional markets, and tapping into suppliers, capital and know-how. In addition, Turkina and Thai (2013) suggest stronger consideration of the social structures and networks in which ethnic entrepreneurs are embedded. The focus then lies not solely on *when* and *how* an ethnic business is founded, but foremost on *who* (groups and individuals) is involved in such an endeavour. In line with the studies by Turkina and Thai (2013), other authors argue that social (actor) networks and social capital impact the creation, the nature and even the success of entrepreneurial activities (Putnam, 1993; Burt, 2005; Kleverbeck et al., 2017). Serageldin and Grootaert (2000) and Putnam (1993) define (social capital) resources as collective norms, networks and organizations. The most recent definitions by Durlauf and Fafchamps (2004, p. 5) state, "[. . .] social capital is [. . .] network-based processes that generate beneficial outcomes through norms and trust". Based on this, we argue that this also refers to ethnic entrepreneurs and even more strongly to informal ethnic entrepreneurs, where trust is at the core of the business.

Informal ethnic business model canvas

Methodological approach

In order to gain better insights into the formation and unfolding of an informal ethnic cross-border business, and to shed light on the motives, incentives and barriers of such an endeavour, as well as its changes over time, a case study of a Polish informal ethnic entrepreneur was undertaken. Access to the informal ethnic entrepreneur was gained through the weak ties of personal networks of the authors. The narrative interview was conducted with the involvement of a third party. Due to the informality of the entrepreneurship, the informal ethnic entrepreneur did not accept personal invitations for an interview. Additional information on, for example, framework conditions was provided by further Polish network members in Germany, who participate as co-ethnic workers in similar businesses or are part of the Polish diaspora. To gain information on informal ethnic entrepreneurship, particular attention was given to transnational flows of knowledge, goods and ideas, as well as to network building since the EU opening of borders between Germany and Poland. To get a better overview of informal ethnic entrepreneurship the case was analysed at two points in time: before and after EU enlargement.

Business model canvas

According to Osterwalder and Pigneur (2010) a business model describes the rationale of how an organization creates, delivers and captures venture. Consequently, the nine building blocks of a business model are the descriptions of customer segments, value proposition, channels, customer relationships, revenue stream, key resources, key activities, key partnerships and cost structure. Thus, the business model canvas is a tool including these nine blocks, allowing everyone who is business oriented or involved in any entrepreneurial activity to picture a new or an existing business model. In this way, a business model canvas also allows the illustration of untypical, disruptive business models such as, in this case, informal ethnic entrepreneurship. These are often poorly understood, but frequently transform societies and build new competitive fields of action interlinking sectors, countries and industries. Applying two *informal ethnic business model canvases* to the case of a Polish informal ethnic entrepreneur in Germany before and after EU enlargement, we argue that the opening of the EU's borders and especially transnational or cross-border undertakings lead to innovative entrepreneurial activities, which also concern informal ethnic businesses.

The case of a Polish informal ethnic entrepreneur in Germany

Background information

It is a popular notion, not least in the newspapers, that the cross-border pilfering of cars between Poland and Germany has been a huge deal for decades (Spiegel Online, 2018). Cross-border vehicle theft is only one consequence of the enormous informal car and car parts industry that is an unwelcomed, but well-established, cross-border informal ethnic business sector between these two countries. This chapter does not discuss illegal activities in detail, but indicates that there is also this side of the coin to the informal car sector.

The beginnings of the car and car parts industry in Poland dates back to socialist times when Western goods, products, ideas and practices were not allowed and were not even available. Moreover, possession of a car (Eastern product only) involved a long process including the placing of one's name on an order list without any guarantee of getting the car, and certainly not for many years to come. In addition to the order list and the waiting time, only a few citizens in the socialist Poland possessed the financial means to pay for such a luxury product as a car. Mostly, it was individuals living on the remittances of their emigrant family members in Western countries who were able to access the finances to afford these expenses.

The demand for cars as luxuries and especially Western trademarks such as BMW, Mercedes or VW increased constantly. These trademarks not only symbolized luxury goods for Polish citizens, but also a way of life oriented towards Western countries, policies and ideologies. Such cars were a rebellion against the socialist system and a symbol of the illusion of a non-existent freedom.

After the transformation of the political system, it was to be expected that the demand for Western car brands decreases, as these goods started to be available in Poland, especially after EU enlargement and the EU opening of borders. But, on the contrary, demand further increased, driven by the wage and quality of life differences, and the opportunities which were created by cross-border and transnational co-operations to satisfy people's wishes. At the same time, the demand in Germany for cheaper cars, car parts and especially car services and repairs grew. Cheaper services were in particular demand among the Polish ethnic group in Germany. From the time in Poland before their emigration they were used to car services and car repair not always being a recognized profession, but rather something of a hobby or a semi-profession. Therefore, it was cheaper, often informal and uncertified.

Market niche before and after the opening of EU borders

Against this background, the informal ethnic entrepreneurship described in-depth here started originally with the business idea of buying and selling cars/car parts and offering car-related services and repairs below German market prices. To make this possible, cars and car parts were offered second-hand or damaged, but if required could be restored to their original state by semi-professional car mechanics. The main customer group for the business were Polish ethnics belonging to the immigrant group of ethnic German resettlers. They were open to such business ideas, knowing the car sector structures and prices of their home country.

After the opening of EU borders the business idea extended. Due to new possibilities of cross-border mobility and new technologies, buying and selling cars/car parts as well as car services and repair became cheaper, and offered enhanced opportunities. Also, the frequencies of the buying and selling of goods increased and the customer circle grew. How exactly this plays out will be presented in the following by applying a business model canvas to this case.

The case of the Polish informal ethnic entrepreneur

The informal ethnic entrepreneur in the case studied is a Polish man aged 40 years. He is a member of the immigrant group of ethnic German resettlers and immigrated to Germany at the age of 11. Due to the migration process he went through, per definition he still is part of the first generation of immigrants. He is married to a Polish wife who grew up in Poland where she completed her education. As is shown in the following this marriage is part of the entrepreneur's business and probably the strongest cross-border connection to Poland and the migration networks. It is important to note that the informal ethnic entrepreneur holds dual nationality, which is by no means the exception for ethnic German resettlers. He thus enjoys privileges that play out positively for his business. He, for instance, can be a car holder in Germany with a car registered at lower costs in Poland. Moreover, he can formally and very quickly enter both labour markets without language barriers and start a formal business in both countries.

As regards his educational biography, he finalized comprehensive school in Germany and an apprenticeship in the insurance sector. For about three years he worked as an insurance salesman focusing on the ethnic group of Poles living in Germany, selling car insurance in his community. These interactions with the Polish ethnic group laid the ground for his later customer base, naturally spinning strong connections in his ethnic community by business relations and trust building. It is hard to determine whether he already started his informal ethnic entrepreneurial activities by selling car insurance informally, or if his ethnic customer group opened up the path to this new sector.

His main motivation to start the informal business was twofold. After losing his job at the insurance office, it was driven by necessity. Later, after the business was established he was motivated by the opportunity to earn "quick money". Moreover, he always struggled with full acceptance as an immigrant in Germany. The narrative he inherited involved the early job loss of his father, whose qualifications were never recognized after the immigration to Germany and who was thus not integrated into German society; this brought him to the point of questioning himself. The feeling of being not accepted and being a second-class citizen in Germany (his own perception) was a downward spiral in his career path and at the same time the beginning of even stronger activities in the Polish community. Since then, each disappointment in business and his personal life was connected to his origin and ethnicity. The more he failed in German society, the more successfully he actively grew his informal business in the Polish ethnic German resettlers' community, and with further associated groups of immigrants and individuals who ideologically fit his mind set.

BMC before the opening of EU borders

The following business model canvas (BMC) applies to the beginning and the first years of establishment of the informal ethnic business before the opening of EU borders. Informal in this case means avoidance of tax payments and paying low or below-average wages to co-ethnic employees. Also, the wage payments are irregular, and only are incurred when an order is accomplished.

The BMC (cf. Figure 5.1) clearly shows that before the possibilities of cross-border entrepreneurial activities, the informal business was strongly focused on the Polish ethnic community in the host country, i.e. Germany. It addresses a niche market by offering possible car services in a low-price segment for the immigrant group of ethnic German resettlers from Poland in the host country. Their needs and demands are met by cheap prices, day and night services, smaller services for free and all-round service using the key resource of the entrepreneur, i.e. his abilities as a network builder and a middleman. The informal ethnic entrepreneur is not involved in the process of car repairs personally. For these activities, he employs co-ethnic workers. He concentrates solely on the buying and selling of cars, but acts in the background. The buying and selling arrangements are also outsourced to further co-ethnic entrepreneurs, to whom he pays a commission for the official arrangement process.

In order to guarantee fast and cheap car services as well as car repair, the main key partners at this stage are co-ethnic co-workers, family members and other entrepreneurs (so-called co-opetitors – a horizontal and vertical networking of companies of the same kind) in Germany, belonging to the same ethnicity and providing the key entrepreneur with illegal employment, low wages, no wages at all and a safe, trust-based environment. The key activities offered are buying and selling second-hand used cars, car parts and car services and repairs. All services are offered licence- and tax-free without invoices. In addition, due to contacts to former colleagues in the insurance sector, on demand car insurance could also be offered. Inquiries into channels of communication and advertisement used for the informal ethnic entrepreneurship made clear that free information management is impossible because of the informal status of the business. In this case communication occurs via direct channels. The usage of personal contacts and hearsay among the ethnic customers, as well as the Polish church diaspora, were the two main communication tools used to increase the customer base.

BMC after the opening of EU borders

With the opening of the EU borders the informal ethnic business introduced in the previous section changed (cf. Figure 5.2). It seems almost as if the ethnic part of the business opened up and became a cross-border and even a transnational informal business. With reference to the informal parts of the business, there are strong overlaps with formal activities, especially with regards to the value proposition. The possibility of cross-border activities enabled formal, certificated car services to also be offered at low prices because there are still immense differences in maintenance expenses and wages between Poland and Germany. In consequence, buying a damaged car in Germany and repairing it in Poland is a cross-border win–win situation for the customer, the middleman and the car mechanic. This is especially the case when the car is sold at a higher price in Germany after repair. Moreover, with the increase of the customer base from ethnic

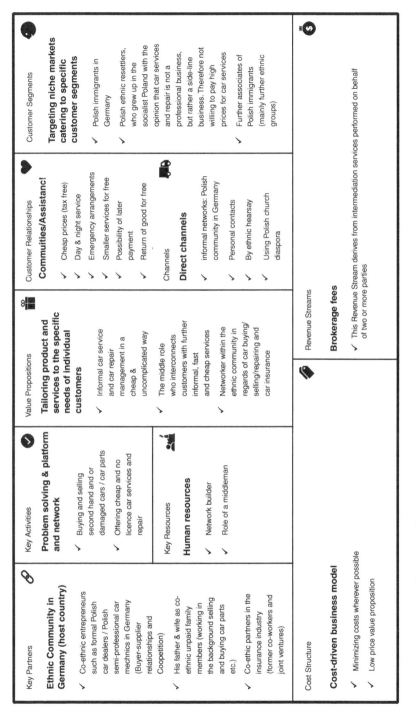

Key Partners	Key Activities	Value Propositions	Customer Relationships	Customer Segments
Ethnic Community in Germany (host country)	**Problem solving & platform and network**	**Tailoring product and services to the specific needs of individual customers**	**Commuities/Assistanc!**	**Targeting niche markets catering to specific customer segments**
✓ Co-ethnic entrepreneurs such as formal Polish car dealers / Polish semi-professional car mechnics in Germany (Buyer-supplier relationships and Coopetition)	✓ Buying and selling second hand and or damaged cars / car parts	✓ Informal car service and car repair management in a cheap & uncomplicated way	✓ Cheap prices (tax free)	✓ Polish immigrants in Germany
	✓ Offering cheap and no licence car services and repair		✓ Day & night service	✓ Polish ethnic resettlers, who grew up in the socialist Poland with the opinion that car services and repair is not a professional business, but rather a side-line business. Therefore not willing to pay high prices for car services
			✓ Emergency arrangements	
			✓ Smaller services for free	
		✓ The middle role who interconnects customers with further informal, fast and cheap services	✓ Possibility of later payment	
			✓ Return of good for free	
	Key Resources		**Channels**	
✓ His father & wife as co-ethnic unpaid family members (working in the background selling and buying car parts etc.)	**Human resources**	✓ Networker within the ethnic community in regards of car buying/ selling/repairing and car insurance	**Direct channels**	✓ Further associates of Polish immigrants (mainly further ethnic groups)
	✓ Network builder		✓ informal networks: Polish community in Germany	
✓ Co-ethic partners in the insurance industry (former co-workers and joint ventures)	✓ Role of a middleman		✓ Personal contacts	
			✓ By ethnic hearsay	
			✓ Using Polish church diaspora	

Cost Structure	Revenue Streams
Cost-driven business model	**Brokerage fees**
✓ Minimizing costs wherever possible	✓ This Revenue Stream derives from intermediation services performed on behalf of two or more parties
✓ Low price value proposition	

Figure 5.1 Business model canvas before opening of EU borders

Source: Own compilation

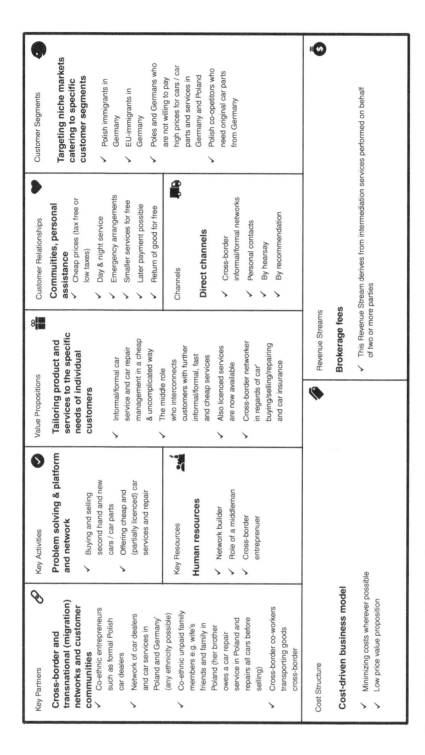

Figure 5.2 Business model canvas after opening of EU borders

Source: Own compilation

Polish communities in Germany to German and Polish EU citizens in Germany and Poland and also in other EU countries the numbers of orders increase, networks are expanded and the role of the informal ethnic entrepreneur moves to the interface between informal and formal.

Innovation in informal ethnic entrepreneurship – conclusion

The comparison of the two informal ethnic business models before and after the opening of the EU borders, utilizing a business model canvas, helped to gain insights into the development trajectories induced by changing framework conditions. The opening of the borders within the EU gave leeway to further develop the business model, i.e. to innovate, in terms of cross-border and transnational business activities and new network connections. Ratten et al. (2017), along with Dimitratos et al. (2015), have already emphasized the importance of transnational entrepreneurs as a new business phenomenon, representing a fluid context in which established arrangements may be expected to change. In our example, we tried to illustrate precisely these changes with new arrangements among cross-border and transnational business partners and a broader customer base. By the creation of new common transnational social capital, including new actor networks (customers and partners), former co-operation and business activities are transformed. David (2015) cites Putnam (1993) and Serageldin and Grootaert (2000) who considered social capital as potential and resources that play out beneficially for all parties involved. As these benefits refer to collaborations between individuals and groups, such social actor networks have value (Putnam, 2000). In this vein, this case of an informal ethnic entrepreneur is a good example of how transnational and cross-border entrepreneurship can bring more value and benefit to the informal parts of a business and all parties involved. Through transnational activities the informal gains a higher profile and the informal ethnic entrepreneur, having been considered as a kind of outsider in the host country and the middleman within his ethnic community, suddenly becomes the crux of the matter, centrally placed in the transnational network. The activities formally regarded as bordering the shadow economy now reveal possibilities of change into formal shapes of entrepreneurship. Here new institutional framework conditions need to come into effect, which cover transnational business law.

This chapter envisioned not only to illustrate the innovative character of informal ethnic entrepreneurship but also to illustrate potential paths from informal to formal activities. In this regard, we first can conclude from the narrative interview that the motivation of the informal ethnic entrepreneur to change from informal to formal entrepreneurship rather is low due to his social status: In the German system, he still acts informal, but has established ways of surviving beyond established structures and institutions. By the ethnic community, in contrast, he is recognized as a middleman, gaining appreciation through his networking capacities. The dark side of such a position is that, for example, the German tax system cannot get hold of his business activities. Equally important is the loss of his implicit knowledge and channels of cross-border knowledge flows. In Poland, the situation is quite opposite, as he enjoys the status of a successful *businessman*, which especially to the elder Polish generations is an aspired position and even profession.

It remains an open question to what extend future regulatory frameworks can facilitate the formalization of informal ethnic entrepreneurial activities. Particularly, this question arises in countries (see here the example of Poland) where informal business still is considered legitimate, and thus enjoys high acceptance in society. This in turn raises the question whether declining acceptance in combination with supportive measures cloud function as a trigger for a self-motivated transition from informal to formal ethnic entrepreneurship. Due to the limitation of our research with just one case, this question cannot be answered yet, but may stimulate future research in this field.

References

Aiyar, S., Barkbu, B., Batini, N., Berger, H., Detragiache, E., Dizioli, A., Ebeke, Ch., Lin, H., Kaltani, L., Sosa, S., Spilimbergo, A., and Topalova, P. (2016). The Refugee Surge in Europe: Economic Challenges. IMF Staff Discussion Note. International Monetary Fund.

Bertelsmann Stiftung/Sachs, A., Hoch, M., Münch, C., and Seidle, H. (2016). Migrantenunternehmen in Deutschland zwischen 2005 und 2014. Ausmaß, ökonomische Bedeutung: Einflussfaktoren und Förderung auf Ebene der Bundesländer.

Bourdieu, P. (1983). Ökonomisches Kapital – Kulturelles Kapital – Soziales Kapital. In R. Kreckel (eds.), *Soziale Ungleichheiten.* Soziale Welt Sonderband 2, Göttingen, 183–198.

Burt, R.S. (2005). *Brokerage and Closure: An Introduction to Social Capital.* Oxford and New York: Oxford University Press.

Castells, M., and Portes, A. (1989). World underneath: The origins, dynamics and effects of the informal economy. In A. Portes, M. Castells and L. Benton (eds.), *The Informal Economy: Studies in Advanced and Less Developing Countries.* Baltimore: John Hopkins University Press, 1–19.

Clark, K., and Drinkwater, S. (2000). Pushed out or pulled in? Self-employment among ethnic minorities in England and Wales. *Labour Economics,* 7(5), 603–628.

David, A. (2017). Migrantisches Unternehmertum: eine Chance der Arbeitsmarktintegration für geflüchtete Menschen? Internet-Dokument. Gelsenkirchen: Inst. Arbeit und Technik. Forschung Aktuell, Nr. 02/2017.

David, A. (2015). *Human Capital and the Role of Networks: Migration, Inclusion and New Qualification for a Sustainable Regional Economy.* University of Twente.

David, A., and Coenen, F. (2017). Immigrant entrepreneurship – A chance for labour market integration of refugees? In A. David and I. Hamburg (eds.), *Entrepreneurship and Entrepreneurial Skills in Europe: Examples to Improve Potential Entrepreneurial Spirit.* Leverkusen: Barbara Budrich Publishers, 77–101.

Dimitratos, P., Buck, T., Fletcher, M., and Li, N. (2015). The motivation of international entrepreneurship: The case of Chinese transnational entrepreneurs. *International Business Review,* In Press.

Durlauf, S.N., and Fafchamps, M. (2004). Social Capital. Working Paper 10485. National Bureau of Economic Research, Cambridge.

Fregetto, E. (2004). Immigrant and ethnic entrepreneurship: A U.S. perspective. In H.P. Welsch (ed.), *Entrepreneurship: The Way Ahead*. New York: Routledge, 253–268.

Granovetter, M. (1973). The strength of the weak ties. *The American Journal of Sociology*, 78(6), 1360–1380.

Greene, P., and Owen, M. (2004). Race and ethnicity. In W.B. Gartner, K.G. Shaver, N.M. Carter and P.D. Reynolds (eds.), *Handbook of Entrepreneurial Dynamics: The Process of Business Creation*. Thousand Oaks, CA: Sage Publications, 26–38.

Haberfellner, R. (2011). Entrepreneurship von Migrant Innen. AMS Info 191/192. Retrieved from: www.forschungsnetzwerk.at/downloadpub/AMSinfo191_192.pdf [Accessed 6 March 2018].

Huijnk, W., and Andriessen, I. (2016). Integration in sight? A review of eight domains of integration of migrants in the Netherlands, Social Cultural Planning Bureau the Netherlands SCP Report 2016–32.

Institut für Mittelstandsforschung (ifm), Universität Mannheim/ Leicht, R., Berwing, S. (2017). Gründungspotenziale von Menschen mit ausländischen Wurzeln. Entwicklungen, Erfolgfaktoren, Hemnisse, Studie im Auftrag des BMWi, Kurzfassung.

Kaas, L., and Manger, Ch. (2010). Ethnic discrimination in Germany's labour market: A field experiment. Discussion Paper. Institute for the Study of Labour, IZA DP No. 4741.

Kaczmarczyk, P. (2008). Arbeitsmigration und der polnische Arbeitsmarkt. Working Paper: Die Zukunft des Europäischen Wirtschafts- und Sozialmodells.

Kleverbeck, M., Terstriep, J., Deserti, A., and Rizzo, F. (2017). Social entrepreneurship: The challenge of hybridity. In A. David and I. Hamburg (eds.), *Entrepreneurship and Entrepreneurial Skills in Europe*. Leverkusen: Barbara Budrich Publishers, 47–76.

Kloosterman, R., and Rath, J. (2003). *Immigrant Entrepreneurs: Venturing Abroad in the Age of Globalization*. New York: Berg.

Knuth, M. (2016). Arbeitsmarktintegration von Flüchtlingen. Arbeitsmarktpolitik reformieren, Qualifikationen vermitteln. WISO Diskurs, Friedrich-Ebert-Stiftung, 21/2016.

Krastev, I. (2017). *After Europe*. Philadelphia: University Pennsylvania Press.

Lee, E.S. (1966). A theory of migration. *Demography*, 5(1), 47–57 and in J.A. Jackson (eds.), *Migration*. Cambridge: Cambridge University Press, 1969, 282–297.

Maloney, W.F. (2004). Informality revisited. *World Development*, 32(7), 1159–1178.

Metzger, G. (2016). Migranten überdurchschnittlich gründungsaktiv – Arbeitsmarkt spielt große Rolle. KfW Research Fokus Wirtschaft, Nr. 115.

Nowicka, M. (2013). Positioning strategies of polish entrepreneurs in Germany: Transnationalizing Bourdieu's notion of capital. *International Sociology*, 28(I), 29–47. doi:10.1177/0268580912468919.

OECD (2015). *Policy Brief on Informal Entrepreneurship. Entrepreneurial Activities in Europe*. Luxembourg: Publications Office of the European Union.

Oltmer, J. (2017). Migration. Geschichte und Zukunft der Gegenwart. Konrad Theiss Verlag, Darmstadt.

Osterwalder, A., and Pigneur, Y. (2010). *Business Model Generation: A Handbook for Visionaries, Game Changers, and Challengers*. Indianapolis: Wiley.

Pekkala Kerr, S.P., and Kerr, W.R. (2016). Immigrant Entrepreneurship. Working Paper 17–011. Harvard Business School.

Pries, L. (2001a). The approach of transnational social spaces: Responding to new configurations of the social and the spatial. In L. Pries (eds.), *New Transnational Social Spaces. International Migration and Transnational Companies in the Early Twenty-First Century*. London: Routledge, 3–33.

Pries, L. (2001b). *Internationale Migration*. Bielefeld: transcript Verlag.

Pries, L. (2001c). *New Transnational Social Spaces: International Migration and Transnational Companies*. London: Routledge.

Pries, L. (2011). Transnationale Migration als Innovationspotenzial. In K. Engel, J. Großmann and B. Hombach (eds.), *Phönix flieg!: Das Ruhrgebiet entdeckt sich neu*. Essen: Klartext.

Putnam, R. (1993). The prosperous community: Social capital and public life. *The American Prospect*, 13, 13–45.

Putnam, R. (2000). *Bowling Alone: The Collapse and Revival of American Community*. New York: Simon and Schuster.

Ratten, V., Dana, L.-P., Ramadani, V., and Rezaei, S. (2017). Transnational entrepreneurship in a Diaspora. In S. Rezaei, L.-P., Dana and V. Ramadani (eds.), *Iranian Entrepreneurship, Deciphering the Entrepreneurial Ecosystem in Iran and in the Iranian Diaspora*. Switzerland: Springer, 181–194. doi:10.1007/978-3-319-50639-5_10.

Sassen, S. (1996). Metropolen des Weltmarkts. Die neue Rolle der Global Cities. Campus Verlag.

Saxenian, A. (2007). *The New Argonauts: Regional Advantage in a Global Economy*. Cambridge, MA: Harvard University Press.

Saxenian, A. (2012). The new argonauts, global search and local institution building. In P. Cooke, M.D. Parrilli and J.L. Curbelo (eds.), *Innovation, Global Change and Resilience*. Cheltenham: Edward Elgar Publishing, 25–42.

Serageldin, I., and Grootaert, Ch. (2000). Defining social capital: An integrating view. In P. Dasgupta and I. Serageldin (eds.), *Social Capital: A Multifaceted Perspective*. Washington, DC: World Bank.

Schmidt, D. (2000). Unternehmertum und Ethnizität. Ein seltsames Paar. *Prokla. Zeitschrift für kritische Sozialwissenschaft*, 30(3), 335–362.

Schmiz, A. (2011). *Transnationalität als Resource? Netzwerke vietnamischer Migrantinnen und Migranten zwischen Berlin und Vietnam*. Bielefeld: transcript Verlag.

Smallbone, D., Welter, F., and Xheneti, M. (2012). Entrepreneurship in Europe's border regions. In D. Smallbone, F. Welter and M. Xheneti (eds.), *Cross-Border Entrepreneurship and Economic Development in Europe's Border Regions*. Cheltenham: Edward Elgar, 1–20.

Simmel, G. (1950). The stranger. In K. Wolf (ed.), *The Sociology of Georg Simmel*. Glencoe IL: Free Press.

Smelser, N.J., and Swedberg, R. (2010). *The Handbook of Economic Sociology*. Princeton: Princeton University Press.

Terstriep, J., et al. (2015). Comparative report on social innovation across Europe. Deliverable D3.2 of the project 'Boosting the Impact of Social Innovation in Europe through Economic Underpinning' (SIMPACT), European Commission – 7th Framework Programme. Brussels: European Commission, DG Research and Innovation.

Ther, Ph. (2017). *Die Außenseiter, Flucht, Flüchtlinge und Integration im modernen Europa*. Berlin: Suhrkamp Verlag.

Turkina, E., and Thai, M.T.T. (2013). Social capital, networks, trust and immigrant entrepreneurship: A cross-country analysis. *Journal of Enterprising Communities: People and Places in the Global Economy*, 7(2), 108–124.

Volery, T. (2017). Ethnic entrepreneurship: A theoretical framework. In L.-P. Dana (ed.), *Handbook of Research on Ethnic Minority Entrepreneurship: A Co-Evolutionary View on Resource Management.* Cheltenham: Edward Elgar, 30–41.

Wagner, M., Fialkowska, K., Piechowska, M., and Lukowski, L. (2013). *Deutsches Waschpulver und polnische Wirtschaft. Die Lebenswelt polnischer Saisonarbeiter. Ethnographische Beobachtungen.* Bielefeld: transcript Verlag.

Waldinger, R., Aldrich, H., and Ward, R. (1990). Opportunities, group characteristics and strategies. In R. Waldinger, H. Aldrich and R. Ward (eds.), *Ethnic Entrepreneurs: Immigrant Business in Industrial Societies.* London: Sage, 13–48.

Weber, M. (1930). *The Protestant Ethic and the Spirit of Capitalism.* New York: Scribner.

Williams, C.C. (2009). The motives of off-the-books entrepreneurs: Necessity- or opportunity-driven? *International Entrepreneurship and Management Journal,* 5(2), 203–217.

Yildiz, Ö. (2017). *Migrantisch, weiblich, prekär? Über präkere Selbständigkeiten in der Berliner Friseurbranche.* Bielefeld: transcript Verlag.

Online references

Eurostat. Retrieved from: http://appsso.eurostat.ec.europa.eu/nui/submitViewTable Action.do [Accessed on 27 Mai 2018].

Bundesamt für Migration und Flüchtling (BAMF), Freizügigkeitsmonitoring: Migration von EU-Bürgern nach Deutschland, Jahresbericht 2016. Retrieved from http://www.bamf.de/SharedDocs/Anlagen/DE/Publikationen/Broschueren/freizuegigkeitsmonitoring-jahresbericht-2016.pdf?__blob=publicationFile [Accessed 18 June 2017].

Spiegel Online, Cross Border Pilfering, Slow Progress in Battle against Polish Car Thieves. Retrieved from: www.spiegel.de/international/europe/cross-border-pilfering-slow-progress-in-battle-against-polish-car-thieves-a-806979.html [Accessed 4 March 2018].

6 Exploring the excellence in socially responsible human resource practices

A case study from Spain

Jesus Barrena-Martinez, Macarena Lopez-Fernandez and Pedro Romero-Fernandez

> We are what we repeatedly do. Excellence, then, is not an act, but a habit.
> —Aristotle (384–322 BC)

Introduction

In the last few years, the proliferation of socially responsible rankings of companies such as 100 Best Companies to Work For, Great Place to Work and Top 50 socially responsible corporations give evidence of an awareness of measuring to what extent their Human Resource Areas are behaving in a responsible way, and consequently what is the contribution of a responsible orientation in the HRM area.

One relevant example of a company located in the first position of these rankings is Google. The giant multinational has a great positive reputation in terms of their human capital. In this case, the firm is not only concerned with the attraction of talent, retaining a great number of US employees (44,862), but also tries to offer them broader perks. For instance, according to the index 100 Best Companies to Work For, Google offers paid time off for volunteering, an onsite fitness centre, discounted gym memberships, an onsite medical care facility and college tuition reimbursement to employees, among other benefits. Additionally, the company provides a wide flextime programme for their workers, with holidays (13 days), vocational programmes (15 days) and sick days (unlimited). Surprisingly, the salary of the chief executive officer and director of Google in 2013 was merely $1. The market in recent years is reading the signals of companies like Google, where the number of job applicants has been considerably over one and a quarter million. In this way, the company is sending a clear message to their competitors and different companies in other sectors: the employee is the key for unlocking the value of companies, and consequently the employee's needs and satisfaction should be one of the primary aims, which surely makes a difference.

Based on the stakeholder theory it is important to consider 'any group or individual who can affect or be affected by the decisions and the achievement of corporate objectives' (Freeman, 1984, p. 25). Given the multiple parties involved in organizational activities, Freeman and authors such as Clarkson (1995) suggest that it is necessary to differentiate and prioritize them according to one criterion in order to properly meet their requirements with a logical order. These previous works use as a consensus a double distinction of stakeholders regarding their nature and the relationship established with the organization: (1) a **primary group**, which usually has a formal contract with the firm and is essential for its proper functioning (owners, shareholders, employees, unions, customers, suppliers, etc.) and (2) a **secondary group,** which, despite not being directly involved in the economic activities of the company and not having a contractual relationship with it, can exercise a significant influence on its activity (citizens, competitors, local community, the government, public, etc.).

Considering the employee as a key and primary stakeholder for their contribution to business success, a socially responsible company should take into account their needs and requirements in order to generate a positive output from their commitment, engagement and performance. But the case of Google is not new. For decades, organizational strategies and actions have been adapted to requirements and environmental pressures. For example, one study by Drucker (1954) reflects the need to take public opinion into account in the decision-making process of any organization. According to the author, this idea is based on the experiences of multinationals such as Ford and General Motors, which in the mid-1950s received criticism from the press, media and various national regulatory institutions due to their developing irresponsible behaviours which did not consider the interests of their community. These companies had to develop further actions to regain the trust of their stakeholders (creating customer channels of attention, collaborating with environmental organizations, implementing a social volunteer programme for employees, etc.).

Considering this argument, the response to the context in which companies operate, keeping their actions and behaviours consistent with principles demanded by external and internal context, is considered vital for organizational survival (Campbell, 2006). This internalization process of a set of norms, beliefs, values and principles accepted by society and the community allowing organizations to achieve the support and backing of their activity is known as legitimacy (Suchman, 1995). On these grounds and as a continuation of the open systems theory developed by Von Bertanlanffy and Katz and Khan, the institutional approach emerges to explain how organizations should act according to a system of social values and the rules of the game in tune with society's expectations. Among the advantages of this process, it is noted that those organizations which can achieve greater legitimacy than their competitors can have more efficient access to resources from certain stakeholders – investor funds, support from government, increased sales and customer loyalty, access to the negotiation of contracts with different suppliers and distributors, obtaining the respect and commitment of employees, etc. This process can help to improve organizational economic and financial performance.

Coming back to the case of Google, its revenue in 2014 reached $55.5 billion. Despite the current economic and financial situation, where many countries are immersed in a crisis state, most companies want to experiment with the Google situation of being a leader in responsible and human terms. The question is, what are the ways to design and formulate socially responsible strategies and policies able to improve and maximize employees' efforts, commitments and performance? Some recent contributions such as those of Jamali et al. (2015) offered some clues in clarifying the important role, objectives and synergies between HRM and CSR in a co-creation model (Figure 6.1).

From the Google experience and according to the co-creation model it is noted that the expected improvements in talent motivation and retention, employee commitment, their trust and loyalty, the visibility of the company's actions, and the specificity are addressed as we can perceive from different press articles, news and opinions from different Google workers.

CinoBoo: I've been there for about five years. You can read about the good parts anywhere, so I'll try to offer a counterpoint based on having worked at other software companies. A common problem is that it's easy to become spoiled by all the perks. Several offices have developed distinct cultures of entitlement, and people whine about the quality of the fudge on the free brownies. It's embarrassing to be around people who've become like spoiled children. An engineering-specific problem there is that there's a lot of support for operations – that is, lots of people whose job it is to keep the systems running. Engineers don't habitually carry pagers and are on-call relatively infrequently. The plus side is that they can focus on development, get adequate sleep and be more productive. The downside is that they can easily lose touch with what's really going on in the data centres and sometimes even their customers. It's a trade-off. Google is at least aware of it and uses incentive programmes to entice engineers to spend time in ops roles. Last, the company is big into 'generating luck', which means trying a whole bunch of stuff in the hopes that a few efforts will pay off.

GoogleEmployee22k: Google is a great place to work. These are the things I like about my job:

1 Everyone is super smart.
2 Eighteen different cafes
3 Free breakfast, lunch, dinner
4 The food is gourmet quality (e.g. omelette bar, chefs that make custom sandwiches for you, sashimi, free drinks 24/7, free snacks of all sorts 24/7).
5 The seven-person conference bicycles
6 Every Friday, Larry, Sergei, or Eric takes questions from us (in person), and we get free beer (e.g. Downtown Brown).

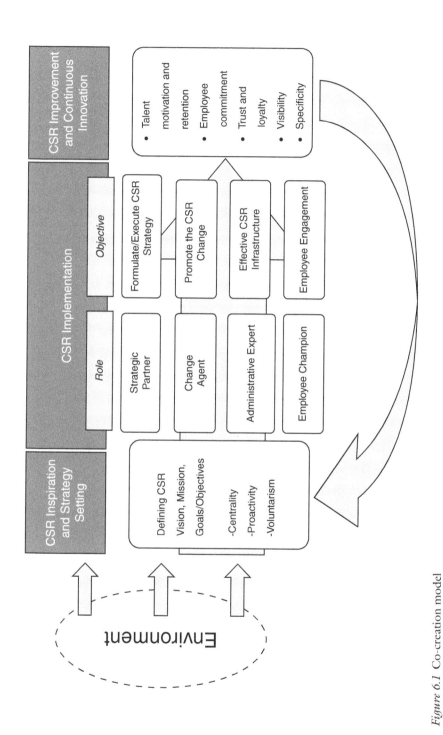

Figure 6.1 Co-creation model

Source: Jamali et al. (2015)

Following the supported evidence of Jamali et al. (2015), this chapter seeks to capture the relevance of socially responsible human resource policies able to improve the organization and employees' performance. At an institutional level, two relevant CSR indices are widely implemented throughout the world by companies: the Global Reporting Initiative (Appendix I) and ISO 26000. The first appendix shows how to measure the implementation of a CSR orientation in the HRM area.

The Global Reporting Initiative is a leading organization in the sustainability field. GRI promotes the use of sustainability reporting as a way for organizations to become more sustainable and contribute to sustainable development. Specifically, the review of the labour section in GRI allows the researcher to identify six management policies of management workers (employment, labour relations management, labour and occupational safety, training and development of employees, diversity and equal opportunities, equity compensation). These policies represent a consistent basis to complete the review of the literature and develop a set of human resource policies with a socially responsible orientation.

Moreover, ISO 26000 is based on an international consensus among experts in CSR, which encourages the application of a set of best practices in social responsibility worldwide. The application of ISO 26000 (Figure 6.2) in accordance

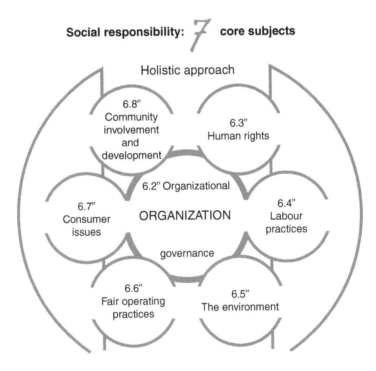

Figure 6.2 ISO 26000 core subjects

Source: www.iso.org/iso/home/standards/iso26000.htm

with different socially responsible behaviours analyses seven business key areas of the organization: organizational governance, human rights, labour practices, the environment, fair operating practices, consumer issues and active participation and community development.

The analysis of the ISO26000 labour management section extracted two additional human resource policies (working conditions and social protection, social dialogue and communication) that complemented the previous six identified in the review of the GRI. Thus, a range of eight socially responsible human resources policies was finally put together after examining the contents of social management and labour standards GRI and ISO 26000 (see Table 6.1).

Academia reflects a wide variety of benefits resulting from the individual and collective previous classifications of different countries (Sharma et al., 2009), shedding light on the fact that most workers prefer to work for socially responsible companies that respect human and social rights. The results in most of these companies are an increase of loyalty, motivation and commitment in these workers, which ultimately affects the stability of the workforce.

To understand the effects of CSR actions on business results it is necessary to comprehend the nature of the concept of organizational performance, coined by Venkatraman and Ramanujam (1986, p. 803), as

> indicators that reflect whether a company has achieved its objectives in terms of comparison with other companies by: (1) financial results, which include economic or accounting indicators such as sales growth, the rate of profit, return on investment, return on sales, return on equity and earnings per share; or by (2) non-financial results, which consider other non-economic aspects such as participation of the company in different markets, the introduction of new products, the quality of production processes and business services, marketing and distribution, efficiency and technological efficiency or innovation.

The improvement on results derived from CSR actions is associated in literature with various causes such as: the efficient and responsible management of

Table 6.1 Consensus of human resource policies obtained through the analysis of corporate social responsibility standards

Socially Responsible Human Resource Policies (SR-HRP)	GRI	ISO 26000
Employment	✓	✓
Management of labour relations	✓	✓
Occupational health and safety	✓	✓
Training and development	✓	✓
Diversity and equal opportunities	✓	✓
Pay equity	✓	
Working conditions and social protection		✓
Communication and social dialogue		✓

Source: Barrena-Martinez et al. (2012).

a company's processes and resources (Barrena-Martinez et al., 2011; Guenster et al., 2011); the reduction of negative impacts on social and environmental business in the environment, and thus the enhancement on firm's reputation (Garay and Font, 2012); or the recognition and legitimacy received by its stakeholders (Liu et al., 2010).

Other institutions like the Commission of the European Communities (2011) argue that initiatives in corporate social responsibility help to improve both the financial and non-financial ratios of companies through (1) reducing the risk of legal penalties, criminal prosecution, litigation and damage to business reputation; (2) the creation of a culture of ethics and morality in management to assist in the decision-making process of the company; (3) the increase in sales and building of a brand that enjoys greater loyalty and credibility among consumers; (4) the achievement of a more human relationship with employees, leading to greater productivity and satisfaction thereof; and (vi) the attraction and retention of skilled labour.

Academics like Hastings and Bartels (2008), in a comparative study in Europe and the United States for the professional consultant KPMG, have mentioned that social responsibility activities can positively affect financial and non-financial performance due to several factors: (1) market differentiation based on their strategy and commitment to stakeholders; (2) a better understanding of the expectations and market risks; (3) their commitment to workers; and (4) access to favourable financing conditions, as well as obtaining a 'licence to operate', which gives more freedom in transactions and exchanges with their environment.

Moreover, professional studies such as those developed by the Spanish association Forética (2011) complement these previous academic arguments, supporting the important and positive effects for companies implementing actions arising from social responsibility, and classify them into four types: (1) the optimization of human capital; (2) operational efficiency; (3) generation of profits; and (4) financial costs – reduced access to capital costs – as shown in Figure 6.3.

Forética research, based on a survey of Spanish directors and managers of large companies, broadly shows a high percentage consensus regarding the benefits of implementing social responsibility actions, showing that these activities help to:

- reduce the access cost to capital and obtain funding (42 percent); a significant decrease in the risk premium organizational risk (51 percent), and the fiscal costs (59 percent);
- achieve greater transparency and accountability, reducing investment risks and ensuring access to new sources of funding (65 percent). According to the Forética Committee these aspects favour the development of good corporate governance, hence high consensus exists regarding the same among directors (70 percent);
- improve the reputation and brand image of the company (60 percent), increasing customer loyalty (77 percent), and facilitating access to new markets (77 percent);

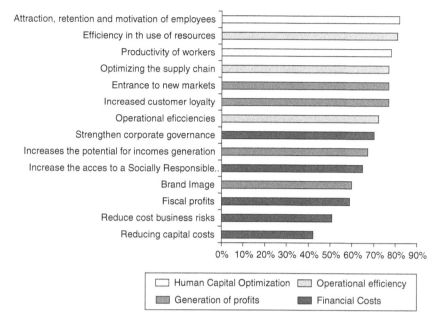

Figure 6.3 Study of Forética in Spain aimed at knowing the effects of CSR actions
Source: Adapted from Foretica Report (2011)

- improve operational efficiency (72 percent), the optimization of the supply chain (77 percent), and the resources and raw materials of the company (81 percent);
- optimize human capital, consecrating it as the most valued by respondents, who perceived CSR as an efficient method of attracting, retaining and motivating people (82 percent), subsequently being able to improve their performance and productivity (78 percent).

The findings and the degree of consensus reached by the managers surveyed by Foretica underlie direct and indirect relationships between social responsibility activities and organizational performance. However, it is necessary to obtain a greater consensus on the theoretical and empirical nature (positive, negative or neutral) of the relationship between CSR and organizational performance, since there is high heterogeneity and inconsistencies in the literature, as Orlitzky et al. (2003):

1 the lack of consensus surrounds a single theoretical framework, which contributes to the theoretical dispersion phenomenon;
2 the use of a wide variety of population (sizes, sectors, countries), which avoids the generation of inferences in statistical terms;

3   methodological shortcomings in measuring the impact of social responsibility actions on financial performance. Considering that CSR represents an intangible construct, it is very difficult to find practical tools to provide an efficient support by researchers to compare the results of these actions on the profitability and performance of the company;

4   the need to analyse the longitudinal basis of the relationship between social responsibility activities and performance indicators. The reason is that these social actions, until they are perceived and treated as actions that create value for stakeholders, require a ripening period, which necessitates measuring this reaction in a large temporary space, which can be about two or three years.

To help clarify this relationship, this chapter is focused on the Spanish experience of different executives who report what are the main socially responsible human resource policies and practices implemented by companies, as well as the main factors which affect them plus the benefits resulting from it.

SR-HRP in the practice: interview with a manager

The qualitative study method represents a deep reflexive process as Maxwell (2008) states, going beyond a quantitative unique value, letting respondents be open about their opinions on a topic. In this way, a culture of Corporate Social Responsibility integrated into Human Resource Management strategies, policies and practices could be better defined and interpreted in qualitative terms by practitioners through interviews. In order to achieve this purpose, a semi-structural interview was made between the months of June and July 2015, ensuring the anonymous participation of respondents. However, the profile of the company (size, age of respondent, gender, industry, description of the business and position) was measured to contextualize the results.

In order to show the value of experience in Corporate Social Responsibility and Human Resources Management, and to systematize knowledge and draw generalized conclusions, the conversations were recorded for the Company A. The questionnaire of the study is provided as follows.

Questionnaire

1   Is there a person in charge of the functions and/or Corporate Social Responsibility actions?

2   Are there committees or groups of people known within the company, who make decisions about corporate social responsibility matters?

3   Do you consider that laws within the legal scope are sufficiently developed to guide companies in terms of social responsibility?

4   Does the company voluntarily undertake these actions in terms of corporate social responsibility? Or do they respond to the environment and specific interest groups? If so, which groups?

5   Does your company guarantee transparency and visibility in terms of social responsibility? Have you published or do you plan to publish annual reports which collate CSR actions?

6   Are the activities carried out in terms of corporate social responsibility linked to core business operations? Or, otherwise, are these activities implemented as isolated actions (for instance, environmental preservation; donations to educational projects or NGOs).

7   Does the company implement Corporate Social Responsibility actions in the area of Human Resources? If so, do you think that there are human resource policies and practices that integrate a socially responsible orientation within the company? Could you list some of them?

8   Considering the preceding question, do you believe that within a human resources strategy, an adjustment is necessary with the corporate social responsibility strategy? If so, what might be the potential benefits to the employees of this setting? Example: commitment, sense of belonging to the company, etc.

Company A

Description of the firm: the activity of the Spanish company, which pertains to a multinational firm of the tertiary sector, is aimed at collecting and moving containers from a terminal (port) to the earth. The terminal is capable of handling the latest and future generations of container vessels with an equipment of Ship To Shore Cranes, Automatic Stacking Cranes and Shuttle Carriers. The number of employees is 88. The human resource manager was interviewed according with the previous questionnaire.

Regarding the first question, the interviewed said that there is not a person in charge of the Corporate Social Responsibility functions. In this line, in the cases in which the company applied some CSR actions, these were performed in an isolated way by the commercial and marketing department. Consequently, the Marketing Manager was the person who had participated in the decision-making process about the implementation of CSR activities within the company.

Regarding the third question the interviewed explains that they are helpless and do not know how to implement actions in terms of social responsibility, according to current laws or regulations. For them, and for the director of the company both nationally and internationally, social responsibility is a future challenge. They would like to implement it, but unfortunately they do not have knowledge or strong fundamentals that will help them to move forward and consolidate this area. Hence, they must have caution regarding the legal interpretation of CSR.

However, according to the fourth question, the head of human resources stated that the CSR actions undertaken since the creation of the company till now are voluntary. In some specific cases, the organization had responded to any specific stakeholder like customers, who have asked us about the use of corporate social responsibility policies in order to collaborate and share knowledge on this specific area. For example, in the environmental area there is a special concern of customers, which demands the use of standards that minimize negative impacts on the environment (use of fuels, renewable and efficient energy, etc.).

In terms of transparency and visibility, the head of human resources ensures that there is nothing developed at a corporate level. In fact, the manager thinks that many actions that can be classified as socially responsible and were conducted in isolation do not cause any effect on its stakeholders because there are not properly disseminated. In this moment, the company is not thinking about publishing CSR activities in reports or memories due to this are not a priority.

Taking into account the potential link between CSR actions and the core operations of the business the human resource manager states the CSR actions implemented till now are definitely isolated.

Going inside the human resource area and the implementation of socially responsible practices, the manager considers that despite the fact that they are doing advances in this field, they do not collect them within an integrated plan although they would like to. Currently, only two people are working in the human resources department of the company, and among their responsibilities is not measuring socially responsible human resource policies or practices. Additionally, the manager describes in detail two socially responsible human resource practices:

1   Breakfast with employees: a breakfast between employees, human resource manager and the CEO of the company ensures a good process of communication. With an informal tone, it is expected to encourage employee participation in order to have a general impression about the operations of the company, the employment status of workers, conditions to improve, etc.

2   Event (strategic meeting): consists of two days together at the end or at the beginning of the year in which employees, along with speakers, the managers of the company, and trainers make a series of immersive activities explaining the general performance of the company and the achievement of objectives (day 1). The second day fosters a competition of innovative ideas among employees. A formal gala dinner closes the event and recognize the best initiatives.

Finally, about the adjustment between CSR and HRM, the human resource manager believes that this adjustment is needed. He also demands the collaboration of the University to facilitate an understanding and implementation of CSR actions. In conclusion, the manager thinks the human resource department should be integrated within a general CSR department, as a consequence of the global character of this area, and HR should be a necessary appendage within CSR aimed at managing and optimizing the human capital.

References

Barrena-Martinez, J., Lopez-Fernandez, M., and Romero-Fernandez, P.M. (2011). Research proposal on the relationship between corporate social responsibility and strategic human resource management. *International Journal of Management and Enterprise Development*, 10(2–3), 173–187.

Barrena-Martínez, J., López-Fernández, M., and Romero-Fernández, P.M. (2012). Towards the seeking of HRM policies with a socially responsable orientation: A comparative analysis between Ibex-35 firms and Fortune's top 50 most admired companies. *Encontros Científicos-Tourism& Management Studies*, (2), 488–501.

Campbell, J. L. (2006). Institutional analysis and the paradox of corporate social responsibility. *American Behavioral Scientist*, 49(7), 925–938.

Clarkson, M. (1995). A stakeholder framework for analyzing and evaluating corporate social responsibility. *The Academy of Management Review*, 20(1), 92–118.

Drucker, P.F. (1954). *The Practice of Management*. New York: Harper & Row.

European Commission.(2011, October 25). A Renewed EU Strategy 2011–14 for Corporate Social Responsibility. Brussels. Retrieved from: http://ec.europa.eu/enterprise/policies/sustainable-business/files/csr/new-csr/act_en.pdf.

Forética. (2011). Report of Forética. Retrieved from: www.foretica.org/sala-de-prensa/noticias/1190-presentado-el-informe-foretica-2011?lang=es.

Freeman, R.E. (1984). *Strategic Management: A Stakeholder Approach*. Boston: Pitman.

Garay, L., and Font, X. (2012). Doing good to do well? Corporate social responsibility reasons, practices and impacts in small and medium accommodation enterprises. *International Journal of Hospitality Management*, 31(2), 329–337.

Guenster, N., Bauer, R., Derwall, J., and Koedijk, K. (2011). The economic value of corporate eco-efficiency. *European Financial Management*, 17(4), 679–704.

Jamali, D.R., El Dirani, A.M., and Harwood, I.A. (2015). Exploring human resource management roles in corporate social responsibility: The CSR-HRM co-creation model. *Business Ethics: A European Review*, 24, 125–143. doi:10.1111/beer.12085.

Liu, G., Liston-Heyes, C., and Ko, W.W. (2010). Employee participation in cause-related marketing strategies: A study of management perceptions from British consumer service industries. *Journal of Business Ethics*, 92(2), 195–210.

Maxwell, J.A. (2008). Designing a qualitative study. *The Sage Handbook of Applied Social Research Methods*, 214–253.

Orlitzky, M., Schmidt, F., and Rynes, S. (2003). Corporate social and financial performance: A meta-analysis. *Organization Studies*, 24(3), 403–441.

Sharma, S., Sharma, J., and Devi, A. (2009). Corporate social responsibility: the key role of human resource management. *Business Intelligence Journal*, 2(1), 205–213.

Suchman, M.C. (1995). Managing legitimacy: strategic and institutional approaches. *The Academy of Management Review*, 20(3), 571–610.

Venkatraman, N., and Ramanujam, V. (1986). Measurement of business performance in strategy research: A comparison of approaches. *The Academy of Management Review*, 11(4), 801–814.

7 The post-mining boom: what next?

The innovation agenda of Fortescue Metals Group: a qualitative case study

Ethan Samuel Miller and
Joanna Poyago-Theotoky

Introduction

Ensuring a viable and sustainable mining industry is of great economic, social and environmental importance to Australia. Despite widespread belief that the boom days of iron ore are over, the reality is far different. The post-mining boom lull has lasted longer than anticipated, forcing iron ore exports between 2014 and 2015 to fall from 20.2 percent to 15.4 percent of the nation's total trade. But, the resource still dominates Australia's exports, claiming the top spot (DFAT, 2014; Austrade 2016).

Provoked by low ore prices, miners have drastically cut operating costs through innovation. Academic literature has not kept up with the dynamic of Australia's iron ore giants, except for Boulter and Hall's 2015 study into mine site communication systems. Little to no academic publication focusses on strategies employed by iron ore producers to cut costs. The researcher believes, to the best of his knowledge, that this work at the time of submission is one of the most up-to-date bodies of work encompassing the innovation agenda of one of Australia's 'Big Three' iron ore producers.

This research consists of a qualitative case study utilising a Glaserian Grounded Theory approach of the innovation agenda at Fortescue Metals Group. It investigates how the company aims to battle current issues facing the industry, outlined by extant research through means of innovative practices. In December 2016, the independent mining sector rating agency *Metalytics Resource Sector Economics*, titled Fortescue Metals Group as the world's lowest cost seaborne iron ore exporter, fulfilling one of the company's goals to be "the safest, lowest cost and most profitable iron ore producer" (Wells, 2016; Fortescue Metals Group Ltd, 2016, p. 24). This study aims to shed light on how Fortescue achieved this goal from the perspective of employees involved in innovative planning and operations on a day-to-day basis.

The study firstly provides a comprehensive review of literature regarding Australia's iron ore and resources industry to contextualise current issues, market conditions, practices and themes. Following the review, the methodology section explains sampling, justification for using Grounded Theory, research design, and research limitations.

The results section presents data collected from the research sample, providing commentary on the relationships and interactions between prevalent themes and sentiments revealed through the data analysis. The three discussion paragraphs form the main body of the work. Firstly, catalysts driving Fortescue to innovate, exploring innovative practices and strategies of Fortescue in detail, and finally presenting participant's perceptions of the culture of the organisation and their subsequent impact on the company's innovation agenda. The final section provides reflection by the researcher of the issues and concepts discussed in the research, presenting a theory by means of a Grounded Theory method as to what truly in his view enables Fortescue Metals Group to innovate successfully.

Literature review

Though many argue the age of the resource boom is over, evidence suggests that Australia will rely on the extraction of raw minerals as a key export for many decades to come (CSIRO, 2014; de Krester and Forrestal, 2012; Maxwell and Guj, 2006; Mudd, 2010). This review explores current trends in literature surrounding Australian mining. Firstly, through a general background of the industry, then examining articles on topics of social impact factors in Australian mining organisations and communities. Last, it will consider the research covering current and future technological innovation in Australia's mining organisations and the greater industry.

Post global financial crisis (GFC), the Chinese government stimulus programme skyrocketed commodity prices to record highs in 2011. The flow on effect had great impacts on Australia's economic policy, keeping Australia out of recession (Robson, 2015 p. 308). In 2016, with iron ore prices more than halving in value, the nation's key export industry was at dire crossroads. Prior et al. (2013) in *Geoforum* stated that there are four key issues concerning Australian mining:

1 Potential constraints of future production due to environmental, social and economic factors.
2 Falling levels of productivity in a sector that is generally expanding.
3 The Dutch Disease and the Resource Curse.
4 The need for sustainable operations.

The 'Dutch Disease' or 'Resource Curse' is one of the main challenges that Australia faces with regards to the resources industry. It is a constant theme amongst the literature with six key articles explaining the phenomenon (Auty, 2007; Larsen, 2006; Goodman and Worth, 2008; Papyrakis and Gerlagh, 2003; Shaxson, 2007; Stevens and Dietsche, 2008). Mohr et al.'s (2015) article in *Natural Resources Research* argues that the production of world iron ore has been projected to enter a period of stagnation around the end of this decade at approximately 4.5 gigatonnes of output per year until early 2040s.

Mudd's 2010 article in *Resources Policy* states the need to consider how the industry can remain viable, reduce costs to society and environment (Mudd, 2010, p. 111). Mudd's list of key 'mega-trends' of mining: increased production at the end of last decade and the demise thereafter, declining grades of iron ore, issues of how to better access these resources, how to deal with the ever-increasing wastage, potential problems of mine rehabilitation, sustainability reporting and CSR (Corporate Social Responsibility) practices.

After the National Peak Minerals Forum in 2010, Prior et al. (2013) found the major outcome of the summit was that the nation's miners severely lacked direction and strategy. Liew (2012, p. 542) in *Australian Journal of International Affairs* argued that Australian policy makers effectively used the hyper-prosperous years of the mining boom to postpone the necessity for innovation development.

Published academic literature surrounding innovation in Australia's mining industry is scarce. There is a much lower volume when compared to CSR, ethics and sustainability in Australian mining. The most recent and relevant works on innovation and technology are within grey literature.

Boulter and Hall (2015, p. 370) in the *International Journal of Mining, Reclamation and Environment*, document the growth of WiFi and wireless network utilisation in mining. Mine site networks allowed mines to be self-sufficient, operating their own LTE system. Two main systems which Boulter and Hall detailed were DISPATCH™ and Caterpillar's MineStar™. The article explored potential impacts of 'Big Data' in the mining industry. They found it greatly increases efficiencies in production and maintenance (Boulter and Hall, 2015, p. 373).

Mudd put forth how the lack of innovations and new discoveries in Australia is having an adverse effect on the industry's ability to mine lower grade ores (Mudd, 2009). In 2010, Mudd's article in *Resources Policy* addressed the need for innovation in diesel technologies because of high fuel transport costs, as well as addressing the need for reducing CO_2 (Mudd, 2010).

Redrup's piece in *Australian Financial Review (AFR)* gives further credence to Liew's 2012 argument that Australian innovation levels are dire, stating Australia has fallen from 17th to 19th in the Global Innovation Index.

The 2016 industry report *Productivity and Innovation in Mining Industry*, by Matysek and Fisher on behalf of BAEconomics, provided insight into innovation in Australian mining. Citing multifactor-productivity (MFP) was falling, they explain that if company MFP declines, that usually indicates that the organisation is not exploiting resources as efficiently as possible (Matysek and Fisher, 2016, p. 20).

Through Australian Bureau of Statistics analysis into the resources sector in 2015, the report uncovers that MFP for the 15-year period from FY 2000/01– 2014/15 fell approximately 14 percent (cited in Matysek and Fisher, 2016, p. 20). Matysek and Fisher's analysis of the Bureau of Resources and Energy Economics discussion paper 2013 discovered that "efficiency and scale effects contributed positively and significantly to Australian mining MFP. . . (But) their analysis finds no positive effect of technological change was observed over the study period" (Matysek and Fisher, 2016, p. 22; Bureau of Resources and Energy Economics 2013).

The pair further add that volume-based strategies were a result of the commodity boom, when it made fiscal sense to seek high volume output targets to suffice the demand that the Chinese market presented (Matysek and Fisher, 2016, p. 23). The article cites IQPC's 2014 findings that mining investment in information technology was projected to increase fivefold by 2017 (Matysek and Fisher, 2016, p. 41). Ernst and Young argue the scale of the issues facing the industry are so great that orthodox solutions will not suffice, rather systematic bloc changes need to occur in mining to improve (Ernst and Young, 2015, p. 4).

Mining industry

PwC's 2016 mining industry report *Mine 2016 Slower, Lower, Weaker . . . But Not Defeated* paints a similar picture to that of Ernst and Young's. Whilst still focussing on the demise of mining globally, it highlighted organisational cutbacks rather than needing to innovate (PricewaterhouseCoopers, 2016). The findings are rather sombre in terms of the overall feasibility of the industry. Declaring that the last financial year was the first on record for PwC where the top 40 producers have seen an ongoing degradation of their overall viability (PricewaterhouseCoopers, 2016, p. 19).

When considering Australia's big three (BHP, Rio Tinto and Fortescue) the only recently published work focussing on cost reduction strategies through innovation is noted in the previously mentioned 2016 BAEconomics report. The authors provide an in-depth focus into Rio Tinto's Australian iron ore operations, with insights into the cost reduction and efficiency strategies of the firm (Matysek and Fisher, 2016). They find that the company is involved in the prototyping and development of automated technologies utilising wireless communication networks. According to the report, Rio Tinto's automated hardware is now a permanent fixture of the company's Pilbara assets (Matysek and Fisher, 2016, p. 25). BAEconomics also found that automation is being implemented across Rio Tinto's logistics and mining assets (Matysek and Fisher, 2016, p. 25).

The Committee for Economic Development Australia's (CEDA) report *Australia's Future Workforce?* illustrates that Rio Tinto as early as 2011 deployed autonomous drilling located at the West Angelas mine in 2011. CEDA notes that Rio Tinto's West Angelas is the first mine in the world able to run all its main drills fully autonomously (CEDA, 2015, p. 73). The report finds Rio Tinto realised numerous windfalls from autonomous systems (Matysek and Fisher, 2016, p. 26). At the time of publication (2016), Rio Tinto was counted to employ 71 autonomous haulage trucks within its Pilbara operations (Matysek and Fisher, 2016, p. 27). The trucks use on-board navigation composed of radar, laser and GPS technology to provide information on the position of other vehicles and to circumnavigate the mine site (Matysek and Fisher, 2016, p. 27).

The report further discovers that the autonomous vehicles on average see 14 percent higher efficiency than their manned counterparts. Rio Tinto could achieve noteworthy savings from the application of this technology (Matysek and Fisher, 2016, p. 27). Autonomous haulage systems also saw improvements across multiple areas, including lower costs, higher safety, greater efficiency from the absence of worker breaks, as well as seeing higher outputs in the manned fleet partly due to the manned fleet competing with higher targets set out by the autonomous vehicles (Matysek and Fisher, 2016, p. 27).

The pair additionally found that driverless vehicles are in the development stages across BHP sites, and fully operational systems are in place by Fortescue Metals Group at the company's Solomon hub (Matysek and Fisher, 2016, p. 27). Further reporting on BHP and Fortescue installations are scarcely published. Moreover, the authors report that Rio Tinto's automation systems spans multiple hardware systems. The implementation of Mine of the Future™ is a noteworthy installation; a joint venture between Rio Tinto and global mine research bodies with the aim to automate all aspects of the mine face and Rio Tinto's newly developed AutoHaul® fully autonomous heavy haulage rail network (Matysek and Fisher, 2016, pp. 28–29).

Regarding Fortescue and BHP, there is very little currently published academic or grey literature regarding their aims for technology development. In Fortescue's 2015 annual report, the company stakes its claim to become the world's leading iron ore producer in terms of safety, sustainable production, as well as operating the lowest cost and most profitable mine (Fortescue Metals Group, 2015, p. 24). Fortescue has needed to sustain immense levels of output to post profits as the price in iron ore has plummeted in recent times.

Jacob Greber, economics correspondent in *The Australian Financial Review* reported that Andrew Forrest (Fortescue's chairman and founder) believes that the iron ore industry is "very close to the bottom of a very major cycle", and that "there will still be insane overproduction in vital commodities which will drive down income everywhere" (Greber, 2016, p. 6). Forrest's statements provide an interesting perspective into how the industry is still battling the issue of low demand, negative growth in MFP and oversupply. Fortescue in its FY15 annual report states, "Having fully completed its capital expansion programme in FY15, Fortescue is not planning to invest in any additional production capacity. Capital expenditure in FY16 will be limited to sustainably support the existing operations, estimated at US$2/wet metric tonne" (Fortescue Metals Group, 2015, p. 32).

BHP, in the same way as Fortescue, posts much less data surrounding efficiency improvements due to technological advancements; it focussed rather on high outputs. Like the two other key players, BHP is concentrating on efficiency gain through haulage, but with less emphasis seen on automation. Located at their Escondida mine, the company benchmarked production times for its truck performance and maintenance services (BHP Billiton, 2015, p. 17). After completion, the firm saw a new benchmark of truck utilisation time in FY15 of 83 percent from 78 percent in the previous financial year. Throughout the rest of the report, BHP does not seem to disclose further information regarding innovative or technological ventures surrounding their iron ore business.

Examining the literature, themes of sustainable operations, climate change, innovation needs, CSR, low grade ore issues, new technology, indigenous affairs, social impact assessments, and future strategies were most prevalent. Published academic literature is vastly lacking in the space of technology and innovation, specifically regarding Fortescue Metals Group and BHP Billiton. As Australia comes to grips with a plateauing of its exports of iron ore to Asia, understanding how to guide the industry for the coming decades is pertinent. Therefore, areas for future research should investigate questions of: Where the economy is heading post-mining boom and where should the nation invest? Which technologies can gain the most efficiency in the mining sector? What specific practices and strategies are Fortescue Metals Group and BHP, two of the largest producers of iron ore in Australia, going to undertake in terms of increasing market share, competitiveness and efficiency gains? How can innovative practices create shared value for communities and organisations? How best shall Australian mining policy makers market our product? What is the strategic direction of our mining industry?

Fortescue Metals Group was justified as the researcher felt that BHP Billiton is unlikely to undertake radical change in terms of R&D and new mining technologies (BHP Billiton, 2015, 2016). Conversely, Fortescue clearly states a desire to innovate and progress their mining technologies, evidently seen by their mission statement:

> Fortescue's operations are absolutely focussed on the key areas within the company's control that support the strategy to become the safest, lowest cost and most profitable iron ore producer.
>
> (Fortescue Metals, 2016, p. 24)

The researcher decided that a qualitative case study into Fortescue Metals Group would contribute to the literature in understanding the research and development and innovation agenda of Fortescue Metals Group.

Research methodology

Using a Glaserian strain of Grounded Theory was preferred as there is currently no direct theory surrounding innovation agendas in mining organisations. The researcher wished to understand from an employee's perspective of why and how Fortescue innovated. From data collected the researcher would discover a theory behind the company's innovation agenda. Barnie Glaser and Anselm Strauss, the two fathers of Grounded Theory first published the theory in 1967 in their seminal work *The Discovery of Grounded Theory: Strategies for Qualitative Research*. The theory is a research tool predominantly used in qualitative research which aims to deduct meaning through concept creation and enable discovery (Glaser and Strauss, 1967; Glaser, 1978). Reason why the Glaserian style was preferable, was due to the Glaserian paradigm being more open and flexible in design.

The study used semi-structured interviews face-to-face and by phone. The choice of semi-structured interviews was made as the researcher wanted the participant to be able to take control of aspects of the interview, resulting in guided conversations (Kallio et al., 2016). Conducting the interviews face-to-face would have been ideal, but logistical issues arose as Fortescue's operations are based in Western Australia, and the researcher in Melbourne. Individual interviews were chosen as the participants are very skilled, highly educated, and could provide rich data without the stimuli of focus groups (Gibbs, 1997). Furthermore, as each participant had differing roles within Fortescue's operations, a focus group in this application would not provide fruitful results.

Data was attained from a sample of seven employees from Fortescue Metals Group who currently work within areas of innovative operations and R&D practices at the organisation. The sample included six males and one female; positions ranged from senior management to operations control located at both Fortescue's Solomon and Chichester hubs. Some of the participants worked previously for Fortescue's competitors, others had not worked in mining before their employment at Fortescue.

Participants were recruited with the help of the University Western Australia's Dean of Business School, Professor Phillip Dolan. Dolan's network with Fortescue Metals Group enabled the first contact with Fortescue Metals Group. The researcher alongside supervisor Professor Joanna Poyago-Theotoky liaised with Fortescue's corporate affairs team to contact certain individuals based on their role at the organisation. As this is not a large-scale qualitative research, it was not possible for the researcher to contact and interview many within Fortescue that work in the field of research.

Interviews ranged from 30 minutes to over an hour. The initial interview was conducted at a mutual meeting point at the International Mining and Resources Conference (IMARC) in Melbourne, the remaining six were phone interviews. In addition to handwritten notes being taken, each interview was audio recorded and subsequently transcribed for data analysis.

After transcripts were certified by Fortescue, they were uploaded to software program NVivo. Hutchison, Johnston and Breckon in *International Journal of Social Research Methodology* (2010) provided a helpful guide on using the NVivo program when conducting a Grounded Theory Study. Explaining, the researcher should code data into nodes (subsets of themes which are prevalent in the data) on the proviso of not forcing concepts into pre-determined categories, in line with the Glaserian style (Glaser, 1992; Hutchison et al., 2010).

The researcher analysed and compared different themes and sentiments held by participants which produce an emerging theory using nodes, mind maps and hierarchy charts within NVivo. The researcher made sure to adhere to the teachings of Glaser by constantly comparing the data between participant responses without stimuli from external sources.

Negligible and low-risk approval was granted by the Senior Human Ethics Officer, La Trobe University Human Ethics Committee after the researcher could ensure all relevant ethical issues were addressed. All reasonable steps were taken by the researcher to ensure that no interviewee could be identifiable in accordance with La Trobe University ethics guidelines. All respondents in the discussion paragraphs received a number in lieu of their name, in order of their respective interviews.

Three limitations were found: Time constraints from a lengthy ethics process, lack of comparison to Fortescue's competition, and absence of other academic texts on the research topic.

If more time was allocated to interview members of the organisation, a larger sample may have been used. Secondly, due to limitations of an honours thesis, the researcher was not able to cross compare findings from Fortescue with competitors. Although every step was taken by the researcher to avoid presenting biased results, focussing on one organisation may omit alternative perspectives. Finally, the researcher holds the sentiment that without extant academic publications on the research topic, it was difficult to construct the research design without reference. Whilst the researcher felt that the choice of methodology and research design for this study is adequate, other academic approaches could be more fitting for this study.

Use of NVivo software allowed the researcher to classify different significant themes and sentiments held by respondents into groups or nodes. Comparing nodes, key aspects of each interview were coded into areas of interest. Nodes were clustered into individual groups and examined through multiple models using NVivo software.

Results

Most nodes were found to interlink with one or more other node. Indicating attributes of the area researched were not mutually exclusive. Nodes were clustered by their respective word similarities, using Pearson's Correlation Coefficient. Interconnectedness can be seen in Figure 7.1 which illustrates that 11 separate clusters were found across a total of 35 separate nodes. Whilst nodes from different clusters can interact, nodes that share the same cluster indicate a stronger relationship or interdependence with one another. The three most striking cluster groups are discussed next.

The yellow cluster shows a relationship involving nodes: *appetite for risk, difference to Fortescue's competition, lack of bureaucracy, openness to people and their ideas, speed of returns on investment, strategic planning* and *stretch targets*. This cluster indicates a link between Fortescue Metals Group's difference to competition, lack of rigidity and openness to people. The brown cluster also shows a noteworthy relationship involving: *auto haulage trucks, financially viable projects, innovation agenda, natural attrition, negatives of automation, resistance to change* and *safety*.

This cluster helps explain the link between Fortescue's automation operations, innovation agenda, change management and financial viability. The dark blue cluster illustrates a correlation which helps to give relevance to the cluster analysis model. Consisting of the nodes *wet processing, ore grade* and *waste reduction*, this

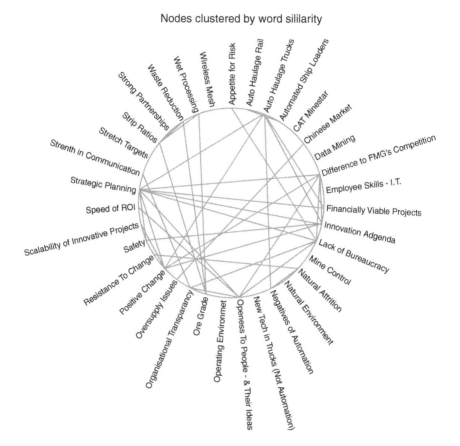

Figure 7.1 Nodes clustered by word similarity

group illustrates links pertaining to how wet processing helps to reduce waste and address ore grade issues.

The hierarchy tool displays topics and themes found in data transcriptions. Ordering how many times nodes were referenced against how many sources cited them. Size of the nodes in the hierarchy chart is determined by how many times the node has been coded. Level of colour saturation within each node is dependent on how many interviewees raised the topic of the node. With 29 items coded, cited by all respondents *financially viable projects* was the second largest node. However, this node pertains exclusively to respondent answers in interviews, inviting the researcher to further investigate the concept as part of the formation of theory to explain the research question. Figure 7.2 illustrates this hierarchy. Whilst the hierarchy chart does not explain why these nodes were most common, it does provide a useful indication as to which thematics were most prevalent.

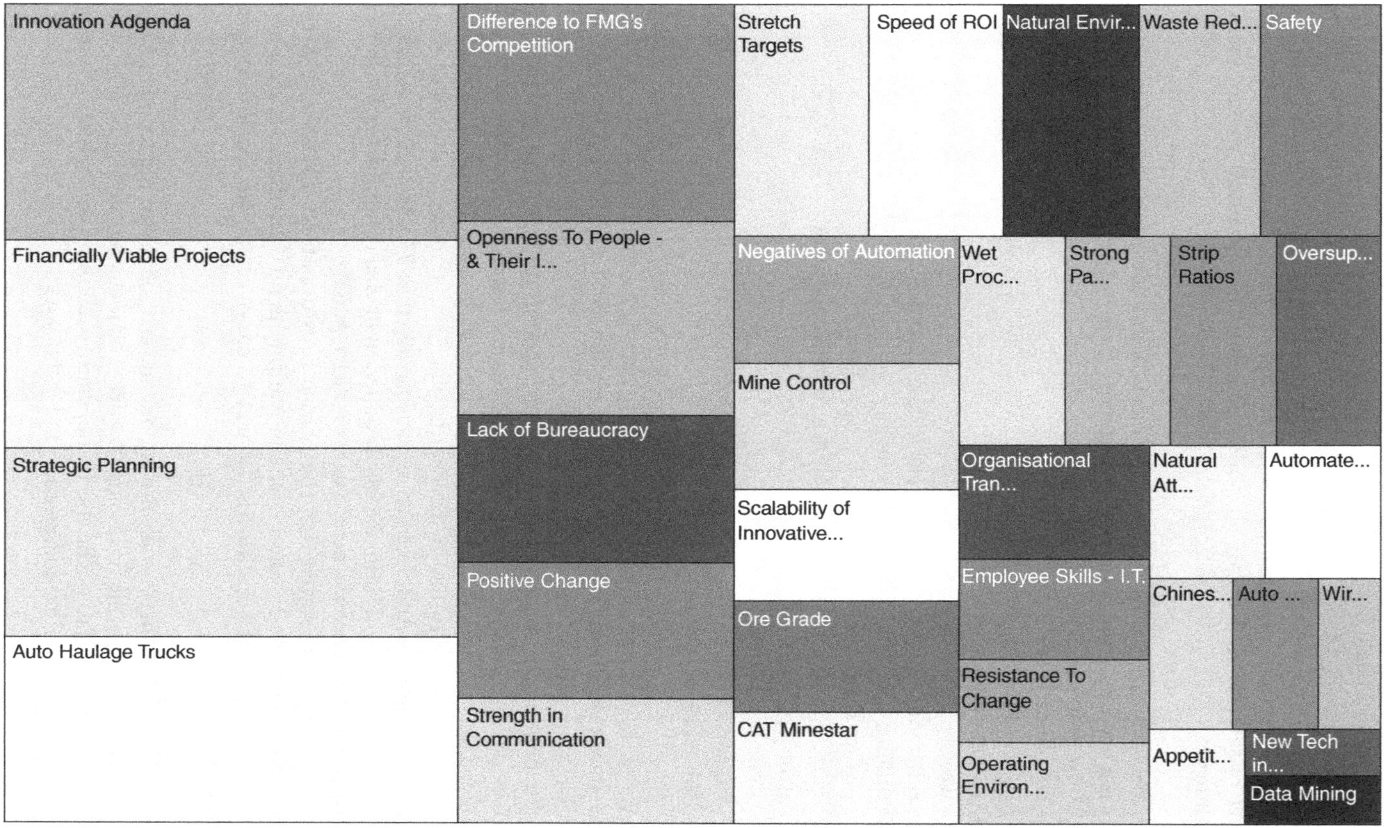

Figure 7.2 Hierarchy chart: nodes compared by number of coding references

Three hundred fifty-seven different references were cited from 35 individual nodes. Each node was created in accordance with a topic, theme or sentiment raised by a participant during the interview process. The results gathered shared the common theme that most topics and concepts discussed with interviewees proved not to be mutually exclusive, resulting in a high level of interrelation across all nodes. The most pronounced themes raised included:

- the financial viability of innovative projects and operations
- the need for rapid return on investment
- how to lower costs
- stretch-targets
- issues of oversupply
- automated haulage in trucks
- wet ore processing
- other innovative technologies (including automated ship loaders, automated drilling operations, rail cruise control)
- project scalability
- Fortescue Metals Group's difference to its competitors
- strong partnerships
- strategic planning
- organisational culture (openness to communication and idea sharing)
- low levels of bureaucracy

Above themes and concepts discovered in data forms foundation for a theoretical framework. The framework explains the catalysts of innovative practices used by Fortescue Metals Group.

The preliminary discussion paragraphs present an in-depth analysis into core factors driving innovative practices employed by Fortescue. In early 2016 the market saw iron ore prices at less than a third of those at the peak of Australia's iron ore boom earlier in the decade. Fortescue founder and current non-executive chairman, Andrew Forrest, last year stated in *The Australian Financial Review* "there will still be insane overproduction in vital commodities which will drive down income everywhere" (Greber, 2016, p. 6).

Five participants stated that the market pressures forced Fortescue Metals Group to pursue an aggressive innovation agenda. Participants reasoned that in lean market conditions, the way to survive is to be the lowest cost producer.

> . . . The thing that is really driving our automation is cost reduction . . . The market is driving the technology harder. The focus is really on C1 cost. The way to survive is to be the cheapest operator . . . I think the market is creating more urgency around innovation and technology.
>
> (Interviewee 1)

Interviews expanded on market pressures and its relation to previous conditions of market 'fatness'. One interviewee seemed pleased that market conditions had reversed, as it created a healthier, competitive and stimulating market.

> . . . In my opinion, during the last 10 years we had been very fat because we've been making so much money and you make money irrespective of what you do you can be very fat and lazy. Whereas now those days are gone and so it's forcing the companies now to re-think.
>
> (Interviewee 5)

The described 'fatness' of the industry aligns with notions put forth by Liew (2012) and Redrup (2016), stating, Australia has ridden on the coat-tails of the mining boom for too long. The lean iron ore market reported by participants forced organisations to lower cost through innovation.

A second impetus for innovation suggested by interviewees was lean organisational strategic planning and 'stretch-targets'. Every participant noted that Fortescue's vision is upheld across departments, forming the main influence of efficiency in the company. Fortescue, on the 8th December 2016, attained its goal of being recognised as the lowest cost supplier of iron ore to China. Metalytics Resource Sector Economics priced Fortescue's operations at $15.43 per wet metric tonne (WMT), down from US$48/WMT in 2012 in their November 2016 report (Wells, 2016, p. 1). Interviewees expressed that Fortescue relied on lean business modelling, enabling innovation and outside the box thinking. Stretch-targets were described as a systematic goal-setting system under continual revision aiming to achieve seemingly unobtainable goals set by Fortescue.

> It's lean to the point where they don't have enough people to do the job. They have to go innovate and change the process . . . We keep going through and making sure that the organisation is not fat . . . That's how we drive innovation targets, they really seem unobtainable . . . You have to go and find something different that drives innovation and change. And it's just a way of life for Fortescue, it never stops.
>
> (Interviewee 1)

> The stretched targets put a natural tension in the organisation to continue to improve.
>
> (Interviewee 5)

> Setting stretched targets is one of Fortescue values and it is a challenging work environment. If you work for Fortescue you've sort of got to go in with eyes wide open, it's very satisfying but it's also very challenging.
>
> (Interviewee 2)

Three participants were asked as to whether the organisation employs a structured strategy driving innovation, answering that the company applies an organisation wide approach.

> We don't necessarily have a very structured strategy around technology . . . The strategy really is around just driving continuous improvement in efficiency and safety. Senior executives on our board do really promote technology where we can use it and try to promote people looking at it. But we're not trying to drive this technology strategy.
>
> (Interviewee 1)

> We haven't got an official R&D and technology innovation group which is a different thing. I think that it works quite well . . . It's embedded in the culture of the organisation.
>
> (Interviewee 7)

The third set of driving factors discovered from interviews and subsequent data analysis was the importance of lowering costs and the rapid ROI required on new investments. All interviewees shared their sentiments and thoughts on why Fortescue innovates, but three raised the importance of driving down costs and very rapid ROI needs.

> Time value of money. Time value of money . . . that's why we've pushed the development so fast, is that time value of money is often more critical than getting it exactly right two years later.
>
> (Interviewee 1)

> . . . You've got to have a very short return on your capital investment. That's the challenge, and that drives the fact that any innovation or technology you implement needs to get up to speed and operating effectively quite quickly so you can realise that return on your investment.
>
> (Interviewee 2)

Interviewee 3 when reflecting on the same issue noted that Fortescue's need for rapid ROI is not just a cultural aspect, but is required to great levels repay market debt.

> I would say turn arounds are short because our bottom line is driven by paying back the debt which we have out in the market.
>
> (Interviewee 3)

Participants indicated technological innovations are key components of lowering C1 costs and net debt. Consequently, lowering costs is one of the most pertinent incentives of innovation. Discovered in the data analysis, all concepts regarding cost, ROI and innovation draw strong links, as lowering costs and debt requires innovation with respect to above average levels of ROI.

Participant perceptions into catalysts of innovation has highlighted numerous factors. Whilst it can be argued that market forces dictate organisational innovation strategy, interviewees expressed pressures by Fortescue's organisation culture have naturally pushed for innovation. Most of the research sample noted oversupply across the industry, forcing producers to cut costs or incur profit loss. The entire sample suggested that Fortescue genuinely upholds the company vision and the organisation drives creativity and innovation to combat low iron ore prices through stretch-targets. Lastly, respondents illustrated that the rapid ROI needs of Fortescue Metals Group to combat market debt levels further stimulates innovative technologies at Fortescue. This itemises and discusses in detail participant responses regarding innovative technologies operated by Fortescue and assess if they added or detracted value to the company.

All seven participants cited autonomous haulage systems (AHS) as a core component of Fortescue's focus for cost reduction and innovation. AHS was first implemented at the Solomon mine hub in 2013. The Solomon hub consists of two mines and produces 73 mtpa, 27 mtpa of which mined at Kings and 46 mtpa at Firetail, respectively (Fortescue Metals Group Limited, 2016, p. 28). Haulage at the Kings mine became fully automated in October 2015. The fleet currently comprises of 54 Caterpillar Command for Hauling© mining trucks run by the Caterpillar MineStar™ wireless mesh. The trucks navigate mine sites through on-board Lidar, Radar and GPS systems. Autonomous trucks retain a redundant driver cab as manufacturers have not yet released fully driverless models.

> Solomon where I am . . . we've got a lot of automation. We run a fleet of 54 autonomous ore trucks . . . It's now to a point where it's a full blown autonomous mine.
>
> (Interviewee 2)

Interviewees 2 and 3 described that fleet command and communication to the autonomous is through the MineStar™ mesh. All info regarding vehicle positioning, fault identification, load types is communicated through the mesh between vehicles, mine site and head office in real time through fibre optic connections.

> Each mine has a mesh that all the mining equipment, light and vehicles – it's essentially connected to the mesh. It's quite an investment.
>
> (Interviewee 2)

> It talks to every machine, which relays back to the office what the dirt is that the truck is carrying, what the dirt is like that the diggers are digging, where it's gotta go.
>
> (Interviewee 3)

Interviewees cited higher needs of communication, management, discipline, technical know-how, precision planning, and changes to the overall mine model were all required to ensure smooth operation of a wirelessly driven haulage system.

> (Autonomy makes operations) more pressured . . . The truck, it's just a computer on wheels. It does pretty much whatever it's told. To make them effective, your communication with your workforce around operational discipline needs to be high.
>
> (Interviewee 2)

Five of the interviewees commented on the benefits of autonomous haul. Themes focussed around cost reduction, efficiency gains and safety improvements. One participant's response highlighted a different issue regarding personnel:

> It's predictable, the safety systems are ironclad, the truck always does what it's supposed to do. There's multiple levels of layers of redundancy and autonomous trucks don't get fatigued . . . They're very, very predictable.
>
> (Interviewee 2)

Participants noted efficiencies are seen in overall speeds across a haul cycle attained by the autonomous fleet.

> Our best driver can do a cycle better than an AHS truck, but only within the first hour of a shift before he gets tired. On average across the shift the AHS cycles better than the manned drivers, because of variability and fatigue.
>
> (Interviewee 1)

Fortescue reports its autonomous fleet attains 20 percent more total productivity over manned trucks (Fortescue Metals Group Limited, 2016, p. 31). This figure, when compared to Matysek and Fisher's findings of Rio Tino's 14 percent efficiency gains, rates 6 percent higher haulage efficiency (Matysek and Fisher, 2016, p. 25).

Interviewees 1, 2 and 4 cited safety benefits of the automated haulage system. One such advantage was the automated system's ability to communicate through the MineStar™ mesh. Each vehicle, manned or not, transmits its position in relation to others in the haul cycle, keeping a constant safe distance.

> They (AHS trucks) have a predicted path technology . . . we install the system on any vehicle that works in the mine. The system controls the truck speed, maximum acceleration, turning radius of every vehicle in the mine. If it calculates a probability at an intersection, the truck will slow down and eventually it will stop.
>
> (Interviewee 2)

Interviewee 2 stated that by taking the driver out of the cabin, human error had been eliminated. The issues that manned fleets once bore such as blind spots and reaction times are no longer present.

> (From the) human behaviour perspective; reaction times, . . . blind spots on the truck, you couldn't allow the trucks to operate in that way because of the drivers but now you don't have that limitation.
>
> (Interviewee 2)

Participants described the main negative effect of AHS is that automated fleets will generate job losses. These beliefs are in congruence with findings by Matysek and Fisher (2016), CEDA (2015) and Tuffley (2015).

Conversations regarding redundancies driven by autonomous haul proved not to be despondent. Five interviewees mentioned that Fortescue manages redundancies well by using long-range planning, high transparency, natural attrition, and by re-employing staff in different roles within the organisation.

> Managing (redundancies) is critical . . . Firstly, to have a long-range plan, manage it through attrition, through short term contracts, re-employ, re-train people. Where we do end up with redundancy, the impact on the culture and the company is minimised by being highly transparent about what you're doing well in advance.
>
> (Interviewee 1)

> We're using a contractor right now which fills gaps in place, rather than employing someone on the books where . . . a time where the scenario could be changing.
>
> (Interviewee 3)

The second issue noted was the level of difficulty which autonomy poses for mine management. Interviewees mentioned that the level of discipline required to handle the complexity of the autonomous system can be challenging.

> It's more difficult to run a mine now autonomously than what it is manned. The level of operational discipline required is much higher from a maintenance perspective and an operational perspective.
>
> (Interviewee 2)

> The humans working there are still going to have a lot more input to do than a computer so it's important to keep that in mind as well.
>
> (Interviewee 6)

> I think the perception is that you become less reliant on people but the opposite is true. You have less people, but the people you do have become more critical and have a huge influence over the success of the technology.
>
> (Interviewee 2)

The second most common innovative cost reduction strategy mentioned was wet ore processing. Ore processing operation is the core component of mine ore processing facilities (OPFs), where raw ore is separated from tailings, producing a sellable product. Increasing efficiencies in OPFs are also an area previously unchallenged by many Australian ore producers (CEDA, 2015; Mudd, 2009, 2010; Matysek and Fisher, 2016; PricewaterhouseCoopers, 2014).

By increasing OPF effectiveness, miners yield more sellable iron ore from total material unearthed, resulting in lower strip ratios and C1 costs. Strip ratios are defined as volume of waste material required to be extracted by the total amount of saleable ore.

> They're like big washing machines, they will wash away the impurities and upgrade the product. That lets you mine a much lower-grade material, wash it out and get the same result.
>
> (Interviewee 5)

> They upgrade the portion of the ore and essentially remove contaminants like silica, alumina and clay. It upgrades ore so you can put a lower grade product in one end and get a higher-grade product.
>
> (Interviewee 2)

> Take Chichester five years ago, it was facing a strip ratio about 5.1:1, and now runs about 1.2:1
>
> (Interviewee 1)

In conjunction with cost saving, respondents illustrated that wet ore processing made reductions in Fortescue's environmental footprint. CO_2 output, wastage and overall mine size have been reduced.

> You end up with an 85 percent recovery. With the strip ratio now of 1.1:1, everything goes into backfill. And because we don't have to build all the waste dumps, the area of impact is smaller . . . It's reducing the waste.
>
> (Interviewee 1)

The researcher found Fortescue's innovation agenda extends further than haulage and ore processing. Innovations included remote mining, rail and port control systems, autonomous drilling in Solomon hub, rail cruise control, task assignment software systems and automated ship loaders.

Five participants shared experiences working day-to-day in remote control centres located at Fortescue's headquarters in Perth. The five interviewees work in port, rail and Cloudbreak mine control. In 2016, Cloudbreak and Christmas Creek mine control were relocated to the Perth head office, transferring around

30 personnel. Participants illustrated the move did not intend to realise initial cost savings, but augment the information flow and cross-skill between control centres.

> Having those control functions co-located, we see significant improvements throughout our supply chain. We're the main interface between our marketing teams and our shipping teams with the operations teams.
>
> (Interviewee 5)

> (Relocating benefited) due to cross-skill. Rather than have three control rooms, you can have one big control room in Perth, your operators or controllers can be cross-skilled across all the sites.
>
> (Interviewee 7)

> Money saved is very minimal . . . You have big savings in the information flow that has all the people working in the same area. For example, the operator that's running the train loaders on the port and the train controller that controls the trains sit next to each other. They can organise maintenance on trains, manage scheduling . . . That information is more valuable than anything that the money saving could do.
>
> (Interviewee 6)

Interviewees spoke of rail cruise control, a new initiative which partially automates the company's heavy haul rail infrastructure. The system retains a driver in the cabin, gaining efficiency through eliminating human variability along the route.

> Savings on autonomous rail are on the cycle time. Taking the variability out of it. (For example,) at this point you need to accelerate it, that point you need to brake . . . and they (drivers) all do it differently. What you want to do is automate it. Automation accelerates and brakes exactly how it's supposed to.
>
> (Interviewee 1)

Further conversation on autonomous technology raised auto drilling, ship loaders, and plans to automate entire processing plants.

> We started conversion of our first autonomous drill last week. A team is working on a fully automated process plant at one of the mines as well.
>
> (Interviewee 1)

Interviewee 2 remarked that autonomous drilling, similarly to AHS, is first prototyped and tested at the Solomon hub before being considered for the remainder of Fortescue's mines. The autonomous drills at Fortescue use comparable technology to those implemented by Rio Tinto, as reported by CEDA (2015) and Matysek and Fisher (2016).

> We've proven that autonomy in trucks can be very successful and is a lower cost option. We'll do the same thing for the drills.
>
> (Interviewee 2)

More than the technology itself, participants provided insight into scalability of innovative projects. Interviewee 6 noted with their experience in Fortescue's project implementation, the organisation greatly consistently considers scalability.

> . . . The reason they do stuff is because it's scalable . . . Every time they do things, they do think forward to see if they can scale it up if they need to.
>
> (Interviewee 6)

Interviewees carefully stated, upscaling large projects requires addressing several key issues. Notably cultural changes would present the largest barrier in terms of implementing AHS into Fortescue's Chichester manned hub.

> Solomon has always had the plan to be autonomous, that's always been part of the psyche out there. It's the people and the process around the existing mine that will be the biggest challenge.
>
> (Interviewee 5)

> I don't think we should trivialise the challenges faced with upscaling. And again, it's people . . . getting change in people's mindset, and how they work. That's the biggest limitation.
>
> (Interviewee 1)

Capital needs and size constraints were also recognised as factors to be considered when upscaling AHS systems.

> Initial upfront investment will determine the scalability . . . It could cost a million dollars to convert a machine from manned to an autonomous. If you only do it for say, 5 pieces of mining equipment, the ROI will be very long.
>
> (Interviewee 2)

Inquiry into technologies behind Fortescue's innovation agenda provided insight into how the organisation aims to achieve goals surrounding C1 cost and efficiency. The two most dominant themes were AHS and wet ore processing as part of Fortescue's OPFs in the Solomon hub. Respondents mentioned Fortescue's actively attempts to limit redundancies through reskilling and natural attrition. The scalability of these systems, interviewees demonstrated, is dependent on strong management of cultural change, large capital outlay and physical limitations of mine sites.

Discussion

This section explains how prevalent themes and concepts arisen from the research of Fortescue's innovation agenda relate to the philosophy of the organisation. Constructing theory to answer the research question utilising the grounded theory approach.

Four interviewees shared the view that one of the fundamental factors of Fortescue's culture was its dependency on people. Interviewees suggested that the requirements of employees are higher than other mining organisations, but delegated responsibility is greater likewise.

> Particularly in my group, it's super critical about people. We're very heavily dependent on people. But they like working there because they have such opportunity to use their capabilities.
>
> (Interviewee 1)

Participants remarked that they had a strong sense of belief instilled in them by Fortescue. Commenting management trusts individual judgement and that the company is prepared to take new ideas on board.

> They really trust the people and they trust people's judgment . . . We employ people who are technically very competent at what they do and let them make decisions.
>
> (Interviewee 1)

> It's a challenging work environment. It's very satisfying but it's also dynamic. On the flipside, Fortescue from an executive leadership point of view is very supportive of trying new things.
>
> (Interviewee 2)

> It's because people take ownership in the company . . . We're all on the same page. We all want to achieve the same goal . . . We take on people's ideas, we review them, and are prepared to give it a crack. That's one of the sayings, it's that we're prepared to give it a crack.
>
> (Interviewee 7)

Participants explained the 'give it a crack' mentality is a result of Fortescue founder and non-executive chairman, Andrew Forrest's own attitude.

> Forrest has a tongue-in-cheek comment that he makes all the time. 'You can have a risky plan-A but you've got to have a bullet-proof plan-B.' That's how we do it, so we're always looking for plan A to be a stretch, a challenge.
>
> (Interviewee 1)

Interviewee 1 further commented that Fortescue's appetite for risk began at the outset.

> Fortescue pretty much grew from nothing, took some big risks in the early days in terms of debt . . . Instead of starting off small with small mines growing and them, it started off as huge mine from day one and developed those. Definitely its appetite for risk is one of the biggest in the industry.
>
> (Interviewee 2)

Interviewee 7 shared the same view, claiming Fortescue's management is unlike others, as it does not stick to methods tried and true.

> . . . The other big companies in management tend to stick to a tried and true method . . . We give it a shot. Other companies have, I suppose aged thinking.
>
> (Interviewee 7)

Fortescue's culture of calculated risk-taking aids the explanation of how the organisation innovates. It could be argued that association between risk appetite and rapid innovation is critical to the success of the company.

Interviewee 1 highlighted the organisation's openness to new partnerships through an open-door policy.

> What we've found is, lots of people come because they know that we'll talk to them. We say these are our 5 biggest problems, which have the biggest potential to improve our business, so what can you do to help us in these areas. The conversation becomes very structured.
>
> (Interviewee 1)

A third common belief held by participants demonstrated the importance of strong corporate partnerships at Fortescue. Interviewees revealed from past experiences working at the company's competitors that dogma plagued decision making by sticking to in-house unoriginal practices. The case of collaborative R&D alongside Caterpillar with autonomous haulage systems was especially documented.

> Larger mining companies probably still have this entrenched belief that "we know better than they do and we'll do our own way because we're a huge company, therefore we must be smarter and know more about it than everyone else." I've worked with some of those companies and the mentality typically is "no we're not going to do what they're doing because we are who we are and the way we do things."
>
> (Interviewee 2)

Interviewee 1 explained, successful and timely implementation of the AHS would have arrived much later without Caterpillars involvement.

Speed's everything . . . No, we wouldn't have hit our targets if we didn't have our partnership with Caterpillar.

(Interviewee 1)

Additionally, Caterpillar's involvement in the partnership was spoken to be rigorous and thorough. Interviewees 1 and 2 mentioned reverence is shared between both parties, and the relationship spans from executives through to operations management. According to interviewee 2, this results in a great amount of shared benefits to both organisations.

It's one of the best partnerships in my thirty years in the mining business. The respect at all levels right through the companies. The two companies, all the senior executives know each other. The partnership is not down here, it goes right through to Andrew Forrest and works down through all levels.

(Interviewee 1)

That's probably the difference between Fortescue and the other companies; really working with the suppliers, or Caterpillar. Caterpillar have access to all our databases, we get huge databases of all their production information and we share . . . and work jointly on it. We want to have a partnership here that's going to be beneficial for both parties. The pace of development is much higher than what it would have normally been.

(Interviewee 2)

The final collectively held theme of Fortescue's culture demonstrated openness and low levels of organisational bureaucracy. Participants note the company has allowed creative thinking to flourish, communication flow, and regarding the innovation agenda, fast implementation of new ideas.

. . . The thing I like about Fortescue is it's just very pragmatic, it keeps it simple. It just makes simple obvious decisions quickly and moves on.

(Interviewee 1)

(With) Other miners . . . I've worked for one of them and yes there's so much more, I suppose red tape to get a result. With Fortescue, they implement change very quickly and they start trials very quickly.

(Interviewee 7)

Pragmaticism and openness between operations and management was reported to travel throughout the company. This approach is not commonplace in the industry, as reported by Interviewee 1.

The CEO gets around every site, every month. It's an organisation, not a big conglomerate. It's a lean organisation with significant interaction with the

CEO, and even down to a managerial level in the business . . . With the large companies, I think the executive gets very, very divorced from the operation.

(Interviewee 1)

The connection between the organisation's approach of fast and effective action was also attributed to the lack of paper shuffling. Participants cited previous experiences working with Fortescue's competition other miners, highlighting that decision-making processes were much slower and entirely different to that of Fortescue's.

I worked in the same position as I am now in one of the other companies, I applied at Fortescue because I couldn't achieve what I wanted to achieve due to red tape.

(Interviewee 7)

Discoveries throughout work further signified findings by Posner (2010) and Sheehan and Isaac (2014) illustrating the importance of corporate culture and employee empowerment. Links were deduced between the ethos behind Fortescue, and its ability to realise fast and pragmatic decisions. Themes and sentiments relating to organisational culture focussed on calculated risk, pragmaticism and quick decision making, autonomy in the workplace and fast implementation of ideas. Additionally, strong corporate partnerships, openness and the unbureaucratic nature of Fortescue were cited as core components.

INTERVIEWEE 1: . . . It's a different company (Fortescue). I think it'll be very, very hard to replicate. It was created by Andrew (Forrest) . . . Neville Power (the company's CEO) has really been instrumental in taking that philosophy from Andrew.

RESEARCHER: So it's a continuation?

INTERVIEWEE 1: It is . . . I feel that these successful companies are created by individuals, there's no doubt. It's very, very hard to replicate.

The researcher proposes that Fortescue has pursued its innovation agenda due to the philosophy which underpins the organisation, irrespective of external factors. Envisioned by its founders, the company's culture permits the company to expand at a rapid rate through taking financial risks requiring innovative thinking and practices. Participants stated, the leanness of the organisation naturally encouraged innovative and creative thinking through the stretch-targets initiative. The researcher contends that Fortescue's unique company culture and design enables the organisation's strong competitive advantage (Porter, 1990), resulting in Fortescue being named the world's lowest cost seaborne producer of iron ore by Metalytics in December 2016 (Wells, 2016).

Using a Glaserian Grounded Theory approach, this study has uncovered reasoning behind Fortescue Metals Group's innovation agenda. Understanding current innovation trends helps to flag potential growth areas and strategic direction of the nation's iron ore giants. The research found catalysts that forced Fortescue to rapidly cut costs throughout its operations.

Innovative practices focussed predominately on two areas: automated truck and rail haulage, and wet ore processing in the OPF functions. Interviewees noted vast cost and environmental benefits were realised by use of innovative technologies and strategies. Participant's attitudes concerning job losses brought on by AHS revealed that Fortescue management is actively seeking alternate plans to mass workforce reductions.

Further findings presented sentiments regarding the culture of Fortescue. The researcher argues Fortescue's unique philosophy and design were the key enablers of its current innovation strategy. This was achieved through calculated but risky decision making, fostering employee idea creation, low organisational bureaucracy and lean organisational design.

Conclusion

Although this research is not intended to provide detail on future strategies of the organisation, it offers preliminary academic insight into the key themes and issues surrounding Fortescue's innovation agenda. The author hopes to encourage further academic research into the field of innovation strategies of Australia's resource producers. The researcher uncovered the emergence of several key areas from the interviews which warrant further investigation: innovation agendas of Fortescue's competitors to benchmark the industry, an update on Mudd's 2010 review of looming constraints and mega trends of Australia's resources sector, and in-depth inquiry into the effects of automation across Australia's mining and resources industry. This research has attempted to shed light on how one of Australia's iron ore giants has innovated to remain viable amongst a long and turbulent mining supercycle.

References

Austrade. (2016). Australia's export performance in 2015, Australian trade and investment commission, Canberra. Retrieved from: www.austrade.gov.au/news/economic-analysis/australias-export-performance-in-2015 [Accessed 12 September 2016].

Australian Bureau of Statistics. (2015). Estimates of industry multifactor productivity Australia, cat. no. 5260.0.55.002. Retrieved from: www.abs.gov.au/ausstats/abs@.nsf/mf/5260.0.55.002 [Accessed 17 October 2016].

Auty, R. (2007). Natural resources, capital accumulation and the resource curse. *Ecological Economics*, 61, 627–634.

BHP Billiton. (2015). Annual report 2015, BHP Billiton. Retrieved from: www.bhpbilliton.com/~/media/bhp/documents/investors/annual-reports/2015/bhpbillitonannualreport2015.pdf [Accessed 4 August 2016].

Boulter, A., and Hall, R. (2015). Wireless network requirements for the successful implementation of automation and other innovative technologies in open-pit mining. *International Journal of Mining, Reclamation and Environment*, 29(5), 368–379.

Bureau of Resource and Energy Economics (BREE) (2013), Productivity in the Australian Mining Sector, BREE Discussion Paper Series 13.01, March 2013, Canberra.

Committee for Economic Development Australia. (2015). Australia's future workforce, CEDA, Melbourne. Retrieved from: http://adminpanel.ceda.com.au/FOLDERS/Service/Files/Documents/26792~Futureworkforce_June2015.pdf [Accessed 2 September 2016].

Commonwealth Scientific and Industrial Research Organisation. (2014). Australian attitudes toward mining, citizen survey 2014 results, CSIRO, Brisbane. Retrieved from: people.csiro.au/~/media/ . . . /M/K/ . . . /CSIRO_MiningReport_Aus. ashx [Accessed 29 April 2016].

de Krester, A., and Forrestal, L. (2012, August 24). Boom has longer to run: Miners. *The Australian Financial Review*. Retrieved from: www.afr.com/p/futureforums/boom_has_longer_to_run_miners_TFKSzlBWONWVDWYoecep0L [Accessed 19 August 2016].

Department of Foreign Affairs and Trade. (2014). Australia's trade at a glance top 10 exports and imports, DFAT, Canberra. Retrieved from: http://dfat.gov.au/trade/resources/trade-at-a-glance/Pages/html/top-goods-services.aspx [Accessed 13 October 2016].

Ernst & Young. (2015). Business risks facing mining and metals, industry report. Retrieved from: Ernst & Young database [Accessed 12 September 2016].

Fortescue Metals Group Ltd. (2015). Annual report 2015, Fortescue metals group limited. Retrieved from: http://fmgl.com.au/media/2590/fortescue-annual-report-fy15.pdf [Accessed 25 August 2016].

Fortescue Metals Group Ltd. (2016). Annual report 2016, Fortescue metals group limited. Retrieved from: http://fmgl.com.au/media/2862/fy16-fortescue-annual-report-final-with-cover.pdf [Accessed 27 August 2016].

Gibbs, A. 1997, 'Focus Groups', *Social Research Update*, 19(8), 12–14.

Glaser, B. (1978). *Theoretical Sensitivity*. Mill Valley, CA: The Sociology Press.

Glaser, B. (1992). *Basics of Grounded Theory Analysis: Emergence v. Forcing*. Mill Valley, CA: The Sociology Press.

Glaser, B., and Strauss, A. (1967). Th*e Discovery of Grounded Theory: Strategies for Qualitative Research*. Chicago: Aldine.

Goodman, J., and Worth, D. (2008). The minerals boom and Australia's resource curse. *Journal of Australian Political Economy*, 61, 201–219.

Greber, J. (2016, October 12). Andrew Forrest says commodity prices have hit bottom. *The Australian Financial Review*. Retrieved from: www.afr.com/news/economy/andrew-forrest-says-commodity-prices-have-hit-bottom-20161012-gs0bcw#ixzz4YRw2MwPL [Accessed 12 October 2016].

Hutchison, A., Johnston, L., and Breckon, J. (2010). Using QSR-NVivo to facilitate the development of a grounded theory project: An account of a worked example. *International Journal of Social Research Methodology*, 13(4), 283–302.

Kallio, H., Pietilä, A.-M., Johnson, M., and Kangasniemi, M. (2016). Systematic methodological review: Developing a framework for a qualitative semi-structured interview guide. *Journal of Advanced Nursing*, 72(12), 2954–2965.

Larsen, E.R. (2006). Escaping the resource curse and the Dutch Disease? *American Journal of Economics & Sociology*, 65(3), 605–640.

Liew, L. (2012). As Asia's quarry: Implications for Australia. *Australian Journal of International Affairs*, 66(5), 542–553.

Matysek, A., and Fisher, B. (2016). Productivity and innovation in the mining industry, industry research report, BA Economics Pty Ltd. Retrieved from: BAEconomics publications database [Accessed 20 September 2016].

Maxwell, P., and Guj, P. (2006). *Australian Mineral Economics: A Survey of Important Issues*. Carlton, Victoria: The Australian Institute of Mining and Metallurgy.

Mohr, S., Giurco, D., Yellishetty, M., Ward, J., and Mudd, G. (2015). Projection of iron ore production. *Natural Resources Research*, 24(3), 317–327.

Mudd, G. (2009). The sustainability of mining in Australia: Key production trends and their environmental implications for the future. Research Report No. RR5, Dept. of Civil Engineering, Monash University and Mineral Policy Institute.

Mudd, G. (2010). The Environmental sustainability of mining in Australia: Key mega-trends and looming constraints. *Resources Policy*, 35(2), 98–115.

Papyrakis, E., and Gerlagh, R. (2003). The resource curse hypothesis and its transmission channels. *Journal of Comparative Economics*, 32, 181–193.

Porter, M. (1990). The competitive advantage of nations. *Harvard Business Review*, 68(2), 73–93.

Posner, B. (2010). Another look at the impact of personal and organizational values congruency. *Journal of Business Ethics*, 97(4), 535–541.

PricewaterhouseCoopers. (2014). Mining for efficiency, industry report. Retrieved from: PwC database [Accessed 20 August 2016].

PricewaterhouseCoopers. (2016). Mine 2016 slower, lower, weaker . . . but not defeated, Industry report. Retrieved from: PwC database [Accessed 20 August 2016].

Prior, T., Daly, J., Mason, L., and Giurco, A. (2013). Resourcing the future: Using foresight in resource governance. *Geoforum*, 44, 316–328.

Redrup, Y. (2016, August 16). Australia drops in global innovation index. *The Australian Financial Review*. Retrieved from: www.afr.com/technology/australia-drops-in-global-innovation-index-20160815-gqsiou [Accessed 19 September].

Robson, A. (2015). The Australian economy and economic policy during and after the mining Boom *Economic Affairs*, 35(2), 307–316.

Shaxson, N. (2007). Oil, corruption and the resource curse. *International Affairs*, 83(6), 1123–1140.

Sheehan, N., and Isaac, G. (2014). Principles operationalize corporate values so they matter *Strategy & Leadership*, 42(3), 23–30.

Stevens, P., and Dietsche, E. (2008). Resource curse: An analysis of causes, experiences and possible ways forward. *Energy Policy*, 36(1), 56–65.

Tuffley, D. (2015, June 17). Australia must prepare for massive job losses due to automation. *Australian Mining*. Retrieved from: www.australianmining.com.au/features/australia-must-prepare-for-massive-job-losses-due-to-automation/. [Accessed 8 October 2016]

Wells, I. (2016). Fortescue – Debt reduction to continue as Fortescue is recognised as lowest cost seaborne supplier of iron ore into China, Company Report, Fortescue Metals Group Limited. Retrieved from: http://fmgl.com.au/media/2927/161208_asx_fortescue-debt-reduction-to-continue-as-fortescue-is-recognised-as-lowest-cost-seaborne-producer/ [Accessed 12 December 2016].

8 Individual innovativeness, entrepreneurial creativity and religious capital

The role of transformational entrepreneurship in Tunisia

Waleed Omri

Introduction

Innovation is widely considered as crucial in the entrepreneurial process and is being increasingly documented as a critical means by which organizations can create meaningful, sustainable value for their different stakeholders in today's dynamically changing environment (e.g., Bessant and Tidd, 2011; Damanpour and Wischnevsky, 2006). Traditional innovation studies have identified that innovation revolves around individuals who creatively engage in new organizational efforts (Scott and Bruce, 1994; Janssen, 2000). In a similar vein, Ireland et al. (2009) added that the innovation behaviors and processes at the organizational member level are central to any corporate entrepreneurship strategy. Therefore, academic research and policy circles are paying increasing attention to how individual innovative behavior can be fostered and triggered (e.g., De Jong et al., 2015; Janssen, 2000; Reuvers et al., 2008). According to De Jong and Den Hartog (2010), innovative behavior at work relates to managers or employees' voluntary willingness to come up with on-the-job innovations; for example, improving work methods, using technology, establishing new plans and strategies, or developing new services or products. Despite innovative behavior having rapidly developed as a new field of research in innovation management, most studies focus on employees in large manufacturing firms and neglect management teams (West and Anderson, 1996). The present study focuses on the role played by owner-managers within the innovation process.

Despite the broadly acknowledged importance of innovation at the individual level in the establishment of successful ventures, the literature lacks evidence on how managers can effectively harness their skills and knowledge in the workplace. The existing literature illustrates that religion can impact the day-to-day work behavior of entrepreneurs, managers, and employees (Drakopoulou Dodd and Gotsis, 2007; Henley, 2017; Judge and Douglas, 2013; Ramadani et al., 2015; Ratten et al., 2017). Other scholars have argued that religious beliefs and practices could affect daily entrepreneurial activities by fostering mental abilities and traits such as creativity, intelligence, and self-efficacy (McCleary and Barro, 2006; Omri and Becuwe, 2014). In the present study, we define religious capital as a set of personal and intangible resources, skills, and competencies that emanate from an individual's religious values, beliefs, practices, and experiences and may be used to increase the quality of economic activities. Iannaccone (1998) highlights that religious beliefs and practices give individuals a religious satisfaction, which can lead them to perform better in the workplace. In addition, religious ethics and practices have been linked to various positive employee outcomes in terms of organizational change, job satisfaction, and entrepreneurial intensity (Dana, 2009; Sabah et al., 2014; Yousef, 2000, 2001). As investigations of their consequences beyond direct task performance are still scarce (Ireland et al., 2009), we explore if religious capital plays a role in managers' innovative behavior. Following Omri and Becuwe (2014), we use both Islamic work ethics (IWE) and Islamic religious practices (IRP) to measure Islamic religious capital.

This study makes at least three contributions to the literature on both individual entrepreneurship and innovation. First, religion has often been identified as a major antecedent of various entrepreneurial activities, yet the discussion on how and why it affects individual innovative behavior remains limited (e.g., Kumar and Che Rose, 2010; Neubert et al., 2017; Omri and Becuwe, 2014). To the best of our knowledge, no study has endeavored to theoretically and empirically establish the effects of Islamic religious capital on entrepreneurial creativity and innovative behavior in the workplace, even though one of the main motivations for studying religious beliefs is its determining role in affecting primary workplace goals and outcomes (Murtaza et al., 2016; Ratten et al., 2017). Second, our study expands on the existing literature (Dorenbosch et al., 2005; Scott and Bruce, 1994) by identifying creativity as a cognitive ability that is not only affected by religiosity but also mediates the relationship between religiosity and innovative behavior. By examining these direct and indirect relationships, this study responds to some of the calls made in the individual entrepreneurship literature (Dana, 2009; MacPherson and Kelly, 2011) to explicitly model the direct effects of individual innovative antecedents and mediated effects through entrepreneurial creativity. Given the important role of creativity in changing a company's entrepreneurial behavior (Khedhaouria et al., 2014), the tendency among managers who use religious criteria to promote entrepreneurial creativity can be considered a path to successful innovation. Finally, *our research also responds to the call* for greater attention toward Muslim-majority countries (Cavanagh, 1999). Our Tunisian sample offers external validity for the theorized relationships in this study.

We test our hypotheses using data gathered from 289 Tunisian small businesses. No direct relationship between IRP and innovative behavior among population has been found. Rather, we find that IRP matter only if managers invest considerable time developing their creative abilities. We also find that managers who are highly sensitive to IWE are likely to be more creative and skilled at problem solving. Nevertheless, these findings do not indicate that the Islamic faith determines creative personality and innovation – the associations we find are nothing more than predispositions – but they point to the value of considering the role of religious beliefs and practices in entrepreneurial activities. Our study also complements other approaches in exploring the role of organizational culture in creativity and innovation. Previous studies have shown that religion (Emerson and Mckinney, 2010; Yousef, 2000) plays a role in both creativity (MacPherson and Kelly, 2011) and innovation orientation (Kumar and Che Rose, 2010; Sabah et al., 2014). Our study does not challenge the importance of either religious ethics or practices in creativity or innovative work behavior. It merely follows Drakopoulou Dodd and Seaman (1998), who argue that to truly explain entrepreneurial behavior, one must also delve deeper into understanding people's way of life, particularly their religious capital.

Theory and hypotheses

Religious capital and individual innovative behavior

Researchers generally concur that entrepreneurial and innovation activities require tolerance for hard work and the capacity to deal with situations of high uncertainty (Bessant and Tidd, 2011; Dana, 2009; Parboteeah et al., 2015). Parboteeah et al. (2015) advocate that belief in the existence of God gives workers useful means to confront uncertainties inherent in innovation (Parboteeah et al., 2015). They added that religion as an important social institution can have a strong norm-setting influence on individuals through its ethics, values, and practices, which set behavior expectations. In the literature, a common starting point to study the relationship between religion and entrepreneurship is the theory of planned behavior (TPB), an offshoot of the theory of reasoned action, by Fishbein and Ajzen (1975). Consistent with the predictions of TPB, an entrepreneur's behavior is guided by social and cultural attitudes, which are central to comprehending human behavior. Under the same framework, religion is considered a background issue that may impact individual attitudes and subjective norms (Ajzen and Fishbein, 2005). To this effect, Parboteeah et al. (2015) added that religiosity could be an important source of personal ethics and values. As values can be a base for the formation of attitudes (Ajzen and Fishbein, 2005; Henley, 2017), religious values and practices are also likely to influence attitudes toward entrepreneurial behaviors such as innovative work behavior. Returning to the open issue of the connection between religion and innovation activity leads to the first main research question: is there an association between religious capital and innovative behavior in an Islamic context?

IWE have been defined as an individual's belief in the likelihood of satisfying God by producing his or her best effort in the workplace (Ali, 1988) and linked to various positive employee outcomes in terms of organizational change (Yousef, 2000), job satisfaction (Yousef, 2001), entrepreneurial intensity (Sabah et al., 2014), and recently, organizational citizenship behaviors (Murtaza et al., 2016). We suggest that individuals with strong IWE tend to have positive attitudes toward their work and believe they are able to successfully generate new and useful ideas and solutions. Several researchers (Kumar and Che Rose, 2010; Omri and Becuwe, 2014; Yousef, 2000) are of the view that IWE can have a positive effect and enhance idea generation, problem solving, and the ability to simultaneously analyze multiple factors and convincingly deal with issues that may arise in a given situation. In addition, Islamic religious practices in the workplace help individuals develop closer links with important aspects of life such as God, people, and family, and thereby, become more effective in their tasks and work environments (Naail et al., 2011). They enable entrepreneurs, managers, and employees to gain a better sense of God's role as well as that of other people in their workplace. Hulusi (2014) suggests that individuals who engage in Islamic spiritual practices, such as prayer and *Dhikr*, have a set of relatively positive emotions and feelings and strive to achieve their objectives even when faced with awkwardness and problems. These practices continually exert formative influences on their behavior until they become entirely conditioned by these influences. Accordingly, we propose the following hypotheses:

H1: Religious capital is significantly positively related to managers' innovative behavior.

H1a: IWE are significantly positively related to managers' innovative behavior.
H1b: IRP are significantly positively related to managers' innovative behavior.

Religious capital and entrepreneurial creativity

Much research shows that creativity is influenced by cognitive factors (Shane and Nicolaou, 2015) as well as individual daily practices and activities (Vygotsky, 1934/1987) related especially to one's religion (MacPherson and Kelly, 2011; Omri and Becuwe, 2014). According to Judge and Douglas (2013), religious capital is an important source of inspiration in identifying problems and thereby, developing creative solutions and ideas. Under the TPB framework (Ajzen, 1991; Ajzen and Fishbein, 2005), previous studies argue that religious resources and norms have the potential to shape mental models that inform motives and behaviors (Henley, 2017). If entrepreneurial creativity resides in individuals, it is tempting to ask whether Muslim owner-managers are more creative when they practice a religion.

Islamic religious inspiration might help individuals quiet their mind and improve their brain's energy efficiency through prayer and contemplation (Ibn Khaldun, 1332–1406). In the Qur'an, positive behavior and entrepreneurial activities such as creativity and innovation are highly encouraged as part of Islam (Murtaza et al., 2016; Yousef, 2001). Indeed, the encouragement of human creativity features widely in the Holy Qur'an (SuratAz-Zariyat, verse number 21: "and also in your own selves; can you not see?"). In these verses (*ayat*), God speaks about the importance of thought in ourselves and in our environment, which contributes to the stimulation of creative ability for all individuals. Various theoretical models predict the significant and positive consequences of religious ethics in terms of work outcomes. Nevertheless, regarding the relationship between IWE and creativity, the literature is far less developed. Omri and Becuwe (2014) show that Islamic ethics might influence people's tendency to develop mental abilities, which can affect the probability of engaging in certain creative work behaviors. On the other hand, true religious practices are those which have the power to improve an individual's brain. Cavanagh (1999) defines factual religious practices as those that might attain the level of an individual's mind and be effective for his or her thinking abilities. In the Islamic context, religious practices have an important role to play in defining, fostering, and developing creative abilities (Kayed and Hassan, 2010; Vargas-Hernandez et al., 2010). They constitute a central resource for the development of the process of spiritual or intellectual progress among Muslim managers and employees. According to Hulusi (2014), true IRP are based on prayer, *Dhikr*, and contemplation, which all related to intellectual activities. A recent empirical study (Omri and Becuwe, 2014) emphasizes that IRP foster creativity and stimulate the development of entrepreneurs' abilities in small businesses. They add that practices, such as prayer and contemplation, can lead people to consistently behave in a more creative manner across various domains including entrepreneurship. Hence, we hypothesize as follows:

H2: Religious capital is significantly positively related to entrepreneurial creativity.

H2a: IWE are significantly positively related to entrepreneurial creativity.
H2b: IRP are significantly positively related to entrepreneurial creativity.

Entrepreneurial creativity and individual innovative behavior

A plethora of academics and scholars concerned with innovation management have stated that innovation behavior is an entrepreneurial process promoted by entrepreneurs and triggered by their entrepreneurial creativity (Amabile, 1997; Shane and Nicolaou, 2015; Zhao and Seibert, 2006). Schumpeter (1934) advocates that the entrepreneur is a creative, driven individual who finds new combinations of production factors to develop a new product, create and expand a new market, or design a new technology.

Dayan et al. (2013) point out that entrepreneurs can harness their creative aptitudes to design unique and useful solutions to economic opportunities, reduce or beat constraints of rare resources, and commercialize and develop businesses. Consequently, creativity is considered critical for entrepreneurial processes, enabling entrepreneurs to compete in a competitive dynamic environment (Dayan et al., 2013; Wu et al., 2014). Zhao and Seibert (2006) add that firm survival and growth require entrepreneurs to be able to discover original ideas; use their creative skills to solve new problems; and create innovative procedures for products, business methods, or strategies. Under the componential theory of creativity (Amabile, 1996, 1997), individuals who have a high level of creativity tend to feel more confident and perceive problems as challenges. Within this framework, Anderson and others (Anderson et al., 2014) have shown that the creative behavior of entrepreneurs can be seen as impacting the entrepreneurial process of generating and implementing innovation solutions that "meet the changing needs of the market and leads to the entrepreneurial event" (Morris and Kuratko, 2002, p. 225). The entrepreneurial event encompasses the launching of a new startup or a new product or service as well as enhancing an existing product, service, or practices within an established organization. Consistent with the same approach, individuals with high creative abilities can mobilize the knowledge, experience, and cognitive resources needed to generate and develop new ideas or solutions. These creative abilities enable individuals to perform specific tasks successfully and achieve organizational innovation goals in the face of obstacles (Anderson et al., 2014; Wu et al., 2014). Thus, we put forth a third hypothesis:

> H3: Entrepreneurial creativity is significantly positively related to managers' innovative behavior.

Mediating role of entrepreneurial creativity

As previously noted, hypotheses 2 and 3 link Islamic religious capital with entrepreneurial creativity and entrepreneurial creativity with individual innovative behavior. This means that the association between religious capital and innovative behavior is hypothesized to be indirect. In other words, entrepreneurial creativity plays the role of an intermediate variable that mediates the relationships between the predictor variable of religiosity and the outcome variable of innovative behavior. As religious beliefs and practices serve as a driving force for an individual's creative ability, these religious variables will have an indirect connection with individual innovation. In particular, entrepreneurial creativity allows both IWE and IRP to function effectively in enhancing individual innovation. In research on innovative work behavior, it is often assumed that antecedents such as Islamic religious beliefs affect individual innovative behavior through changes in individual-level cognitive abilities (Omri and Becuwe, 2014). Islamic religious beliefs and practices not only enable managers to experiment with innovative work practices but also foster their overall creative abilities (Omri and Becuwe, 2014; Yousef, 2000). Drawing on these arguments, the present study tests the extent to which entrepreneurial creativity mediates the relationship between Islamic ethics and practices on the one hand and innovative work behavior on the other, irrespective of full or partial mediation. In other words, the greater an individuals' level of religious beliefs and practices, the more they will develop their creative ability (Allen, 1978), which in turn will positively affect innovative behavior. Thus, we propose the following hypotheses:

> H4: Entrepreneurial creativity mediates the relationship between religious capital and managers' innovative behavior.
>
>> H4a: Entrepreneurial creativity mediates the relationship between IWE and managers' innovative behavior.
>> H4b: Entrepreneurial creativity mediates the relationship between IRP and managers' innovative behavior.

Research method

Sample selection and survey procedures

The sampling frame, constructed from the databases of the Tunisian agency for the promotion of industry and innovation (APII[1]), offers relatively complete coverage of Tunisian firms. A random stratified sampling method was used to select 620 small companies from the APII database. The characteristics of the sample companies are presented in Table 8.1.

Small business owner-managers[2] were approached and invited to participate in the survey. The questionnaire was pilot tested on a convenience sample of 12 owner-managers. All selected respondents were encouraged to provide comments or re-write items in the questionnaire they felt were ambiguous or problematic. The feedback collected from the pilot test was used to modify the first version of the questionnaire. The final copy of the questionnaire, which was preceded by an introductory letter, was sent to participants. This letter briefly described the aims of the research and explained how the study itself would be of benefit to respondents and their company. A total of 412 companies qualified to participate in the study on the basis of email and telephone pre-surveys and the availability of their owner-managers. Twenty days following the initial email, personal phone calls were made to remind each participant about the questionnaire survey. Twenty days after the initial telephone contact, we sent a second copy of the questionnaire to non-respondents. A total of 296 questionnaires were collected, and after excluding those with missing data and unclear or contradictory answers, 289 questionnaires were used for the data analysis. The manager response rate was 70 percent. Their tenure ranged from 0.8 to 35.6 years. The average age of the sample was 41 years. All participants (100 percent) held a university diploma.

Measures

Dependent variable: innovative behavior

The measurement of individual innovation behavior (eight items) is adopted from Scott and Bruce (1994) and Janssen (2000) and has been used and

Table 8.1 Sample distribution by industry

Industry	Number of firms	Percentage of total sample
1. Manufacturing	102	35.0
2. Services	81	28.0
3. Agro-alimentary	39	14.0
4. Trade	32	11.0
5. Telecommunications	17	6.0
6. Health	11	4.0
7. Other	7	2.0
Total	289	100

validated in previous studies (Reuvers et al., 2008; Omri, 2015). The innovative behavior scale is designed to elicit answers from managers regarding
behaviors through which they contribute in the innovation process of their
companies. In the present research, we use a one-dimensional measurement of
innovative behavior, encompassing both the generation and implementation
of ideas. The scale comprises eight items and respondents rate each item on a
seven-point Likert scale, ranging from "strongly disagree" to "strongly agree."
The coefficient alpha for this scale was 0.897, denoting a high level of internal
consistency.

Independent variable: religious capital

The two measures of Islamic religious capital were focused on the concept of religiosity developed in the previous literature (Ali, 1988; Arslan, 2001; Iannaccone,
1998). We chose this scale because it has been validated by Omri and Becuwe
(2014) and it assesses the importance of an individual's religious work ethics and
religious practices under the same dimension. We measured IWE using five questions with respect to the respondents' conception of time management and their
view of group work and behaviors regarding consultation. We then measured
IRP on the basis of five items, indicating the importance they attribute to private
prayer, recitation of the holy Qur'an, visiting parents and other family members,
and contemplation. Each item was rated on a seven-point Likert scale, ranging
from one (strongly disagree) to seven (strongly agree). For the first scale (IWE),
Cronbach's alpha was at a satisfactory level of 0.847. For the second scale (IRP),
Cronbach's alpha was also satisfactory at 0.895.

Mediator variable: entrepreneurial creativity

In this study, seven items adopted from Zhou and George (2001) were employed
to measure entrepreneurial creativity. These seven items had the highest factor
loadings in their study and had previously been used to reflect entrepreneurial
creativity in several management studies (Dayan et al., 2013). For each item,
informants were asked to provide an assessment on a seven-point Likert scale,
ranging from one (strongly disagree) to seven (strongly agree). Cronbach's alpha
for the seven items was acceptable at 0.853.

Control variables

In our analysis, we controlled for two variables that might influence a manager's innovative behavior. Control variables used in the analysis are age and level
of education. The existing literature suggests that older managers are likely to
be more innovative (Yuan and Woodman, 2010). Existing empirical research
(Bessant and Tidd, 2011; Fayolle, 2007) also suggests that managers with a high
education level display significantly more favorable attitudes toward entrepreneurial activities.

Data analysis and results

Validation of measurements

We use structural equation modeling (SEM) with a robust maximum likelihood estimation to explore the relationships among the above-described variables. SEM is applied using the SPSS software package (version 18.0) because it can be used for exploratory factor analysis (EFA) and includes AMOS 18.0 to measure both the confirmatory factor analysis (CFA) and structural model. AMOS 18.0 was also used to assess the overall fit of the models using the maximum likelihood method.

Similar to relevant studies (e.g., Abstein et al., 2014; Scott and Bruce, 1994), we followed Anderson and Gerbing's (1988) two-step approach to validate the measurement model prior to the structural model. A principal component analysis (PCA) was initially conducted to ensure the unidimensionality of the scales measuring each concept in our conceptual model and show the loadings of items on the corresponding construct. Following Flynn et al.'s (1994) recommendations, items should be deleted if they load on more than two factors or the difference between factor loadings is less than 0.10 across factors. As shown in Table 8.2, the EFA results demonstrate that unidimensionality is ensured.

Table 8.2 Exploratory factor analysis

Constructs	Variables	Factor loadings		
Islamic work ethics	IWE 1	0.740		
	IWE 2	0.817		
	IWE 3	0.793		
	IWE 4	0.781		
	IWE 5	0.814		
Islamic religious practices	IRP 1		0.762	
	IRP 2		0.873	
	IRP 3		0.829	
	IRP 4		0.869	
	IRP 5		0.860	
Entrepreneurial creativity	ECR 1			0.687
	ECR 2			0.630
	ECR 3			0.727
	ECR 4			0.749
	ECR 5			0.787
	ECR 6			0.804
	ECR 7			0.735
Innovative behavior	INB 1			0.743
	INB 2			0.744
	INB 3			0.701
	INB 4			0.769
	INB 5			0.803
	INB 6			0.762
	INB 7			0.788
	INB 8			0.808

Note: N = 289 observations; INB: innovative behavior; IWE: Isamic work ethics; IRP: Islamic religious practice; ECR: entrepreneurial creativity

Following Fornell and Larcker (1981) and Anderson and Gerbing (1988), we evaluated the reliability and validity of our variables using CFA. Table 8.3 summarizes the results of our confirmatory assessment of the measurement model. Bagozzi and Yi (1988) recommend computing values for Cronbach's alpha (CA), composite reliability (CR), and average variance extracted (AVE) to assess scale reliability. As Table 8.3 illustrates, the values for CA in each case are higher than the recommended 0.70 threshold and indicate that the scales are reliable (Fornell and Larcker, 1981; Nunnally, 1978). The generally accepted threshold for CR is 0.70 (Bagozzi and Yi, 1988) and our results show that the CR coefficients were above the recommended level, indicating that all latent variables are reliable for this research. In addition, the AVE coefficient was also used to assess the reliability of each construct. This coefficient serves to complement the CR measurements (Hair et al., 1998). Results, shown in Table 8.3, showed that all

Table 8.3 Confirmatory factor analysis

Chi-square ratio = 1.274; RMSEA = 0.031; NFI = 0.906; TLI = 0.975; CFI = 0.978; IFI = 0.978

Constructs	Item code	Factor loading	t-value	C.A. value	C.R. value	AVE
Islamic work ethics	IWE 1	0.649	11.908	0.847	0.832	0.500
	IWE 2	0.697	11.669			
	IWE 3	0.725	12.089			
	IWE 4	0.699	11.501			
	IWE 5	0.702	11.777			
Islamic religious practices	IRP 1	0.724	13.446	0.895	0.833	0.500
	IRP 2	0.833	16.963			
	IRP 3	0.769	15.108			
	IRP 4	0.877	18.109			
	IRP 5	0.810	16.271			
Entrepreneurial creativity	ECR 1	0.613	10.834	0.853	0.874	0.500
	ECR 2	0.557	09.638			
	ECR 3	0.684	12.460			
	ECR 4	0.690	12.594			
	ECR 5	0.748	14.055			
	ECR 6	0.775	14.789			
	ECR 7	0.674	12.211			
Innovative behavior	INB 1	0.699	13.085	0.897	0.889	0.502
	INB 2	0.701	13.143			
	INB 3	0.650	11.904			
	INB 4	0.729	13.865			
	INB 5	0.770	14.981			
	INB 6	0.717	13.539			
	INB 7	0.756	14.597			
	INB 8	0.780	15.255			

Note: N = 289 observations; RMSEA: root mean square error of approximation; NFI: normed fit index; CFI: comparative fit index; TLI: Tucker-Lewis index; IFI: incremental fit index; CA: the Cronbach's alpha statistic; CR: composite reliability; AVE: average variance extracted; INB: innovative behavior; IWE: Islamic work ethics; IRP: Islamic religious practice; ECR: entrepreneurial creativity. All factor loadings are significant at the p < 0.001 level.

latent variables AVE values were greater than or equal to the acceptable threshold of 0.5 recommended by Hair et al. (2013). Consequently, the research scales are sufficiently reliable.

Bagozzi and Yi (1988) recommend assessing convergent validity using both factor loadings and t-statistics with values greater than 0.5 and 2.0, indicating strong validity. As shown in Table 8.3, the standardized lambda coefficients for each individual item are all significant and exceed the 0.50 threshold, with values of 0.56 or greater. All individual items load significantly on their corresponding factors, with t-values ranging from 9.64 to 18.11 (see Table 8.3). This shows that all study constructs have sufficient convergent validity. According to Fornell and Larcker (1981), discriminant validity determines the extent to which a latent variable is empirically different from other latent variables in the path model. As shown in Table 8.4, CFA results lend strong support to the discriminant validity in our research model because the square roots of the AVEs (mentioned in the diagonal) are all greater than the correlation coefficient between latent variables (mentioned in the off-diagonal; Fornell and Larcker, 1981). Thus, discriminant validity was established for all constructs.

SEM results

We also used SEM analysis to examine the research model. A bootstrapping procedure was used to generate t-statistics and standard errors. Table 8.5 summarizes the results of the hypothesized structural models. Before conducting the analysis, a data screening technique should be used to detect potential data problems, notably in normal distributions. To examine this assumption, we review Mardia's coefficient (a measure of multivariate kurtosis (Mardia, 1970) obtained using AMOS 18.0. In our data, this statistic is equal to 7.657 with a critical ratio of 1.771 (a critical ratio of more than 1.96 signifies departure from multivariate

Table 8.4 Mean standard deviations and correlations of the constructs

Constructs	Mean	S.D.	IWE	IRP	ECR	INB
Islamic work ethics	5.992	0.764	**0.707**			
Islamic religious practices	5.287	0.699	0.007	**0.707**		
Entrepreneurial creativity	5.768	1.201	0.204**	0.256**	**0.707**	
Innovative behavior	5.372	0.823	0.266**	0.107	0.296**	**0.709**

Note: N = 289 observations. INB: innovative behavior; IWE: Islamic work ethics; IRP: Islamic religious practices; ECR: entrepreneurial creativity. Bold values on the diagonal line are the square roots of the average variances extracted (AVEs). All coefficients are significant at the p < 0.01 level.

The measurement model is also assessed for good fit using item-level data. As shown in Table 8.4, goodness-of-fit statistics indicate that the model fits the data well: $\chi2 = 338.949$ ($df = 266$), $p \leq 0.001$, $\chi2/df$ ratio = 1.274; root mean square error of approximation (RMSEA) = 0.031; normed fit index (NFI) = 0.906; Tucker–Lewis index (TLI) = 0.975; comparative fit index (CFI) = 0.978; and incremental fit index (IFI) = 0.978, with all indices at acceptable cut-off ranges (Hair et al., 1998).

Table 8.5 Result of hypothesis testing and structural relationships

Panel A: Structural direct model

Hypothesis	Path	β	S.E	t-Statistic
–	Education → Innovative behavior	0.123	0.052	2.358*
–	Age → Innovative behavior	–0.169	0.055	–3.053**
H1a	Islamic work ethics → Innovative behavior	0.340	0.092	3.701***
H1b	Islamic practices → Innovative behavior	0.086	0.045	1.917[NS]
H2a	Islamic work ethics → Entrepreneurial creativity	–	–	–
H2b	Islamic practices → Entrepreneurial creativity	–	–	–
H3	Entrepreneurial creativity → Innovative behavior	–	–	–
H4a	Islamic work ethics → Entrepreneurial creativity → Innovative behavior	–	–	–
H4b	Islamic practices → Entrepreneurial creativity → Innovative behavior	–	–	–

$R^2_{\text{Innovation behave}}$	0.36
$\chi^2/(df)$	1.932
RMSEA	0.057
NFI	0.890
TLI	0.933
CFI	0.942
IFI	0.943

Panel B: Structural mediated model

Hypothesis	Path	β	S.E	t-Statistic
–	Education → Innovative behavior	0.097	0.051	1.904[NS]
–	Age → Innovative behavior	–0.174	.054	–3.223***
H1a	Islamic work ethics → Innovative behavior	0.277	0.091	3.059***
H1b	Islamic practices → Innovative behavior	0.042	0.046	0.918[NS]
H2a	Islamic work ethics → Entrepreneurial creativity	0.219	0.077	2.831**
H2b	Islamic practices → Entrepreneurial creativity	0.154	0.040	3.804***
H3	Entrepreneurial creativity → Innovative behavior	0.293	0.085	3.444***
H4a (Sobel test)	Islamic work Ethics → Entrepreneurial creativity → Innovative behavior	–	–	2.187*
H4b (Sobel test)	Islamic practices → Entrepreneurial creativity → Innovative behavior	–	–	2.553***

$R^2_{\text{Entrepreneurial creat}}$	0.23
$R^2_{\text{Innovation behave}}$	0.42
$\chi^2/(df)$	1.596
RMSEA	0.046
NFI	0.870
TLI	0.939
CFI	0.945
IFI	0.946

Note: N = 289 observations; S.E: standard error; RMSEA: root mean square error of approximation; NFI: normed fit index; CFI: comparative fit index; TLI: Tucker–Lewis index; IFI: incremental fit index

***p < 0.001, **p < 0.01, * p < 0.05; NS = non-significant. T-statistics are obtained by re-sampling the original sample (800 bootstraps).

normality with 95 percent confidence). Consequently, non-normality was not a major issue for our data (Hair et al., 1998).

We tested the two proposed structural equation models (direct and mediation); the associated fit indices are displayed in Table 8.5. The goodness-of-fit indices for our direct model are as follows: $\chi 2$ = 318.846 (df = 165), p ≤ 0.001, $\chi 2$/df ratio = 1.932; RMSEA = 0.057; NFI = 0.890; TLI = 0.933; CFI = 0.942; and IFI = 0.943. These indices are completely acceptable compared with the threshold values suggested by Hair et al. (1998). As shown in Table 8.5, Panel A, the results of our bootstrapping re-sampling analysis indicate that one of the two hypotheses is supported by the standardized estimate and associated t-value. The relationship between IWE and managers' innovative behavior (II1a) is positive and significant at the 0.1 percent level, as hypothesized with an estimate of 0.34 and t-value of 3.701. Although hypothesized as positive, the relationship between religious practices and managers' innovative behavior (H1b) is non-significant with an estimate of 0.09. These findings offer support for H1a but do not corroborate H1b. Regarding the control variables, the impact of age (β = –0.17, p < 0.01) and education level (β = 0.12, p < 0.05) on individual innovative behavior is statistically significant. Furthermore, our results in Table 8.5, Panel A, show that religious capital explains 36 percent of the variance ($R2$ = 0.36) in individual innovative behavior.

Because our model reveals that entrepreneurial creativity mediates the impact of religious capital on individual innovative behavior, this study follows the procedure used by Baron and Kenny (1986) to confirm the mediating effect of entrepreneurial creativity. Step 1 of the method requires that the predictor variables (IWE and IRP) significantly influence the intervening variable (entrepreneurial creativity). Step 2 requires that the predictor variables directly and statistically influence the criterion variable (innovative behavior). Step 3 allows both the intervening variable and predictor variables to affect the criterion variable with emphasis on the intervening variable statistically influencing the criterion variable. Step 4 determines whether full or partial mediation is identified by comparing the second and third set of results. Full mediation is indicated when a significant correlation between the predictor and outcome is reduced to non-significant after controlling paths running through the potential mediator. Partial mediation is indicated when the association between the predictor variable and outcome variable remain significant after introducing the potential mediator.

The results of the mediation model are presented in Table 8.5, Panel B, and indicate a good fit of the model: $\chi 2$ = 504.486 (df = 316, p ≤ 0.001, $\chi 2$/df ratio = 1.596), RMSEA = 0.046, NFI = 0.870, TLI = 0.939, CFI = 0.945, and IFI = 0.946. In the mediation model, the assumptions can be confirmed by interpreting the structural path coefficients. H2a and H2b propose that entrepreneurial creativity is driven by religious capital-related variables. In line with our claim, we find that IWE and religious practices positively relate to entrepreneurial creativity as follows: β = 0.22, p < 0.01 and β = .16, p < 0.001. Consequently, all the results are as expected: H2a and H2b are supported. To the effect of H1a in the mediation model, which anticipated a positive effect of IWE on innovative behavior, the results reveal a significant positive effect ($\beta = 0.28$, $p < 0.001$) and empirical support for the hypothesis. Nevertheless, the results do not confirm that religious practices have a direct relationship with innovative behavior among managers as the effect is statistically non-significant ($\beta = 0.04$, $p > 0.05$). This rejects H1b in the same model. In addition, our findings show that entrepreneurial creativity positively and strongly relates to individual innovative behavior ($\beta = 0.29$, $p < 0.001$), supporting H3 in the mediation model.

Based on the preceding results, and in line with Baron and Kenny (1986), entrepreneurial creativity can be seen to have a mediating effect in our model. Indeed, the direct relationship between IWE and individual innovative behavior remained, even when creativity was included as an intervening variable, partially supporting H4a. However, the effect of religious practices on individual innovative behavior, after controlling for creativity, was non-significant, thus fully supporting H4b. This finding implies that IRP can influence individual innovative behavior only indirectly through individual creativity. To test whether individual creativity carries over the influence of Islamic religious capital-related dimensions to innovative behavior, a significance test of indirect effect (Sobel, 1982) was conducted. The test for creativity indicated a significant effect ($t = 2.187 > 1.96$; $p < 0.05$), suggesting that entrepreneurial creativity mediates the relationship between IWE and innovative behavior. In addition, the Sobel test also yielded a significant indirect effect of religious practices on innovative behavior through entrepreneurial creativity ($t = 2.553 > 1.96$; $p < 0.001$).

Interestingly, the impact of age on the innovative behavior of interviewees in the mediation model was significant ($\beta = -0.19$, $p < 0.01$), whereas that of education level on innovative behavior was not ($\beta = 0.10$, $p > 0.05$). Finally, our results for the full model indicate that IWE and religious practices together explain the 23 percent variance ($R^2 = 0.23$) in entrepreneurial creativity, while all independent variables explain the 42 percent of the variance ($R^2 = 0.42$) in innovative behavior. Table 8.5 summarizes our results.

Discussion

Findings

In the past few decades, experts – both scholars and practitioners – have shown little interest in intriguing questions related to the antecedents and consequences of individual innovative behavior in the workplace (De Jong and Den Hartog, 2010; Janssen, 2000; Reuvers et al., 2008; Scott and Bruce, 1994; Yuan and Woodman, 2010). The overall purpose of the present study is to disentangle the effect of religious capital on individual innovative behavior to gain a better understanding of how religious beliefs and practices influence managers' innovative work behavior. Importantly, our discussion and implications are based on the view that religious ethics and spiritual practices are germane to what managers feel and, finally, to how they behave in the workplace.

With respect to the first research question on the relationship between religious capital and innovative behavior, we find no relationship between IRP and managers' innovative behavior. This non-significant relationship is surprising since Islamic religion teaches their followers to benefit from spiritual practices, such as prayer and contemplation, to better manage their day-to-day tasks, and thus, complete their work in a perfect and innovative way. This might explain why some religious managers do not link values derived from their religious practices with their business context (Dana, 2009; Parboteeah et al., 2015; Ratten et al., 2017).

Our results also suggest a positive and strong association between IWE and managers' innovative behavior. This positive influence was also identified in other research studies, for example, Kumar and Che Rose (2010), who conclude that IWE can considerably contribute to innovation capability. For the firms investigated, it clearly emerges that religion is not an impediment to entrepreneurial behavior, which reflects Sabah et al.'s (2014) findings. A possible explanation for this positive relationship is that managers who are highly sensitive to IWE are likely to be more innovative and skilled in problem solving. This study suggests that truly innovative managers are those who can harness their ethical beliefs to develop creative problem-solving styles, which in turn, can be imperative for the innovation process. In addition, Islamic teachings encourage the acquisition of knowledge and transformation of this knowledge into creative skills, which can be useful for community welfare (Murtaza et al., 2016). Consequently, our findings endorse earlier scholarly views on the role of IWE in affecting innovation behavior. Islamic sacred texts emphasize the importance of cooperation in both personal and professional domains by encouraging followers to transform their religious values and ethics into useful knowledge that can be shared with other colleagues.

This study is one of the few that examines the impact of religious capital (values and practices) on managers' beliefs regarding their creativity at the workplace. Entrepreneurial creative ability stands out as a key factor, through which Islamic religious capital indirectly affects individual innovative behavior in the workplace. Some clarifying remarks should be made at this point. Religious factors in a manager's environment can affect his or her motivation to invest more creativity in the firm and ability to seize valuable entrepreneurial opportunities. Affirming the Islamic beliefs and practices of workers has the potential to increase the likelihood that they will generate and implement creative ideas. This result supports Ibn Khaldun's assertion that Islamic ethics and practices can develop creativity and enhance human abilities. It also supports Omri and Becuwe (2014) and Rice's (1999) view that a number of religious ethics have been identified and associated with both high creative achievement and increased innovative projects. To further clarify these results, we note that when managers acquire true religious knowledge about work ethics during their careers, they also develop important entrepreneurial creative abilities essential to innovate. Religious traditions support a constructive attitude toward creative and innovative tasks stemming from the idea that each Muslim has a calling to serve God by working creatively and professionally with diverse interest groups to achieve shared outcomes. In conclusion, for small companies competing in an emerging market characterized by limited resources, we find that the creative ability of managers, developed over time through religious capital and training, contacts, and repeated transactions, is the most valuable mechanism in fostering both entrepreneurial creativity and innovative behavior.

Practical implications

Our findings provide direct implications for Muslim entrepreneurs and managers on how to manage Islamic religious capital and creative abilities for innovation. The following practical implications are noteworthy. First, Muslim managers should learn and teach Islamic work values through training and lecture programs to enhance their understanding of the link between religious work ethics and "day-to-day" entrepreneurship within organizations. However, decision makers should be vigilant in respecting religious diversity in the workplace to avoid serious problems arising from discriminatory or biased attitudes and behaviors that are occasionally associated with religious expression and practices. In addition, they should pay attention to the risks related with the implementation of the identical codes of ethics across cultures (Rice, 1999). Second, the results of this study indicate that religious practices can encourage innovative behavior by developing entrepreneurial creativity. Tunisian managers may be more innovative if they combine spiritual practices and creative abilities. If supported by additional research, local and foreign businesses overseeing the work of Tunisian managers may wish to establish systematic policies to encourage and control Islamic work-related values among managers who are morally trustworthy so that their subordinates will view them as ethical and fair. Finally, another important practical implication of this study is that managers should be aware of the strategic potential of their creative thinking skills to reinforce firm innovativeness to outperform competitors. In particular, we found that a manager's creativity is a major factor for a successful innovation process. This is consistent with previous studies (Khedhaouria et al., 2014) suggesting that personality variables may be important factors where entrepreneurship is concerned. According to our results, entrepreneurial creativity is not only an important factor in the innovative process but also in overall firm performance. At the level of higher education, entrepreneurial creativity is seen to play a strong mediating role in the present study, and therefore, it is imperative for universities to maintain and improve students' creativity levels and have a system in place for students to, for example, recommend their courses and training through social media platforms. This will enable students to disseminate their creative ideas within their social circles, which in turn will generate more positive word-of-mouth related to the creative ability in the class or workplace.

Limitations and directions for future research

As with any study, the findings of our research should be viewed in light of its limitations. First, a more accurate understanding of the causal relationships between antecedents and innovative work behavior would require a longitudinal research design. A longitudinal study can help reduce the limitations of our cross-sectional or survey study, particularly the reliance on managers' responses that require post hoc verification to rationalize their capabilities, attitudes, and behaviors. Second, it is perhaps extraordinary that firms with high religious ethics show high innovative behavior at work. Clearly, the impact of religious values and beliefs needs further examination using small businesses from diverse religious traditions. Finally, while religious ethics are generally described as a positive factor in generating beneficial work outcomes, it is possible that they can have an undesirable effect in certain circumstances. Therefore, future research could, for example, compare varying levels of ethics (high vs. low) to discern if there are any differential effects on individual-level workplace innovation.

Notes

1 Tunisian Agency for the promotion of industry and innovation, see www.tunisiein dustrie.nat.tn.
2 Interviewees were conducted on a "one representative per company" basis.

References

Abstein, A., Heidenreich, S., and Spieth, P. (2014). Innovative work behaviour: The impact of comprehensive HR system perceptions and the role of work – Life conflict. *Industry and Innovation*, 21(2), 91–116.
Ajzen, I. (1991). The theory of planned behavior. *Organizational Behavior and Human Decision Processes*, 50(2), 179–211.
Ajzen, I., and Fishbein, M. (2005). The influence of attitudes on behavior. In D. Albarracin, B.T. Johnson and M.P. Zanna (eds.), *The Handbook of Attitudes*. Mawah, NJ: Erlbaum, 173–221.
Ali, A. (1988). Scaling an Islamic work ethic. *Journal of Social Psychology*, 128(5), 575–583.
Allen, D. (1978). *Structure and Creativity in Religion*. The Hague, Paris, and New York: Mouton Publishers.
Amabile, T.M. (1996). *Creativity in Context*. Boulder: Westview.
Amabile, T.M. (1997). Motivating creativity in organizations: On doing what you love and loving what you do. *California Management Review*, 40(1), 39–58.
Anderson, J.C., and Gerbing, D.W. (1988). Structural equation modeling in practice: A review and recommended two-step approach. *Psychological Bulletin*, 103(3), 411–423.
Anderson, N., Potocnik, K., and Zhou, J. (2014). Innovation and creativity in organizations: A state-of-the-science review, prospective commentary, and guiding framework. *Journal of Management*, 40(5), 1297–1333.
Arslan, M. (2001). The work ethic values of Protestant British, Catholic Irish and Muslim Turkish. *Journal of Business Ethics*, 31(4), 321–339.
Bagozzi, R.P., and Yi, Y. (1988). On the evaluation of structural equation models. *Journal of the Academy of Marketing Science*, 16(1), 74–94.
Baron, R.M., and Kenny, D.A. (1986). The moderator-mediator variable distinction in social psychological research: Conceptual, strategic and statistical considerations. *Journal of Personal Social Psychology*, 51(6), 1173–1182.
Bessant, J., and Tidd, J. (2011). *Innovation and Entrepreneurship* (2nd edition). John Wiley & Sons.

Cavanagh, G.F. (1999). Spirituality for managers: Context and critique. *Journal of Organizational Change Management*, 12(3), 186–199.

Damanpour, F., and Wischnevsky, D.J. (2006). Research on innovation in organizations: Distinguishing innovation-generating from innovation-adopting organizations. *Journal of Engineering and Technology Management*, 23(4), 269–291.

Dana, L.P. (2009). Religion as an explanatory variable for entrepreneurship. *The International Journal of Entrepreneurship and Innovation*, 10(2), 87–99.

Dayan, M., Zacca, R., and Di Benedetto, A. (2013). An exploratory study of entrepreneurial creativity: Its antecedents and mediators in the context of UAE firms. *Creativity and Innovation Management*, 22(3), 223–240.

De Jong, J.P.J., Parker, S.K., Wennekers, S., and Wu, C.H. (2015). Entrepreneurial behavior in organizations: Does job design matter? *Entrepreneurship Theory and Practice*, 39(4), 981–995.

De Jong, J., and Den Hartog, D. (2010). Measuring innovative work behaviour. *Creativity and Innovation Management*, 19(1), 23–36.

Dorenbosch, L., Van Engen, M.L., and Verhagen, M. (2005). On-the-job innovation: The impact of job design and human resource management through production ownership. *Creativity and Innovation Management*, 14(2), 129–141.

Drakopoulou Dodd, S., and Seaman, P.T. (1998). Religion and enterprise: An introductory exploration. *Entrepreneurship: Theory & Practice*, 23(1), 71–86.

Drakopoulou Dodd, S.D., and Gotsis, G. (2007). The interrelationships between entrepreneurship and religion. *The International Journal of Entrepreneurship and Innovation*, 8(2), 93–104.

Emerson, T.L.N., and Mckinney, J.A. (2010). Importance of religious beliefs to ethical attitudes in business. *Journal of Religion and Business Ethics*, 1(2), 5.

Fayolle, A. (2007). *Handbook of Research in Entrepreneurship Education, Volume 1 – A General Perspective*. Cheltenham: Edward Elgar.

Fishbein, M., and Ajzen, I. (1975). *Belief, attitude, intention, and behavior: An introduction to theory and research*. Reading, MA: Addison-Wesley.

Flynn, B.B, Schroeder, R.G., and Sakakibara, S. (1994). A framework for quality management research and an associated measurement instrument. *Journal of Operations Management*, 11(4), 339–575.

Fornell, C., and Larcker, D.F. (1981). Evaluating structural equation models with unobservable variables and measurement error. *Journal of Marketing Research*, 18, 39–50.

Hair, J. F., Hult, G. T., Ringle, C. M. & Sarstedt, M. (2013). *A primer on partial least squares structural equation modeling (PLS-SEM)*. Thousand Oaks, CA: Sage Publications Ltd..

Hair, J.F., Tatham, R., Anderson, R.E., and Black, W. (1998). *Multivariate Data Analysis* (5th edition). Upper Saddle River: Prentice Hall.

Henley, A. (2017). Does religion influence entrepreneurial behavior? *International Small Business Journal*, 35(5), 597–617.

Hulusi, A. (2014). *The Power of Prayer: Channeling Brain Waves through Dhikr*. Marston Gate: Amazon.co.uk., Ltd.

Iannaccone, L.R. (1998). Introduction to the economics of religion. *Journal of Economic Literature*, 36(3), 1465–1495.

Ibn Khaldun, A.R. (1332–1406). *The Muqaddimah: An introduction to history* (Princeton Classics). Princeton: Princeton University Press; Abridged edition (April 27, 2015).

Ireland, R.D., Covin, J.G., and Kuratko, D.F. (2009). Conceptualizing corporate entrepreneurship strategy. *Entrepreneurship Theory and Practice*, 33(1), 19–46.

Janssen, O. (2000). Job demands, perceptions of effort-reward fairness, and innovative work behavior. *Journal of Occupational and Organizational Psychology*, 73(3), 287–302.

Judge, W.Q., and Douglas, T.J. (2013). Entrepreneurship as a leap of faith. *Journal of Management, Spirituality, and Religion*, 10(1), 37–65.

Kayed, R.N., and Hassan, K. (2010). *Islamic Entrepreneurship*. London: Routledge.

Khedhaouria, A., Gurau, C., and Torres, O. (2014). Creativity, self-efficacy, and small-firm performance: The mediating role of entrepreneurial orientation. *Small Business Economics*, 44(3), 485–504.

Kumar, N., and Che Rose, R. (2010). Examining the link between Islamic work ethics and innovation capability. *Journal of Management Development*, 29(1), 79–93.

MacPherson, J.S., and Kelly, S.W. (2011). Creativity and positive schizotypy influence the conflict between science and religion. *Personality and Individual Differences*, 50(4), 446–450.

Mardia, K.V. (1970). Measures of multivariate skewness and kurtosis with applications. *Biometrika*, 57(3), 519–530.

McCleary, R.M., and Barro, R.T. (2006). Religion and economy. *Journal of Economic Perspectives*, 20(2), 49–72.

Morris, M., and Kuratko, D. (2002). *Corporate Entrepreneurship: Entrepreneurial Development Within Organizations*. Fort Worth, TX: Harcourt College Publishers.

Murtaza, G., Abbas, M., Raja, U., Roques, O., Khalid, A., and Mushtaq, R. (2016). Impact of Islamic work ethics on organizational citizenship behaviors and knowledge-sharing behaviors. *Journal of Business Ethics*, 133(2), 325–333.

Naail, M.K., Al-Kahtani, A.H., and Bin Sulaiman, M. (2011). The components of spirituality in the business organizational context: The case of Malaysia. *Asian Journal of Business and Management Sciences*, 1(2), 166–180.

Neubert M.J., Bradley, S.W., Ardianti, R., and Simiyu, E.M. (2017). The role of spiritual capital in innovation and performance: Evidence from developing economies. *Entrepreneurship Theory and Practice*, 41(4), 621–640.

Nunnally, J.C. (1978). *Psychometric Theory* (2nd edition). New York: McGraw-Hill.

Omri, W. (2015). Innovative behavior and venture performance of SMEs: The moderating effect of environmental dynamism. *European Journal of Innovation Management*, 18(2), 195–217.

Omri, W., and Becuwe, A. (2014). Managerial characteristics and entrepreneurial internationalization: A study of Tunisian SMEs. *Journal of International Entrepreneurship*, 12(1), 8–42.

Parboteeah, K.P., Walter, S.G., and Block, J.H. (2015). When does Christian religion matter for entrepreneurial activity? The contingent effect of a country's investments into knowledge. *Journal of Business Ethics*, 130(2), 447–465.

Ramadani, V., Dana, L.P., Ratten, V., and Tahiri, S. (2015). The context of Islamic entrepreneurship and business: Concept, principles and perspectives. *International Journal of Business and Globalisation*, 15(3), 244–261.

Ratten, V., Ramadani, V., Dana, L.P., and Gërguri-Rashiti, S. (2017). Islamic entrepreneurship and management: Future research directions. In V. Ramadani, L.-P. Dana, S. Gërguri-Rashiti and V. Ratten (eds.), *Entrepreneurship and Management in an Islamic Context*. Switzerland: Springer, 227–242.

Reuvers, M., Van Engen, M.L., Vinkenburg, C.J., and Wilson-Evered, E. (2008). Transformational leadership and innovative work behaviour: Exploring the relevance of gender differences. *Creativity and Innovation Management*, 17(3), 227–244.

Rice, G. (1999). Islamic ethics and the implications for business. *Journal of Business Ethics*, 18(4), 35–345.

Sabah, S., Carsrud, A.L., and Kocak, A. (2014). The impact of cultural openness, religion, and nationalism on entrepreneurial intensity: Six prototypical cases of Turkish family firms. *Journal of Small Business Management*, 52(2), 306–324.

Schumpeter, J. (1934). *The Theory of Economic Development*. Cambridge, MA: Harvard University Press.

Scott, S.G., and Bruce, R.A. (1994). Determinants of innovative behavior: A path model of individual innovation in the workplace. *Academy of Management Journal*, 37(3), 1442–1465.

Shane, S., and Nicolaou, N. (2015). Creative personality, opportunity recognition and the tendency to start businesses: A study of their genetic predispositions. *Journal of Business Venturing*, 30(3), 407–419.

Sobel, M.E. (1982). Asymptotic confidence intervals for indirect effects in structural equation models, *Sociological Methodology*, 13, 290–312.

Vargas-Hernandez, J., Noruzi, M., and Sariolghalam, N. (2010). An exploration of the effects of Islamic culture on entrepreneurial behaviours in Muslim countries, *Asian Social Science*, 6(5), 120–127.

Vygotsky, L.S. (1934/1987). Thinking and speech. In R. Rieber, A. Carton and L.S. Vygotsky (eds.), *Collected Works*. New York: Plenum, 239–285.

West, M.A., and Anderson N.R. (1996). Innovation in top management teams. *Journal of Applied Psychology*, 81(6), 680.

Wu, C.-H., Parker S.K., and De Jong, J.P.J. (2014). Need for cognition as an antecedent of individual innovation behavior. *Journal of Management*, 40(6), 1511–1534.

Yousef, D.A. (2000). Organizational commitment as a mediator of the relationship between Islamic work ethic and attitudes toward organizational change. *Human Relations*, 53(4), 283–302.

Yousef, D.A. (2001). Islamic work ethic – A moderator between organizational commitment and job satisfaction in a cross cultural context. *Personnel Review*, 30(2), 152–165.

Yuan, F., and Woodman, R.W. (2010). Innovative behavior in the workplace: The role of performance and image outcome expectations. *Academy of Management Journal*, 53(2), 323–342.

Zhao, H., and Seibert, S.E. (2006). The big five personality dimensions and entrepreneurial status: A meta-analytical review. *Journal of Applied Psychology*, 91(2), 259–271.

Zhou, J., and George, J.M. (2001). When job dissatisfaction leads to creativity: Encouraging the expression of voice. *Academy of Management Journal*, 44(4), 582–696.

9 Cultural leadership ideals and cultural practices leading to women's participation in transformational entrepreneurial leadership

Pedro Torres and Mário Augusto

Introduction

The topic of women participating in entrepreneurial leadership has recently received increasingly more attention from academics (e.g., Bullough and Luque, 2015). In this context, it would be helpful to understand which environments encourage women to make such moves. This is important not just to academics but also to policy makers, communities, and organizations around the world. The extent to which national cultures influence entrepreneurial action is still an important research topic, in spite of being a rather old one (e.g., McClelland, 1961). In fact, as reported by Stephan and Pathak (2016), previous research into entrepreneurship and culture has produced mixed findings. In order to make up for the lack of theory development and rigorous empirics in women's leadership literature, Bullough and Luque (2015) studied the effect of culturally endorsed implicit leadership theories (CLTs), i.e. the cultural expectations regarding outstanding, ideal leadership on women's business leadership roles in society. However, they also failed to find enough evidence to support all of their hypotheses.

This study aims to make a contribution to the pre-existing literature on women's leadership by examining the configurations of cultural-related conditions that result in the presence, or absence, of women's self-employment (hereafter designated as WSE or ~WSE, respectively, where the tilde "~" represents the negation). Entrepreneurs are often viewed as leaders (e.g., Vecchio, 2003) and self-employment implies the start-up of new business organizations with their own legal identity, which is considered a definition of entrepreneurship (Woodside et al., 2016). The rates of self-employment have been used in previous studies as a measure of entrepreneurship (e.g., Fairlie, 1999; Lin et al., 2000; Bullough and Luque, 2015).

Self-employment is probably a less likely employment choice for women (Klyver et al., 2013). In fact, prior research has analysed the entry dynamics into and out of self-employment and concluded that men are more "loyal" to self-employment than women (Vejsiu, 2011). Furthermore, drivers of entrepreneurship behaviour do not have the same degree of influence over women as men. For example, women are motivated to a higher degree than equally qualified men to become self-employed for non-pecuniary reasons (Vejsiu, 2011; Georgellis and Wall, 2005). Thus, women's entrepreneurship constitutes an important research stream within entrepreneurship literature.

Women's entrepreneurship literature has increasingly shifted from a focus on socio-demographic factors to a focus on the role of institutions to better understand entrepreneurial decision-making; and questions related to cultural factors provide a fertile area of inquiry regarding self-employment (e.g., Minniti and Naudé, 2010). In recent years, the need for research into the way in which institutions promote or discourage women's entrepreneurship has been emphasized, and its policy implications have been taken into account (Naudé, 2010). Nevertheless, although some studies have tried to predict associations between cultural and entrepreneurial outcomes at national levels, the findings are remarkably inconsistent (Hayton and Cacciotti, 2013). For example, gender equality policies might be expected to have a positive influence on the rate of women's self-employment (Bruton et al., 2010), but in countries that are considered highly egalitarian at an institutional level only women's employment is integrated (Kreide, 2003). This is probably the case because these countries often solely support women's employment rights, thereby promoting women's employment options rather than women's self-employment options (Klyver et al., 2013). Therefore, new approaches may be able to shed additional light on the conditions that favour women's participation in entrepreneurial leadership. Contrary to previous research on this topic, this study considers not only CLTs, but also cultural practices. This is in line with the current trend in the comparative entrepreneurship research stream, which pays more attention to cultural practices than to cultural values (e.g., Thai and Turkina, 2014).

Furthermore, this study acknowledges that each country has a "cultural configuration" that represents its DNA, in line with Woodside et al. (2016), which is another important factor making it different from previous published research. Prior studies analysed and reported net effects of cultural dimensions (e.g., Hechavarria and Reynolds, 2009) rather than the influence of culture as a whole (Woodside et al., 2016). Most of the previous studies employed methods that tend to imply linearity, additive effects, and unifinality. However, cultures represent complex wholes rather than a collection of net effects of individual factors (Woodside et al., 2016). Examining cultures as complex wholes (configurations) provides additional insight into how two countries can achieve relatively high rates of women's self-employment and yet differ in terms of culture. It is also reasonable to assume that cultural configurations indicating low rates of women's self-employment are not necessarily the mirror opposites of cultural configurations supporting high women self-employment. These types of conjunctural causation justify the application of new empirical methods, such as qualitative comparative analysis (Ragin, 2008), which stresses nonlinearity, synergistic effects, and equifinality (Woodside et al., 2016). Qualitative comparative analysis (QCA) executes a systematic cross-case analysis that models relations among variables in terms of set membership using Boolean algebra, which enables the testing of configurations that reflect necessary and sufficient conditions for an outcome of interest (Ordanini et al., 2014).

The present study uses fuzzy-set qualitative comparative analysis (*fs*QCA) and examines combinations of two CLTs, charismatic/value-based leadership (CL), self-protective leadership (SPL), and two cultural practices, uncertainty avoidance practices (UAP) and in-group collectivism practices (ICP), that lead to both high and low rates of women's self-employment. The most important cultural dimensions affecting entrepreneurship are uncertainty avoidance and individualism-collectivism (Hayton et al., 2002), which justifies the use of UAP and ICP. In the same line, CL and SPL were chosen because they are the most important CLTs impacting on entrepreneurship (Stephan and Pathak, 2016). In general, cultures that tolerate and embrace uncertainty and that pursue individual, rather than group, interests are seen as more likely to encourage entrepreneurial behaviour (e.g., Frese and Gielnik, 2014). Regarding CLTs, while CL is seen as effective and desirable (Den Hartog et al., 1999), SPL is often considered to be negative. Nevertheless, some authors point out that SPL may be essential for developing a business (e.g., Stephan and Pathak, 2016).

Considering that CL is performance-oriented, and is grounded on the firmly held values of integrity, self-sacrifice and vision, Bullough and Luque (2015) suggested that CL could be positively related to women's participation in leadership. These authors also hypothesized that women would be discouraged from participating in entrepreneurial leadership in societal environments that endorse SPL. The justification for the latter is based on the assumption that women tend to be authentic (Eagly, 2005), conflict solving (Westermann et al., 2005), gentle (Rudman and Glick, 1999), and sensitive to the needs of followers (Groves, 2005), while SPL is self-centered (associated with behaviours characterized as being status conscious, conflict causing, face saving, and procedural). Although Bullough and Luque (2015) found some evidence of these effects when considering female seats in National Parliaments, their results do not support the claim that SPL is negatively related to women's self-employment (which was used as a measure of women's participation in entrepreneurial leadership). This is not surprising since they argued that women's involvement in these spheres (political and business) is not necessarily related. Therefore, the topic of women's participation in entrepreneurship deserves further study.

The results of the present study indicate that cultural practices may be more important than CLTs in explaining women's participation in entrepreneurial leadership. Excluding Japan and New Zealand, the absence of UAP and the presence of ICP are part of the solutions obtained justifying a higher level of women's self-employment. The findings also support the use of complexity theory and indicate that different configurations of conditions, i.e. different cultures may lead to higher WSE. Furthermore, the complex antecedent conditions indicating ~WSE are not the mirror opposites of antecedent conditions indicating WSE. These findings have significant implications for academics, policy makers, communities, and organizations. Cultures are complex wholes (configurations), which implies that initiatives to encourage women's participation in entrepreneurship should take into account each country's culture. "One size does not fit all", and each country should implement the most suitable actions to achieve high rates of women's self-employment according to their own profile. Furthermore, it becomes clear that one condition alone is not sufficient to obtain this outcome. It is necessary to have a combination of conditions to be effective in promoting women's participation in entrepreneurial leadership.

Following this introduction, Section 2 presents the conceptual background and the tenets for theory construction. Then, Section 3 describes the sample, the data, and the method employed). Section 4 presents and discusses the results. Finally, Section 5 presents the main conclusions.

Background

The topic of women's participation in entrepreneurial leadership has recently received increased attention from researchers (e.g., Bullough and Luque, 2015). The literature regarding women's entrepreneurship has focused mainly on analysing the influence of contexts on women's self-employment, rather than individual factors (Klyver et al., 2013). On the one hand, previous studies noted that if individuals consider they have profiles aligned with individuals' implicit theories regarding entrepreneurs, they are more likely to start an entrepreneurial activity (e.g., Gupta et al., 2008). On the other hand, context influences what is expected of leaders (Stelter, 2002) and leadership includes relationships rooted in social settings (Bryman et al., 1996). Thus, societal culture could help explain rates of women's self-employment.

Culture is an important issue in business research (e.g., Hofstede, 2001) and the GLOBE study conducted by House et al. (2004) identified several cultural dimensions that relate culture to leadership. Culture refers to complex configurations that include knowledge, belief, art, morals, customs, and any other abilities or habits acquired by members of a society (Soares et al., 2007). Leadership may be defined as the ability of an individual to influence, motivate, and enable others to contribute to the success of their organizations (House et al., 2004). Leaders tend to behave according to what is generally expected and accepted by followers (Collinson, 2006). Nevertheless, some authors (e.g., Rosette and Tost, 2010) have suggested that women employ strategies to gain influence that are affected by the problems of resistance and legitimacy that they often face. These limit the use of directive and assertive behaviours and encourage the use of more participative leadership (Eagly and Carli, 2003), i.e. women in leadership roles often tend to include others in decision making and implementation. Moreover, Bullough and Luque (2015) suggested that a societal environment that favours gender equality, which is also future and performance-oriented would encourage women's leadership. However, it has been noted that gender equality policies only favour women's employment options rather than women's self-employment options (Klyver et al., 2013). All in all, the findings in women's entrepreneurship literature are inconsistent, which justifies further analysis and the use of different approaches.

Culturally endorsed implicit leadership theories and women's self-employment

The GLOBE study identified six leadership dimensions: i) charismatic/value-based leadership (which is performance-oriented and inspirational); ii) team-oriented leadership (which emphasizes team building); iii) participative leadership (which implies the involvement of others in decision making and implementation); iv) humane-oriented leadership (which is characterized by compassion and generosity); v) autonomous leadership (which relates to independent and individualistic leadership traits), and vi) self-protective leadership (which is self-focused and competitive). From these six leadership dimensions, CL and SPL emerged as the most related to entrepreneurship (Stephan and Pathak, 2016).

Based on the idea that women should excel in contexts that encourage empathy, cooperation, and sensitivity (Groves, 2005; Rosette and Tost, 2010), Bullough and Luque (2015) hypothesized that CL would have a positive effect on entrepreneurship, while SPL would be a potential barrier, thereby implying that women's leadership would tend to flourish in environments that show strong core values and integrity, express consideration for followers' needs and motivations, and present performance-based rewards. However, they only found evidence of the positive effect of CL on women's leadership participation in business; the negative effect of SPL was not empirically supported. More recently, some authors have suggested that the presence of both CL and SPL could be required because leaders face conflicting demands of cooperation and competition (e.g., Stephan and Pathak, 2016). Women entrepreneurs experience a constant struggle in perceiving themselves as entrepreneurs (Verheul et al., 2005) and are led to develop career paths that are seen by society as being more appropriate for them (Carter et al., 2003). Nevertheless, entrepreneurship is often seen as a deviation from the norms (Garud and KarnØe, 2001). Therefore, in this study it has not been assumed that one type of CLT is more favourable than another, and the presence and absence of each antecedent condition (CL and SPL) has been considered plausible antecedent conditions for women's participation in entrepreneurial leadership.

Cultural practices and women's self-employment

In recent years, comparative entrepreneurship research has started to pay more attention to cultural practices (e.g., Autio et al., 2013). This shift results from the inconsistent findings of prior research into cultural values. Cultural practices reflect descriptive norms of typical behaviour in a culture (Stephan and Uhlaner, 2010) and are expected to have a more direct influence on entrepreneurship behaviour (Stephan and Pathak, 2016). In fact, cultural practices are more closely related to behaviour and societal outcomes (Javidan et al., 2006) because the influence of practices is often tacit and individuals can easily implement what they perceive to be common behaviours (Nolan et al., 2008). Cultural practices were introduced in the GLOBE study, and nine cultural dimensions were identified (House et al., 2004): i) performance orientation (which implies rewarding excellence); ii) assertiveness (that refers to the degree to which individuals are or should be assertive); iii) future orientation (which implies planning and delaying gratification); iv) humane orientation (which values altruism); v) institutional collectivism (which encourages collective action); vi) group collectivism (that refers to the degree to which individuals express pride, loyalty, and cohesiveness in their organizations and families); vii) gender egalitarianism (which involves the minimization of gender inequality); viii) power distance (which corresponds to the degree to which a society accepts and endorses power differences), and ix) uncertainty avoidance (that refers to the extent to which a society relies on social norms, rules, and procedures to minimize unpredictability of future events).

Following Stephan and Pathak (2016), this study focuses on UAP and ICP because individualism/collectivism and uncertainty avoidance have been suggested to be the cultural dimensions that have the most influence on entrepreneurship. In general, participation in entrepreneurial leadership implies the acceptance of uncertainty. Therefore, if cultures embrace uncertainty they should provide a more suitable context for risk-taking and innovative actions (Clercq et al., 2010). However, women tend to have more affinity with future planning (Bullough and Luque, 2015), which could mean that they prefer environments that minimize the unpredictability of future events. Furthermore, it has been suggested in previous research that individualistic cultures could provide a better context for entrepreneurship because they favour proactivity and independent actions (e.g., Baughn and Neupert, 2003). Nevertheless, more recent studies have not supported the relation between individualism and entrepreneurship (e.g., Autio et al., 2013). Moreover, environments that endorse cooperative and collaborative approaches are expected to encourage women's leadership (e.g., Bullough and Luque, 2015).

In light of the preceding, this study shows that different combinations of these cultural practices (UAP and ICP) in conjunction with the CLTs mentioned in the last section (CL and SPL) would lead to the same outcome, i.e. high and low rates of women's participation in entrepreneurial leadership. Thus, the key tenets that have guided this current research are formulated in the next section.

Tenets for women's participation in entrepreneurial entrepreneurship

A recent article from Woodside et al. (2016) noted six principal tenets of complexity theory. Firstly, a simple antecedent condition could have a positive, as well as a negative, relationship to an outcome condition. Secondly, for most antecedent conditions, a case that exhibits a high score in a simple antecedent condition is neither necessary nor sufficient for the case to have a high score in the outcome condition. Thirdly, some complex antecedent conditions (i.e., combinations of simple antecedent conditions) consistently indicate high scores in the outcome

condition in some cases, which means they are sufficient conditions for identifying cases with a high score in the outcome condition. Fourthly, there is more
than one path to the achievement of a desired outcome. Fifthly, the mirror opposites of complex antecedent conditions that lead to consistently high scores of
the outcome condition do not indicate the negation of that outcome condition.
Finally, simple antecedent conditions that are found to be necessary are not sufficient to achieve high scores of the outcome condition.

Therefore, considering the preceding, and the four simple antecedent conditions (CL, SPL, UAP, and ICP) along with the desired outcome condition
(WSE), the following tenets are proposed:

T1: Any simple antecedent condition (CL, SPL, UAP, ICP) could be either
present or absent in the configurations leading to the outcome condition
(WSE).

T2: The presence or absence of a simple antecedent condition (CL, SPL,
UAP, ICP) is neither necessary nor sufficient to obtain the outcome condition (WSE).

T3: A few combinations of simple antecedent conditions (CL, SPL, UAP,
ICP), which may include the presence or absence of specific conditions
could be sufficient to identify countries with high scores in the outcome
condition (WSE).

T4. Any one configuration of antecedent conditions which is sufficient in
identifying countries with high outcome score is not necessary.

T5. The mirror opposites of complex antecedent conditions leading to high
scores in the outcome condition (WSE) do not indicate the negation of the
outcome condition (~WSE).

Methodology

Data and sample

This study uses public data from the World Bank for the outcome condition –
that is women's self-employment (WSE) – and data from the GLOBE study
(House et al., 2004) for the antecedent conditions (CL, SPL, UAP, and ICP). In
line with previous research (e.g., Bullough and Luque, 2015), the percentage of
self-employed females in each country was used as a measure of women's participation in entrepreneurial leadership. The data covered the years (2005 to 2010)
that are temporally close to the GLOBE data (2004), respecting the temporal
ordering.

The rate of women's self-employment was relatively stable throughout the
period under analysis. An average was calculated for each country. A final sample of 20 countries was used combining the two datasets. Table 9.1 describes
the sample and gives the calibrated scores for the antecedent conditions (more
information regarding the calibration method is provided in the next section).
Countries were ranked and ordered according to their percentage of WSE.

Table 9.1 Sample, calibrated scores, and WSE ranking

Country	Code	UAP	ICP	CL	SPL	Rank	WSE %
Greece	GRC	0.04	0.89	0.84	0.91	1	31.06
Portugal	PRT	0.24	0.95	0.23	0.42	2	22.45
Poland	POL	0.10	0.95	0.14	0.93	3	21.05
Italy	ITA	0.17	0.69	0.76	0.68	4	19.55
Argentina	ARG	0.11	0.95	0.74	0.89	5	19.35
Australia	AUS	0.62	0.19	0.95	0.30	6	13.50
Spain	ESP	0.28	0.94	0.46	0.83	7	13.19
Japan	JPN	0.36	0.43	0.04	0.96	8	12.91
Slovenia	SVN	0.16	0.94	0.16	0.96	9	12.89
New Zealand	NZL	0.83	0.06	0.42	0.58	10	12.49
Czech Republic	CZE	0.66	0.02	0.48	0.48	11	11.00
Austria	AUT	0.95	0.61	0.86	0.34	12	10.98
Netherlands	NLD	0.81	0.07	0.73	0.08	13	10.27
Hungary	HUN	0.02	0.88	0.48	0.66	14	9.13
Finland	FIN	0.92	0.16	0.57	0.00	15	8.63
France	FRA	0.65	0.28	0.00	0.05	16	7.47
Ireland	IRL	0.55	0.83	0.95	0.22	17	7.28
Sweden	SWE	0.97	0.06	0.36	0.05	18	5.98
United States	USA	0.43	0.23	0.97	0.52	19	5.76
Denmark	DNK	0.95	0.05	0.82	0.05	20	5.41

Notes: WSE = Women self-employment; CL = Charismatic leadership; SPL = Self-protective leadership; UAP = Uncertainty avoidance cultural practices; ICP = In-group collectivism cultural practices. Values for CL, SPL, UAP, and ICP range from 0 to 1, indicating non-membership and full-membership on corresponding conditions, respectively.

Method

This study uses qualitative comparative analysis (QCA). This method involves the examination of relationships between the outcome of interest and all possible combinations of binary states (i.e., presence or absence) of antecedent conditions to identify configurations that indicate necessary and sufficient conditions for an outcome of interest (Ordanini et al., 2014). In particular, the present research employs fuzzy-set QCA (fsQCA) to identify configurations of conditions that support WSE, and its negation (~WSE).

Unlike multiple regression analysis, this approach takes into consideration the fact that some cases may contradict the main effect, that is, possible asymmetric effects are taken into account. The focus on complex and configurational models rather than additive and linear ones justifies this choice of the method (Schneider and Eggert, 2014). In fact, considering the aim of the present study and follow-ing the arguments outlined by Schneider et al. (2010), fsQCA is the most suitable method because: i) asymmetrical causality is allowed, ii) combinations of antecedent conditions, rather than single conditions, are considered to be linked to the outcome; iii) the idea of equifinality is accepted, and iv) links between the various combinations of causal conditions and the outcome are expressed as necessary and sufficient conditions.

The *fs*QCA method starts with the transformation of the original values of the conditions into fuzzy scores (which are defined in the [0,1] interval), which requires the specification of full membership and full non-membership thresholds, and a cross-over point of maximum ambiguity. Each of these thresholds translates into a specific fuzzy value and it is standard to use the following fuzzy values of 0.95, 0.05, and 0.50, respectively (see Ragin, 2008). In line with previous research (e.g., Ho et al., 2016; Navarro et al., 2016; Ryan and Berbegal-Mirabent, 2016), the thresholds for full membership, non-membership, and for the cross-over point in this study were defined using the 90th, 10th, and 50th percentiles of the values of the original distribution of each condition. After transforming the original values of the conditions into fuzzy scores, an analysis of necessary conditions is required (Schneider and Wageman, 2010). Ragin (2008) proposed two criteria for evaluating the necessary conditions: consistency and trivialness of necessity. The consistency threshold used to assess necessary conditions should be larger than the one used for sufficient conditions. Following Schneider et al. (2010) 0.90 was considered to be an adequate consistency threshold for the analysis of necessary conditions. Moreover, to be considered necessary conditions, it is also required that causal conditions show a non-negligible coverage, thereby indicating that they are not trivial.

Regarding the configurational analysis, several authors recommend avoiding values less than 0.75 for the consistency threshold, and suggest that using values of 0.80 or higher will be preferable (e.g., Ragin, 2009). Thus, only configurations with consistency values above 0.80 will be considered acceptable in this study. Additionally, "core" and "peripheral" conditions are identified, thereby indicating the relative importance of each condition. The importance of distinguishing between core and peripheral conditions has been shown in previous research (for a review see Fiss, 2011). For example, Stuart and Podolny (1996) used the concepts of core and periphery values to classify the technology position of Japanese semiconductor firms in terms of their knowledge areas. To make this distinction both the parsimonious and the intermediate solutions presented in the configurational analysis needed to be considered. According to Fiss (2011, p. 403) "core conditions are those that are part of both parsimonious and intermediate solutions, and peripheral conditions are those that are eliminated in the parsimonious solution and thus only appear in the intermediate solution". This approach enables a better understanding of the causal relationships between the characteristics of a certain configurations and outcomes of interest.

Results and discussion

The analysis of necessary conditions indicates that no simple antecedent condition is necessary in order to obtain a high rate of WSE. All consistency values are below the 0.90 threshold, as can be seen in Table 9.2. Nevertheless, the higher values of SPL, ~UAP, and ICP suggest that these are important conditions for WSE. In fact, in the models obtained for WSE, presented in Table 9.3, these conditions are the most frequent among the different solutions. Regarding ~WSE, UAP and ~SPL emerged as the most relevant conditions.

Table 9.2 Analysis of necessary conditions for WSE and ~WSE

	WSE		~WSE	
	C1	*C2*	*C1*	*C2*
CL	0.65	0.56	0.72	0.69
~CL	0.64	0.67	0.55	0.63
SPL	0.82	0.78	0.45	0.48
~SPL	0.46	0.43	0.80	0.83
UAP	0.45	0.44	0.78	0.83
~UAP	0.83	0.77	0.48	0.49
ICP	0.78	0.73	0.46	0.48
~ICP	0.44	0.43	0.74	0.79

Notes: WSE = Women self-employment; CL = Charismatic leadership; SPL = Self-protective leadership; UAP = Uncertainty avoidance cultural practices; ICP = In-group collectivism cultural practices; C1 = Consistency; C2 = Raw coverage. The tilde "~" represents negation.

Table 9.3 Configurations leading to WSE and ~WSE

Model	WSE			~WSE		
	1	*2*	*3*	*1*	*2*	*3*
CL	⊗	⊗		⊗	●	●
SPL		●	●		⊗	●
UAP	⊗		⊗	●	●	⊗
ICP	●	⊗	●	⊗		⊗
C1	0.86	0.96	0.85	0.95	0.90	0.88
C2	0.49	0.29	0.66	0.40	0.56	0.21
C3	0.05	0.12	0.22	0.13	0.22	0.02
Overall C1	0.85			0.88		
Overall C2	0.83			0.70		

Notes: WSE = Women self-employment; CL = Charismatic leadership; SPL = Self-protective leadership; UAP = Uncertainty avoidance cultural practices; ICP = In-group collectivism cultural practices. The tilde "~" represents negation. C1 = Consistency; C2 = Raw coverage; C3 = Unique coverage. Black circles (●) indicate the presence of a condition; circles with a cross-out (⊗) indicate its absence; blank spaces indicate "don't care". Large circles indicate core conditions and small ones indicate peripheral conditions.

The results of the configuration analysis reveal multiple combinations of simple antecedent conditions that result in consistently high rates of WSE or ~WSE. The notation used in Table 9.3 follows Fiss (2011) with black circles (●) indicating the presence of a condition; circles with a cross (⊗) indicating its absence; blank spaces indicating a situation in which the causal condition may be either present or absent; large circles indicating core conditions, and small circles indicating peripheral conditions.

Three configurations (models) lead to high WSE. All models have acceptable consistency (≥ 0.85) and coverage (≥ 0.29). The overall coverage indicates that the three models account for about 83 percent of membership in this outcome. Both Model 1 and Model 3 combine the presence of ICP and the absence UAP, but the former also requires the absence of CL and the latter the presence of SPL. Model 2 includes two core conditions, the presence of SPL and the absence of CL, and one peripheral condition, the absence of ICP. Model 3 (~UAP, ICP, and SPL) has the highest raw coverage (C2 = 0.66) and unique coverage (C3 = 0.22), indicating that it is the most frequent configuration leading to WSE. The presence of ICP and the absence of UAP are the most frequent core conditions (they are part of the solution in both Model 1 and Model 3), thereby indicating that cultural practices are more important than CLTs in explaining women's rates of self-employment. Moreover, comparing Model 1 to Model 3 reveals that the absence of CL and the presence of SPL, which are peripheral conditions, can be treated as substitutes.

These results support the tenets 1 to 4, proposed in the background section. Different combinations of conditions may lead to high scores of WSE, including either the presence or the absence of any simple antecedent conditions (CL, SPL, UAP, and ICP), and none of them *per se* is necessary or sufficient to achieve the outcome of interest (WSE). Thus, tenets T1 and T2 are supported. Furthermore, three configurations were found to be sufficient to identify countries with high scores in WSE, but none of these models is necessary, which supports tenets T3 and T4.

Regarding the negation of WSE – that is ~WSE – three models were also obtained, explaining 70 percent of this outcome. None of the models is the mirror opposite of those leading to WSE, thereby supporting tenet T5. All models show high consistency (≥ 0.88) and present acceptable raw coverage (≥ 0.21). Model 2 is the most frequent (C2 = 0.56; C3 = 0.22) and includes the presence of CL, the absence of SPL, and the presence of UAP, which is the only core condition in this model. Model 1 also includes the presence of UAP as a core condition, and the absence of both CL and ICP as peripheral conditions. Model 3 is not as frequent; it includes the presence of CL and SPL, and the absence of UAP and ICP, but only the presence of CL and the absence of ICP are core conditions. The most frequent core condition is the presence of UAP (which is included both in Model 1 and Model 2).

An analysis of the countries that present high scores of WSE in each configuration was also performed to further the interpretation of the findings. XY plots were drawn to guide this analysis. The scores of each country in each model were computed and compared with the scores they have regarding WSE. The configuration scores were obtained using the calibration values for the presence, or absence (negation), of the condition. The values for negation of the condition correspond to 1 minus the calibrated value, and the total score for a configuration equals the lowest value appearing among the conditions present in the configuration. Scores above 0.50 indicate membership.

In Figure 9.1, Model 1 leading to WSE that combines ~CL*~UAP*ICP was considered. Five countries achieved scores above 0.50 in this configuration

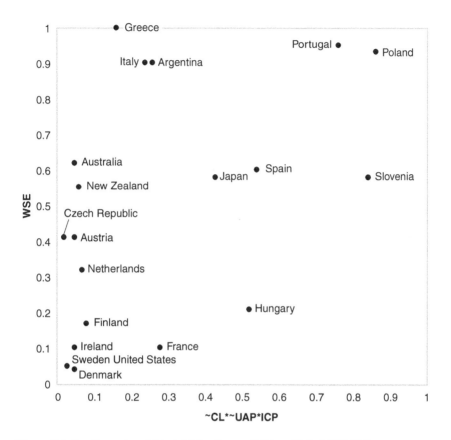

Figure 9.1 Configurational Model 1 leading to WSE: ~CL*~UAP*ICP

Notes: WSE = Women self-employment; CL = Charismatic leadership; UAP = Uncertainty avoidance cultural practices; ICP = In-group collectivism cultural practices. The tilde "~" represents negation.

(Portugal, Poland, Spain, Slovenia, and Hungary), but one of them (Hungary) had a low score regarding WSE. This indicates that the model predicted a high score of WSE in four out of five cases. When using Model 2 all cases with high scores in the configuration ~CL*SPL*~ICP were correctly predicted, but this includes just two countries, Japan and New Zealand, as can be seen in Figure 9.2. This indicates that Model 2 is more specific. In fact, only these two countries achieved relatively high scores of WSE giving more importance to CLTs rather than cultural practices, and they could be considered to be outliers. Moreover, they have a score just slightly above 0.50, which indicates there is room for further development of women's entrepreneurship. Finally, the scores obtained using Model 3 are presented in Figure 9.3. The results indicate that this model (SPL*~UAP*ICP) predicted six out of seven cases. Models 1 and

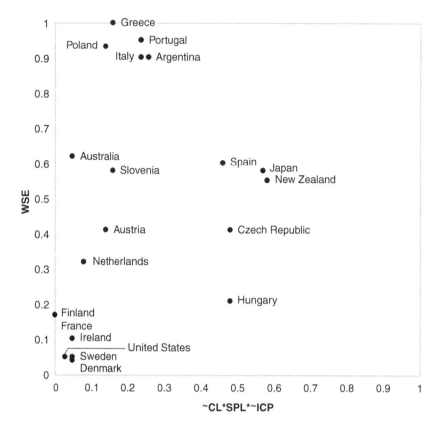

Figure 9.2 Configurational Model 2 leading to WSE: ~CL*SPL*~ICP

Notes: WSE = Women self-employment; CL = Charismatic leadership; SPL = Self-protective leadership; ICP = In-group collectivism cultural practices. The tilde "~" represents negation.

3 both have the same core conditions (~UAP and ICP), but they have different peripheral conditions (~CL in Model 1 and SPL in Model 3). Thus, ~CL and SPL may be seen as substitutes. This difference makes Model 3 work for countries like Greece, Argentina, and Italy, which do not have high scores with Model 1. However, some countries, like Spain and Slovenia, have high scores in the two models. Portugal has a significant difference between the scores obtained in these models; in this case, Model 1 is clearly better in predicting the outcome of interest.

A different angle of analysis indicates which model is the most suitable for countries with low WSE scores. By considering the scores obtained by a given country for each condition of the solution, decision makers could invest in improving the condition that would be more effective in achieving high WSE values. For instance, France presents a higher score using Model 1, which indicates that it could be a better model for building higher WSE. Furthermore, considering that

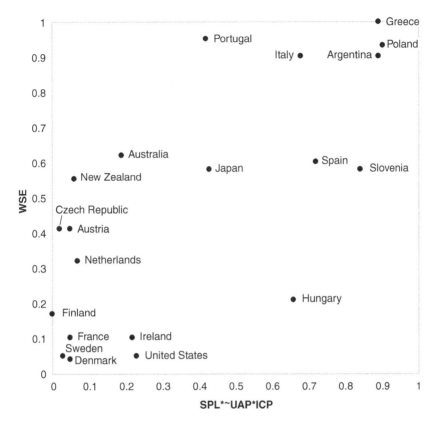

Figure 9.3 Configurational Model 3 leading to WSE: SPL*~UAP*ICP

Notes: WSE = Women self-employment; SPL = Self-protective leadership; UAP = Uncertainty avoidance cultural practices; ICP = In-group collectivism cultural practices. The tilde "~" represents negation.

the lowest score is obtained on ICP, it could be more effective to invest in building up ICP, which reflects the degree to which individuals express pride, loyalty, and cohesiveness in their organizations and families.

Another perspective which has not been addressed in previous research on the topic of WSE is an analysis of what could lead to ~WSE, considering the possibility of asymmetrical causality. Using the same procedure as used for WSE, the scores in each configuration that indicate high scores of ~WSE were computed and the values for each country were plotted. In Figure 9.4 it can be seen that the configuration ~CL*UAP*~ICP explains the high scores of ~WSE for France and Sweden. The scores obtained for the configuration CL*~SPL*UAP are presented in Figure 9.5 and these justify the higher scores of ~WSE observed for Denmark, Netherlands, Austria, Ireland, and Finland. In both Model 1 and

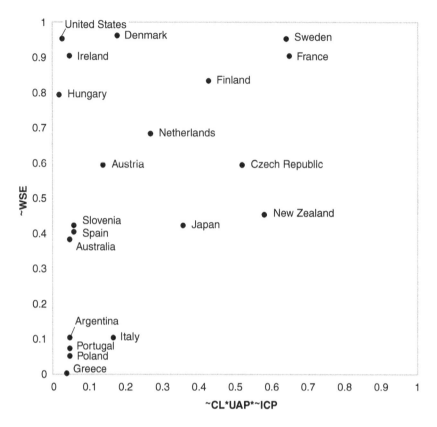

Figure 9.4 Configurational Model 1 leading to ~WSE: ~CL*UAP*~ICP

Notes: WSE = Women self-employment; CL = Charismatic leadership; UAP = Uncertainty avoidance cultural practices; ICP = In-group collectivism cultural practices. The tilde "~" represents negation.

Model 2 leading to ~WSE, the presence of UAP is core, while the absence of UAP is core in the two most represented paths to WSE, which indicates that this is an important factor in explaining women's entrepreneurship. This suggests that women will tend to feel encouraged in participating in entrepreneurial leadership in cultures that embrace uncertainty, which is in line with previous research on entrepreneurship (e.g., Clercq et al., 2010). Thus, it could be inferred that self-employment is a more probable path for women where cultural practices do not try to avoid uncertainty. This could be the case despite women's preference for predictable environments (Bullough and Luque, 2015). Finally, the configuration CL*SPL*~UAP*~ICP, plotted in Figure 9.6, correctly predicts the outcome ~WSE for one country, the United States. This result indicates that this could be a special case and shows that "one size does not fit all". In the model, two conditions are core, the presence of CL and the absence of ICP, which differs

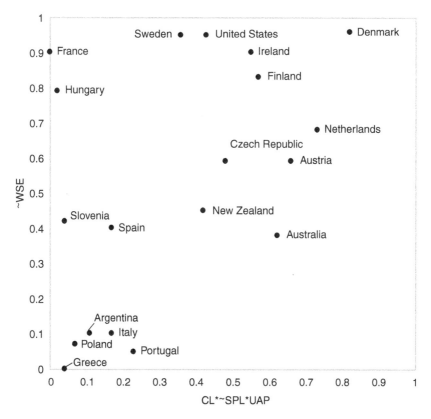

Figure 9.5 Configurational Model 2 leading to ~WSE: CL*~SPL*UAP

Notes: WSE = Women self-employment; CL = Charismatic leadership; SPL = Self-protective leadership; UAP = Uncertainty avoidance cultural practices. The tilde "~" represents negation.

significantly from the other models that lead to ~WSE. In fact, the core condition in Model 1 and Model 2 was the presence of UAP and the presence or absence of CLTs was considered to be peripheral.

The findings of this study regarding WSE are somewhat different from previous research on women's entrepreneurship. For instance, according to Bullough and Luque (2015), women should be more likely to engage in entrepreneurial leadership in societal environments that endorse CL because, among other factors, they tend to be more sensitive to the needs of followers (Groves, 2005). However, this study concludes that CL is not an important condition for obtaining WSE. Furthermore, some models require the absence of this condition, which appears to be a core condition for the existence of ~WSE in the United States. Moreover, contrary to common wisdom, two of the models required the presence of SPL, which is a core condition in one of the models, thereby suggesting that in

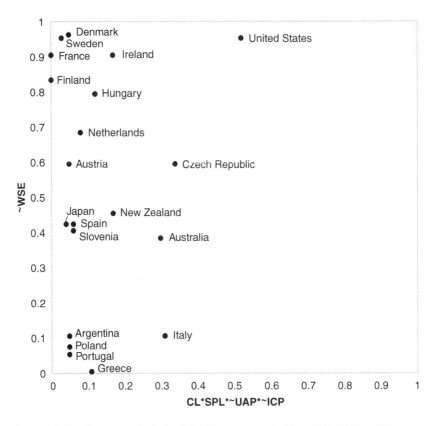

Figure 9.6 Configurational Model 3 leading to ~WSE: CL*SPL*~UAP*~ICP

Notes: WSE = Women self-employment; CL = Charismatic leadership; SPL = Self-protective leadership; UAP = Uncertainty avoidance cultural practices; ICP = In-group collectivism cultural practices. The tilde "~" represents negation.

societal environments that endorse more self-focused and competitive leadership style, the percentage of WSE will tend to be higher. Previous research has suggested that women's leadership tends to be more collaborative, democratic, and authentic (e.g., Eagly, 2005; Eagly and Carli, 2003), which led Bullough and Luque (2015) to argue that SPL was incongruent with women's leadership style. However, these authors could not find empirical evidence to back this idea. In fact, recent research pointed out that entrepreneurs may have to focus on self-interests and exhibit competitive behaviour to successfully create and manage a new business (e.g., Stephan and Pathak, 2016). Moreover, prior studies also suggested that increased competition would provide better opportunities for potential entrepreneurship (e.g., Vejsiu, 2011). In the case of women, the endorsement of SPL by society may favour entrepreneurial leadership because they tend to face a constant struggle in perceiving themselves as entrepreneurs (Verheul et al.,

2005). However, this finding should be relativized because only one configuration leading to WSE shows SPL as a core condition; and the model only fits two cases, i.e. Japan and New Zealand (see Table 9.3, Model 2, and Figure 9.2).

All in all, the results show that women's participation in entrepreneurial action is embedded in culture. On the one hand, although previous research (Stephan and Pathak, 2016) found a positive influence of both CLTs (CL and SPL) on individual entrepreneurship, this study suggests that only the presence of SPL may be part of a solution leading to higher levels of women's self-employment. This indicates that women will need to show a higher degree of self-protective and competitive behaviour in certain societies, which is made possible by cultural endorsement of SPL. On the other hand, the findings indicate that cultural practices tend to have a more important role in encouraging women to be self-employed. In particular, the absence of UAP and the presence of ICP are core conditions in most of the cases exhibiting high scores on WSE. The GLOBE project (House et al., 2004) suggests that in countries characterized by high UAP, more people seek orderliness, consistency, structure, formal procedures, and laws to cover situations in their daily lives. In our view, the absence of UAP may encourage more women to become entrepreneurs because women's self-employment has been seen as an act of institutional disintegration (Klyver et al., 2013). The frequent presence of ICP as a component of the solutions giving high values of WSE, suggests that women tend to be more likely to participate in entrepreneurial leadership in societal environments in which cultural practices promote loyalty and cohesiveness, which is in line with the social and emotional skills at which women excel (Groves, 2005).

Conclusion

This study adds to the stream of research into women's entrepreneurship by identifying configurations of CLTs (CL and SPL) and cultural practices (UAP and ICP) that lead to increased participation of women in entrepreneurial leadership. The findings support the idea that culture plays an important role in promoting or discouraging WSE, in particular cultural practices. With the exception of Japan and New Zealand, the absence of UAP and the presence of ICP are core conditions for solutions leading to higher levels of women's self-employment. The configurations obtained also suggest that in some cases the presence of SPL or the absence of CL are part of the solution. This indicates that women tend to be more encouraged to participate in entrepreneurial actions in societies that endorse a more self-focused and competitive leadership style, rather than in societies that endorse the type of leadership that reflects the ability to inspire, motivate, and that expect high performance outcomes from others based on firmly held core values.

The present study makes a contribution not only to theory but also to policy makers and management practices. The results showcase the advantages of adopting complexity theory and asymmetric analysis to advance the entrepreneurship body of research. Cultures represent complex wholes (configurations) and combinations of different simple antecedent conditions (CL, SPL, UAP, and ICP) may lead to the same outcome: a high percentage of WSE. This idea was not encompassed in previous research that covered the net effects of individual factors. The findings indicate viable paths to high WSE and showcase the combination of conditions that provide the best results in each country. According to these results, country leaders should not only invest in building the right combination of antecedents for their respective countries but also carefully avoid any configurations that might lead in the wrong directions.

This study is not without its limitations. Firstly, contrary to commonly held ideas, the findings show the presence of CL and the presence of SPL are more closely related to solutions leading to high WSE than previously realized. In spite of the justification already provided in the results and discussion section, additional research is necessary to better clarify the role of cultural leadership ideals on women's participation in entrepreneurial leadership. Secondly, the rate of women's self-employment was used as a proxy of women's participation in entrepreneurial entrepreneurship, in line with previous research (e.g., Bullough and Luque, 2015). Although this measure is widely used, it may be misleading if innovative Schumpeterian entrepreneurship is the outcome interest; a systematic cross-country study conducted by Henrekson and Sanadaji (2014) has suggested that the rate of billionaire entrepreneurs correlates negatively with self-employment (meaning that successful "innovative" entrepreneurs tend to replace smaller rivals as they scale up). Thirdly, this study does not distinguish between opportunity-based and necessity-based self-employment; this limits the insights on women's self-employment as a choice, which would be better measured using only opportunity-based entries (Klyver et al., 2013). Future research could explore these issues, use a larger sample, and collect data from different sources in order to improve the generalizability of the findings hereby presented.

References

Autio, E., Pathak, S., and Wennberg, K. (2013). Consequences of cultural practices for entrepreneurial behaviors. *Journal of International Business Studies*, 44(4), 334–362.

Baughn, C.C., and Neupert, K.E. (2003). Culture and national conditions facilitating entrepreneurial start-ups. *Journal of International Entrepreneurship*, 1(3), 313–330.

Bruton, G.D., Ahlstrom, D., and Li, H.-L. (2010). Institutional theory and entrepreneurship: Where are now and where we need to move in future. *Entrepreneurship Theory and Practice*, 34(3), 421–440.

Bryman, A., Stephens, M., and Campo, C. (1996). The importance of context: Qualitative research and the study of leadership. *The Leadership Quarterly*, 7(3), 353–370.

Bullough, A., and Luque, M.S.D. (2015). Women's participation in entrepreneurial and political leadership: The importance of culturally endorsed implicit leadership theories. *Leadership*, 11(1), 36–56.

Carter, N.M., Gartner, W.B., Shaver, K.G., and Gatewood, E.J. (2003). The career reasons of nascent entrepreneurs. *Journal of Business Venturing*, 18(1), 31–39.

Clercq, D.D., Danis, W.M., and Dakhli, M. (2010). The moderating effect of institutional context on the relationship between associational activity and new business activity in emerging economies. *International Business Review*, 19(1), 85–101.

Collinson, D. (2006). Rethinking followership: A post-structuralist analysis of follower identities. *The Leadership Quarterly*, 17(2), 179–189.

Den Hartog, D.N., House, R.J., Hanges, P.J., Ruiz-Quintanilla, S.A., and Dorfman, P.W. (1999). Culture specific and cross-culturally generazible implicit leadership theories: Are attributes of charismatic/transformational leadership universally endorsed? *The Leadership Quarterly*, 10(2), 219–256.

Eagly, A.H. (2005). Achieving relational authenticity in leadership: Does gender matter? *The Leadership Quarterly*, 16(3), 459–474.

Eagly, A.H., and Carli, L.L. (2003). The female leadership advantage: An evaluation of the evidence. *The Leadership Quarterly*, 14(6), 807–834.

Fairlie, R.W. (1999). The absence of the African-American owned business: An analysis of the dynamics of self-employment. *Journal of Labor Economics*, 17(1), 80–108.

Fiss, P.C. (2011). Building better causal theories: A fuzzy set approach to typologies in organization research. *Academy of Management Journal*, 54(2), 393–420.

Frese, M., and Gielnik, M.M. (2014). The psychology of entrepreneurship. *Annual Review of Organizational Psychology and Organizational Behavior*, 1, 413–438.

Garud, R., and KarnØe, P. (2001). Path creation as a process of mindful deviation. In R. Garud and P. KarnØe (eds.), *Path Dependence and Creation*. Lawrence Eribaum Associates, 1–38.

Georgellis, Y., and Wall, H.J. (2005). Gender differences in self-employment. *International Review of Applied Economics*, 19(3), 321–342.

Groves, K.S. (2005). Gender differences in social and emotional skills and charismatic leadership. *Journal of Leadership & Organizational Studies*, 11(3), 30–46.

Gupta, V.K., Turban, D.B., and Bhawe, N.M. (2008). The effect of gender stereotype activation on entrepreneurial intentions. *Journal of Applied Psychology*, 93(5), 1053–1061.

Hayton, J.C., and Cacciotti, G. (2013). Is there an entrepreneurial culture? A review of empirical research. *Entrepreneurship and Regional Development: An International Journal*, 25(9/10), 708–731.

Hayton, J.C., George, G., and Zahra, S.A. (2002). National culture and entrepreneurship: A review of behavioral research. *Entrepreneurship Theory and Practice*, 26(4), 33–52.

Hechavarria, M., and Reynolds, P.D. (2009). Cultural norms & business start-ups: The impact of national values on opportunity and necessity. *International Entrepreneurship and Management Journal*, 5(4), 417–437.

Henrekson, M., and Sanadaji, T. (2014). Small business activity does not measure entrepreneurship. *Proceedings of the national academy of sciences of the United States of America (PNAS)*, 111(5), 1760–1765.

Ho, J., Plewa, C., and Lu, V.N. (2016). Examining strategic orientation complementarity using multiple regression analysis and fuzzy set QCA. *Journal of Business Research*, 69(6), 2199–2205.

Hofstede, G. (2001). *Culture's Consequences: Comparing Values, Behaviors, Institutions, and Organizations Across Nations* (2nd edition). Thousand Oaks, CA: Sage Publications.

House, R.J., Hanges, P.J., Javidan, M., Dorfman, P., and Gupta, V. (2004). *Culture, Leadership, and Organizations: The GLOBE Study of 62 Societies*. Thousand Oaks, CA: Sage Publications.

Javidan, M., House, R.J., Dorfman, P.W., Hanges, P.J., and Luque, M.S.D. (2006). Conceptualizing and measuring cultures and their consequences: A comparative review of GLOBE's and Hofstede's approaches. *Journal of International Business Studies*, 37(6), 897–914.

Klyver, K., Nielsen, S.L., and Evald, M.R. (2013). Women's self employment: An act of institutional (dis)integration? A multilevel, cross-country study. *Journal of Business Venturing*, 28(4), 474–488.

Kreide, R. (2003). Self-employment of women and welfare-state policies. *International Review of Sociology*, 13(1), 205–218.

Lin, Z., Picot, G., and Compton, J. (2000). The entry and exit dynamics of self-employment in Canada. *Small Business Economics*, 15(2), 105–125.

McClelland, D.C. (1961). *The Achieving Society*. New York: The Free Press.

Minniti, M., and Naudé, W. (2010). What do we know about patterns and determinants of female entrepreneurship cross countries? *European Journal of Development Research*, 22(3), 277–293.

Naudé, W.A. (2010). Entrepreneurship, developing countries, and development economics: New approaches and insights. *Small Business Economics Journal*, 34(1), 1–12.

Navarro, S., Llinares, C., and Garzon, D. (2016). Exploring the relationship between co-creation and satisfaction using QCA. *Journal of Business Research*, 69(4), 1336–1339.

Nolan, J.M., Schultz, P.W., Cialdini, R.B., Goldstein, N.J., and Griskevicius, V. (2008). Normative social influence is underdetected. *Personality and Social Psychology Bulletin*, 34(7), 913–923.

Ordanini, A., Parasuraman, A., and Rubera, G. (2014). When the recipe is more important than the ingredients: A Qualitative Comparative Analysis (QCA) of service innovation configurations. *Journal of Service Research*, 17(2), 134–149.

Ragin, C.C. (2008). *Redesigning Social Inquiry: Fuzzy Sets and Beyond*. Chicago: University of Chicago Press.

Ragin, C.C. (2009). Qualitative comparative analysis using fuzzy sets (fsQCA). In C.C. Ragin and B. Rihoux (eds.), *Configurational Comparative Methods: Qualitative Comparative Analysis (QCA) and Related Techniques*. Los Angeles: Sage, 87–122.

Rosette, A.S., and Tost, L.P. (2010). Agentic women and communal leadership: How role prescriptions confer advantage to top women leaders. *Journal of Applied Psychology*, 95(2), 221–235.

Rudman, L., and Glick, P. (1999). Feminized management and backlash toward agentic women: The hidden cost to women of a kinder, gentler image of middle managers. *Journal of Personality and Social Psychology*, 77(5), 1004–1010.

Ryan, J.C., and Berbegal-Mirabent, J. (2016). Motivational recipes and research performance: A fuzzy set analysis of the motivational profile of high performing research scientists. *Journal of Business Research*, 69(11), 5299–5304.

Schneider, C.Q., and Wageman, C. (2010). Standards of good practice in qualitative comparative analysis (QCA) and fuzzy-sets. *Comparative Sociology*, 9(3), 397–418.

Schneider, M.R., and Eggert, A. (2014). Embracing complex causality with the QCA method: An invitation. *Journal of Business Market Management*, 7(1), 312–328.

Schneider, M.R., Schulze-Bentrop, C., and Paunescu, M. (2010). Mapping the institutional capital of high-tech firms: A fuzzy-set analysis of capitalist variety and export performance. *Journal of International Business Studies*, 41(2), 246–266.

Soares, A.M., Farhangmehr, M., and Sholam (2007). Hofstede's dimensions of culture in international marketing studies. *Journal of Business Research*, 60(3), 277–284.

Stelter, N.Z. (2002). Gender differences in leadership: Current social issues and future organizational implications. *Journal of Leadership & Organizational Studies*, 8(4), 88–99.

Stephan, U., and Pathak, S. (2016). Beyond cultural values? Cultural leadership ideals and entrepreneurship. *Journal of Business Venturing*, 31(5), 505–523.

Stephan, U., and Uhlaner, L.M. (2010). Performance-based vs socially supportive culture: A cross national study of descriptive norms and entrepreneurship. *Journal of International Business Studies*, 41(8), 1347–1364.

Stuart, T.E., and Podolny, J.M. (1996). Local search and the evolution of technological capabilities. *Strategic Management Journal*, 17(1), 21–38.

Thai, M.T.T., and Turkina, E. (2014). Macro-level determinants of formal entrepreneurship versus informal entrepreneurship. *Journal of Business Venturing*, 29(4), 490–510.

Vecchio, R.P. (2003). Entrepreneurship and leadership: Common trends and common threads. *Human Resource Management Review*, 13(2), 303–327.

Vejsiu, A. (2011). Incentives to the self-employment decision in Sweden. *International Review of Applied Economics*, 25(4), 379–403.

Verheul, I., Uhlaner, L., and Thurik, R. (2005). Business accomplishment, gender and entrepreneurial self-image. *Journal of Business Venturing*, 20(4), 483–518.

Westermann, O., Ashby, J., and Pretty, J. (2005). Gender and social capital: The importance of gender differences for the maturity and effectiveness of natural resource management groups. *World Development*, 33(11), 1783–1799.

Woodside, A.G., Bernal, P.M., and Coduras, A. (2016). The general theory of culture, entrepreneurship, innovation, and quality of life: Comparing nurturing versus thwarting enterprise start-ups in BRIC, Denmark, Germany, and the United States. *Industrial Marketing Management*, 53, 136–159.

10 Open innovation, knowledge creation and capability building

The case analysis of transformational entrepreneurship at Alibaba and SHOP.COM

Connie Zheng and Cynthia Laurin

Introduction

Nowadays, global market interdependence and hyper-competition are prevailing conditions under which many market-driven firms are operating. Market-oriented firms are defined by Slater and Narver (1998) as those organizations making 'long term commitment to understanding customer needs . . . and to developing innovative solutions that produce superior customer value' (p. 1002). To be successful, market-oriented firms must not only possess superior skills in satisfying their customers (Day, 1994) but also deliver new value propositions with higher and quicker rates of innovation, minimum/low costs and the best differentiation strategy from their competitors (Grant, 1995a; Arrigo, 2012). However, with the complexity of modern technology, it is impossible for a single organization to innovate products and services in isolation without the support and development of external linkage in the innovation process (Arora and Gambardella, 1990; Hamel and Prahalad, 1994; Laursen and Salter, 2006; Arrigo, 2012; Gallego et al., 2013). Successful innovation increasingly depends on the development and integration of external ideas. In particular, market-driven with technology/knowledge-intensive firms have to engage with different types of partners to acquire resources so as to use both internal and external ideas to create new knowledge and advance their technologies via the open innovation process (Grant, 1995a; Chesbrough, 2003; Laursen and Salter, 2006; Gallego et al., 2013).

The concept of open innovation refers to 'a process of using purposive inflows and outflows of knowledge (*among many partners*) to accelerate internal innovation, and expand the markets for external use of innovation'(Chesbrough, 2006, p. 1; words in *italics* are added). In an open market, many partners such as customers, suppliers and competitors interact with market-oriented firms to influence their corporate decisions on innovation. In practice, Arrigo (2012) argues that use of open innovation is one of the best approaches for market-driven knowledge-intensive firms to draw knowledge insights from external partners, share information, and generate new knowledge to further create new products and services. Thus, corporate decisions of this type of market-oriented and knowledge-based firms must be 'purposive', and have intentional and deliberate judgements in order to drive firm innovation and performance (Chesbrough, 2006; Morgan et al., 2009).

Usually, market-driven and knowledge-intensive firms, as argued by Arrigo (2012), are able to develop a global scale learning platform and establish proper channels for their business operation. However, the global learning platform can only be established via an outside-in open innovation management process, whereby firms are able to absorb external knowledge about new products or processes. Available channels for potential global learning can be utilized and these channels are identified as global supply chain, distribution and marketing, and production channels (Arrigo, 2012). In effect, in global markets, a sustainable competitive advantage depends on the firm's ability to obtain, integrate, reconfigure and share knowledge in a little time and to learn faster and better than their competitors. Morgan et al. (2009) claim that firms operating in the global markets must develop specific and distinctive capabilities to anticipate market changes and to manage increased volatility and instability, so as to increase their innovativeness.

In this chapter, we intend to conduct a comparative case analysis of two market-driven and internet-based technology/knowledge-intensive firms: Alibaba from China, and SHOP.COM/Market America, to explore how they have utilized the open innovation process, so as to facilitate their global learning, create new knowledge and develop capabilities, in order to maintain and sustain their global market competitiveness. The rest of the chapter is organized as follows. Section 2 provides a brief literature review on a link between knowledge management and open innovation, with a focus on addressing the challenges of knowledge creation and capacity building as a result of adopting the open innovation process. This is followed by an introduction of two giant internet-based companies in Section 3. Based on the existing literature discussed in Section 2, a comparative analysis of Alibaba and SHOP.COM is subsequently conducted in Section 4, with further discussion on some lessons learnt and implications to other market-based firms. Concluding marks are drawn in Section 5.

Literature review

As argued by many scholars (e.g. Grant, 1995a; Song et al., 2003; Enkel et al., 2009; Taminiau et al., 2009; Tseng et al., 2011; Arrigo, 2012; Moustaghfir and Schiuma, 2013; An et al., 2014; Anand Walsh, 2016), knowledge management, defined as 'a systematic process of managing knowledge assets, processes and organizational environments to facilitate the creation, sharing and utilization of knowledge to achieve the strategic aim of an organization' (An et al., 2014, p. 580), is crucially important for technology-based knowledge-intensive firms. In these organizations, knowledge management is emphasized because collaboration between the firms is achieved by the creation of specific information channels and knowledge flows (Arrigo, 2012). Darroch and McNaughton (2002) purport that effective knowledge management has been regarded as one of proven methods for improving innovation and firm performance (see also An et al., 2014, p. 581). Thus, it is argued that an underlying relationship between knowledge management and firm innovation exists, and that effective management of such relationship is important for market-oriented and knowledge-based firms to maintain innovativeness and sustain global competitiveness.

In theory, the resource and knowledge-based view of the firm (Wernerfelt, 1984; Barney, 1991; 2001; Grant and Baden-Fuller, 1995; Grant, 1996b) argues that the acquisition and development of tangible and intangible knowledge through interfirm collaboration help firms gain unique, rare, valuable and inimitable resources, which lead firms to maintain and sustain competitive advantage in the marketplace. In discussing the link of the unique resources and knowledge with innovation, Tseng et al. (2011) assert that external knowledge from interacting with various partners such as customers, suppliers and competitors is considered to be a learning opportunity for market-based firms. Firms obtaining complementary external knowledge are arguably to be more effective in providing them with a source to review their in-house knowledge in order to innovate (Tseng et al., 2011; An et al., 2014). Resources for which contemporary firms compete in the global marketplaces are increasingly likely to be knowledge rather than the ownership of land and access to capital (Taminiau et al., 2009). From examining the factors for innovation among 29 Dutch consultancy firms, Taminiau et al. (2009) found that informal knowledge sharing with clients, colleague consultants and their experienced superiors is the most fruitful route to innovation.

Anand and Walsh (2016) conclude from an extensive literature review on knowledge sharing in the field of religion, science and management, that generosity helps towards knowledge sharing, subsequently help humanity and firm success. Knowledge sharing is defined by Anand and Walsh (2016, p. 714) as an activity through which knowledge, i.e. information, skills or expertise, is freely exchanged among people, friends, families, communities and organizations, via an open platform. In the context of organizations or market-oriented firms, generous knowledge sharing via formal and informal channels, utilized by firms through their internal relationships and external networks is the key way to innovate more efficiently (Gulati, 1998; Bellantuono et al., 2013; Anand and Walsh, 2016). Chesbrough (2012) simply calls this type of open and generous knowledge sharing inside and outside the organization that leads to accelerate internal innovation of products and services and subsequently expand the market size of the firm as an open innovation process (see also Chesbrough, 2006; Grönlund et al., 2010). Next, we shall further explain the relationship between open innovation and knowledge sharing/creation, and the impact of such relationship on the market-oriented firms as it relates to the case analysis in this chapter.

Open innovation and knowledge creation

The existing literature discusses the concept of 'open innovation' specifically within three core processes: outside-in, inside-out and coupled processes (Enkel et al., 2009; Gassmann et al., 2010; Bellantuono et al., 2013). The outside-in process refers to the activities in which companies monitor the external environment to source knowledge and technologies from stakeholders (consumers, suppliers, etc.) and to license intellectual property from other firms. The inside-out process includes technology transfers by the commercialization of in-house technology; whilst the coupled process combines outside-in and inside-out processes by working together with complementary partners or by participating in other companies.

All the previously mentioned three processes of open innovation complement one another but the outside-in process is regarded as most prevalent among the market-oriented and technology-based companies (Bellantuono et al., 2013). This is because modern technology is so complex that a single firm, even if large, cannot hold the financial resources necessary to develop a new product or process alone. Consequently, external and global networks are created to connect the old internal R&D departments of technology/knowledge-intensive firms and deal with their innovation process across the system of external partners and offshore sites (Huizingh, 2011; Arrigo, 2012).

According to Inauen and Schenker-Wicki (2012), open innovation emphasizes the importance of capturing knowledge from the external environment and converting it into innovative processes, products or services. With a sample of 141 R&D managers, Inauen and Schenker-Wicki (2012) show that firms with a higher openness towards customers are more likely to increase their product innovations. In contrast, firms with more cooperation with suppliers, competitors and other external partners are more likely to increase their process innovation. The reasons are that customers tend to pay increased attention to product attributes and many commercially relevant products were initially conceptualized by lead users rather than manufacturers. At the same time, every firm needs to pay attention and maintain good relationships with partners to enhance its own competitive ability. The partners within the supply chain are one of the most important sources of knowledge applied to develop innovative processes. Therefore, the combination of the company know-how with new knowledge creation by suppliers, customers and external actors can increase the firm's innovativeness.

Several open innovation practices have been commonly adopted by market-driven firms, as listed in Table 10.1. Briefly, firms can adopt a spectrum of the practices ranging from a simple process of making casual contacts and/or organized exchange of information and experiences (Fritsch and Lukas, 2001) to a more complex management decision assessment on adopting open innovation (Huizingh, 2011; Bellantuono et al., 2013).

Mostly, open innovation practices are interfirm collaboration-based. Firms build cooperative relationships via joint use of equipment or laboratories, joint R&D projects (Fritsch and Lukas, 2001); and contractual coordination

Table 10.1 Open innovation practices with specific examples

Open innovation practices	Examples	Sources
Building cooperative relationships	Casual contact and organized exchange of information and experience; involving in planning and operation of projects; pilot use of an innovation; joint use of equipment or laboratories; joint R&D projects, research contracts	Fritsch and Lukas (2001)
Contractual coordination mechanisms	Different types, length and specificity to include long term contracts; strategic alliance agreement, R&D consortia; market-driven transactions (e.g. licensing); intermediate form of governance structures (e.g. joint ventures and consortia)	Sobrero and Roberts (2002)
Inbound and outbound organizational modes and activities	Organizational change associated with, or produced by the introduction of open innovation. Inbound mode would include activities such as purchase of scientific services or in-licensing; outbound refers to activities such as collaboration, supply of scientific services and out-licensing	Chesbrough et al. (2006) Mortara and Minshall (2011); Bianch et al. (2011)
Technology exploitation and exploration practices	Venturing, outward IP licensing, employee involvement in open innovation, customer involvement, external networking, external participation, outsourcing R&D, inward IP licensing	Van de Vrande et al. (2009)
Collective research centre	Company support for external knowledge acquisition and networking activities	Spithoven et al. (2010)
Collaboration exercises	Adoption of both open v. closed partnership An innovation mall or network community is an open place for anyone or company to post a problem and offer solution. An elite circle (or consortium) is a close and selective group of experts/organizations used by the company to address specific problems.	Pisano and Verganti (2008)
Collaborative innovation	Funding licensing, outsourcing, R&D partnership, joint ventures and inter-firm alliance	Lee et al. (2010); An et al. (2014)
Management decisions on open innovation	When, how, with whom, for what purposes and in what way should organizations cooperate with external partners to source, activate, control and coordinate knowledge?	Huizingh (2011); Bellantuono et al. (2013)

mechanism through strategic interfirm alliance agreement (Gulati, 1998), joint ventures and consortia (Sobrero and Roberts, 2002; Lee et al., 2010; An et al., 2014). Interfirm collaboration can also include activities such as in-licensing or out-licensing of scientific services (Chesbrough et al., 2006; Van de Vrande et al., 2009; Mortara and Minshall, 2011; Bianch et al., 2011), and development of collaborative network community or elite consortium (Pisano and Verganti, 2008; An et al., 2014). Open innovation practices with involvement of employees and customers could also range from a very loose form of self-initiated building an open innovation mall, whereby anyone could post a problem and offer solution (Pisano and Verganti, 2008) to a planned exploitation and exploration practices that purposively ask for employees and customers' inputs to explore potential new technology, and/or create new products and services; and to seek feedback (exploitation) from employees and customers in order to further innovate new technology products and services (Van de Vrande et al., 2009). Furthermore, more complex management decision on open innovation must involve employees, customers, suppliers and even competitors in order to effectively share, source, activate, control, coordinate and manage knowledge and innovation (Bellantuono et al., 2013).

In addressing the relationship between knowledge creation and open innovation process, Lichtenthaler (2011) argues that the capabilities are needed at the firm level; and individual attitudes towards knowledge creation in the open innovation process are also required. Therefore, the next subsection is devoted to discuss the challenge of capability building as well as the fruitful outcome of capacity enhancement for those market-driven firms in the process of open innovation and knowledge creation.

Capability building in the process of open innovation and knowledge creation

In line with the concept of open innovation, Day (1994) argues that market-driven firms must possess and/or acquire and develop distinctive capabilities in three core corporate processes: 1) the inside-out processes (such as those of manufacturing, logistics, technology development, and human resource management – HRM); 2) the outside-in processes (such as market sensing, customer linking, channel bonding and technology monitoring); and 3) the spanning processes to integrate both inside-out and outside-in processes that would require capability of delivering quality customer service, developing new products and services, and sensing right pricing and safe purchasing from the market.

Development of the outside-in capabilities is crucially important for market-oriented firms, because these capabilities allow the firm to tie with the external environment so that it can be anticipatory and responsive in satisfying the needs of customers first, as well as much better than competitors, so as to grasp new business opportunities. These capabilities permit the firm to build strong relationships with external customers, distributors and suppliers (Arrigo, 2012).

Internally, Moustaghfir and Schiuma (2013, p. 497) adopted a resource and knowledge-based view of the firm and argued that:

> The core competences of a learning and innovation organization stem from its integrated learning capabilities and organizations covert such learning capabilities into core and distinctive competencies such as product and process innovation, through the active application and utilization of the principles of transformative and absorptive capacities that recognize the value of new, external information, assimilate the information, and then apply the learned knowledge to its own internal product and service outputs.

Developing the inside-out capabilities involves a virtuous cycle of promoting creativity, continuing research & development (R&D) efforts, creating knowledge and applying innovation, which is an important building block of organizational HRM process (Wright et al., 2001). The inside-out capabilities enable organizations to exploit existing internal and external firm-specific competencies to address changing environment. Both inside-out and outside-in capabilities are vital to facilitate firms to look inward to understand their own specific capabilities, and outward to identify their specific opportunities in the world around them (Moustaghfir and Schiuma, 2013). The most critical organizational capability is nonetheless the one to quickly reassess changing market realities, and develop new capabilities to respond to changing market conditions, which are embedded in the spanning process of developing combined capabilities (Kogut and Zander, 1992; Day, 1994), particularly relevant to the two cases presented in this chapter.

In the context of the contemporary knowledge-driven economy, innovation is no longer conceived as a specific result of individual actions. Instead, as identified by Moustaghfir and Schiuma (2013), it is a problem-solving process, an interactive process involving relationships between firms with different actors, a diversified learning process involving the exchange of codified and tacit knowledge, and an interactive process of learning and exchange whereby interdependence between actors generates an innovative ecosystem or cluster. Therefore, a dynamic capability (Teece et al., 1997) developed via organizational learning and learning organization is required to achieve resource configurations and capability combinations (Kogut and Zander, 1992) in order to assist firms to gain a long-term competitive advantage (Teece et al., 1997; Moustaghfir and Schiuma, 2013).

The concept of 'a learning organization' instilled in *The Fifth Discipline* written by Peter Senge (1990) is perhaps more well-known than how a learning organization facilitates organizational learning defined as a process of creating, retaining and transferring knowledge within an organization (Argote, 2011). Whilst a learning organization is an entity for any firms to aspire for, organizational learning is related to organizational capability that successful market-oriented firms must possess. Organizational learning links individual learning with organizational capacity of delivering training and development of skills, and generating and combining internal and external knowledge for new knowledge creation and innovation (Moustaghfir and Schiuma, 2013). Thus, organizational learning signifies an action and capacity building effort of organizations for the continuous development of new knowledge and empowerment for innovation.

Based on the earlier discussion on open innovation, collaborative ability is identified as another important capability required for knowledge creation and open innovation among market-based firms. Using a sample of 1,266 firms, Díaz-Díaz and de Saá Pérez (2014) find that the use of the external sources of knowledge that exploits internal knowledge is helpful for firms to innovate, but open innovation works best when people are collaborating side by side (Díaz-Díaz and de Saá Pérez, 2014). Similarly, An et al.'s (2014) analysis of collaborative innovation in the context of China suggest that China's global competitiveness has increased largely due to its national effort to drive collaborative innovation and organizational promotion, encouragement and enhancement of individual collaborative capabilities. In modern day, the question is not about why to innovate, but how to innovate (Grönlund et al., 2010). Therefore, a firm must decide how to renew its knowledge in order to update its capacity to innovate and thus prevent obsolescence and imitation from its competitors (Zhou and Wu, 2010).

In summary, open innovation is the best channel for market-oriented and technology/ knowledge-intensive firms to acquire external knowledge that complement internal knowledge so as to create necessary new knowledge for further innovation in order to maintain competitive position and survive in the global marketplace. Both inside-out and outside-in capabilities are required for firms to continue innovation and create knowledge. In particular, organizational learning, collaborative capability and innovation capacity must be in place as firms adopt appropriate open innovation practices and implement their knowledge management strategies.

Cases for comparative analysis

We use two large and well-known internet technology/knowledge-intensive and market-oriented companies in the world: Alibaba from China and SHOP.COM/ Market America as cases to compare how these two companies have adopted open innovation process and leverage each other's comparative strengths and capabilities to serve their global customers and succeed in the global online market. Before conducting an in-depth analysis of the open innovation process of these two companies, a brief introduction of the cases is presented first.

Alibaba Group

Established in 1999 by 18 people led by Jack Ma Yun, a former English teacher from Hangzhou, China, Alibaba Group, with a total of 45,000 employees as of 2016, has operated in over 190 countries, enabling small businesses to leverage innovation and technology to grow and compete more effectively in the domestic and global economies. Through its consumer-to-consumer website Taobao (translated to English as 'looking for treasures'), Alibaba has helped small

Chinese exporters, manufacturers and entrepreneurs to sell internationally, at the same time grown itself into a global leader in the online and mobile commerce market. Today the company and its related companies (such as AliCloud, AliExpress, AliPay, AliZila, Ant Financial, Cainiao, Tianmao etc.) lead the wholesale and retail online marketplaces as well as operate businesses in cloud computing, digital media and entertainment, innovation initiatives and others (www.alibaba group.com).

In January 2017, Ma, when meeting with the newly elected President Donald Trump of the USA, promised to create 1 million jobs in America (Booton, 2017). Many are curious about the methods Alibaba would have use to enable innovation and job creation. Capri (2017) provides a brief explanation on how Alibaba's customers' portal Taobao with a billion products, of which ordinary American could instantly become online sellers, business owners or distributors. Capri (2017) implies that it might be just possible for millions of online small businesses to be generated because Alibaba has technical prowess well ahead of its Western counterparts such as Amazon, Google, eBay and PayPal.

In the true spirit of a technology company, Alibaba has formed collaborative partnerships with many Western firms (e.g. AXA, AustPost, Coupa, WCA, even IOC – International Olympic Committee), and also openly sourced its product development, as it continues the joint technology innovation with several tech-companies such as Google's AppScale, Microsoft's cloud, SAP, SUSE, Hitachi Data Systems (HDS), and Yahoo!. Alibaba's global service partners cover five regions: Southwest Asia (e.g. Bangladesh's TradeShi, UAE's Dubai Chamber, Israel's Game on, Pakistan's Origaa); Southeast Asia (e.g. Singapore's Innovation Hub and IGS, S Korea's Yellow Pages); Europe (e.g. Austria's Zeevan, Germany's Kyto, Greece's Line Group, Italy's Eurocall, Russia's Indi Group); South America (e.g. Brazil's Doing B); and Oceania (e.g. Australia's iSynergi Solution) (see these information sources from https://activity.alibaba.com/ggs/Alibaba_Global_Service_Partners.html).

Comparing to Alibaba's strong influences to create small businesses in the developing nations, fewer activities have occurred in the American continent, despite Alibaba investing widely in American technology start-ups, such as Shop-Runner, a San Mateo-based retail shipping company, eBay listing tools Auctiva and Vendio, ridesharing service Lyft, and Tango, a mobile messenger (Gordon, 2014). This is understandable as there exist strong competitors such as Amazon, eBay and Google in the continent. Nonetheless, Yue (2015) reported that in order to get into China and Asia markets more effectively, Amazon trialled a new strategy of building alliance with Alibaba, by opening stores on Alibaba's online shopping site Tmall.com. This Alibaba-Amazon's strategic alliance suggests that American business owners can use Alibaba's Tmall to sell their wares and services, as a result, both companies gain benefits from an increased size of the market cake (Yue, 2015). A personal evidence provided by the second author of this chapter also indicates that SHOP.COM has partnered with Alibaba's overseas online portal, AliExpress as one of its affiliate online stores, thus, the customers of SHOP.COM are able to purchase products on AliExpress and get paid by cashback, while AliExpress, without having to pay for the expensive advertising fees, is able to link their website on SHOP.COM and leverage additional eight million customers of SHOP.COM in North America and worldwide. This online collaborative exercise signifies a good example of benefits of open innovation and rival collaboration in the increasingly globalized online shopping world.

SHOP.COM/Market America

Founded in 1992 and headquartered in Greensboro, USA, Market America is a product brokerage and internet marketing company that specializes in one-to-one marketing and social shopping. JR Ridinger is the CEO and founder of Market America/SHOP.COM. His goal is, by leveraging the collective purchasing power, to create the consumers' own economy. As a result, Ridinger's vision is to help people around the world generate residual income with the UnFranchise Business. As a product brokerage, Market America/SHOP.COM is in a position to move with market trends, which are characterized with Product Brokerage, One-to-One Marketing, Social Shopping, and building shared benefits between business owners and customers, breaking away from the antiquated methods of manufacturing, mass marketing and traditional advertising of products and services. The company is always prepared for building new relationships with extensive suppliers, customers and business owners, and change the buying habits of consumers. By leveraging these paradigm shifts in marketing and customer acquisition, Market America/SHOP.COM has built a unique Unfranchise Business Development System that is aimed at empowering individuals and engaging them to work as a team, in conjunction with other Unfranchise business owners to create the economy of their own, and to take charge of their financial future. The company has employed over 700 people globally as of year 2015, with international operations in Australia, Canada, Hong Kong, Mexico, Singapore, Spain, Taiwan, UK and USA. In recent years, Market America/SHOP.COM has also operated in some emerging markets such as Bahamas, Colombia, Dominican Republic, Ecuador, Jamaica, New Zealand and Panama. Its products can also be accessed by customers from over a hundred countries including China.

In the early stage of development, there was only Market America that had several lines of products as exclusive brokerage, including health and nutrition, home and garden, automotive and personal care, weight management, cosmetics, baby and children's healthcare products, anti-aging and skin care products; as well as services to cover personal financial management (maCapital Resources) and internet marketing services for small to medium-sized businesses (maWebCenters) (www.marketamerica.com). According to the onsite experience of the second author, one of the most advantageous aspects of Market America's business model is that its specific orientation is built around a product brokerage concept. The company does not manufacture any one product or specialize in a single service, which allows the organization to swing with various growing market directions for emerging products and services, so as to swiftly capitalize on current consumer demands. This flexibility ensures the stability, profitability and, most importantly, longevity of the organization.

Initially products and services were sold face-to-face, which limited the sale volume. To expand the market size, in 2010, Market America acquired an internet portal SHOP.COM owned previously by Microsoft Bill Gates (Wauters, 2010). Now, SHOP.COM/Market America has thousands of exclusive products sold online, via its shop consultants or Unfranchise Business Owners. The company has been known to have a proven innovative business model, blending with support, training, technology, products and services to enable individuals to conduct successful businesses. Indeed, the total earnings gained by unfranchised business owners via SHOP.COM reached over US$3.5 billion at the end of 2015. The company's localized operations are best seen in the countries and regions such as Australia, Canada, Hong Kong, Mexico, Singapore, Spain, Taiwan, United Kingdom and USA, however their products have been made available through their global online system to consumers in over a hundred countries.

Apart from the exclusive brands, Market America/SHOP.COM have thousands of retailers that offer over 40 million products and services. Their partners are some of the most famous brands and stores in the world – such as Walmart, Target, Staples, The Home Depot, Nordstrom and Lands' End. They are localized from country to country. Becoming one of Market America's Premier Partners, vendors and manufacturers could take advantage of a unique opportunity, for free, to position their business in front of a world of shoppers who are looking for quality products and services, and to heighten the exposure of their business within an extensive network of over three million preferred customers. This interlocked network of premier partners, vendors and customers appears to be a useful platform for knowledge generation and open innovation.

Different from Alibaba's strengths derived from collaborating with many global service partners, the success of SHOP.COM/Market America appears to be generated from close collaboration between the company and its business owners and customers. Next we outline the similarities and differences of these two cases with reference to their choices of channels for knowledge creation and dynamic capabilities applied in their respective open innovation practices and processes.

Case analysis

Both Alibaba Group and Market America/SHOP.COM represent typical market-oriented firms whereby the organizations aspire for taking a long-term commitment of developing innovative solutions to create added-values to customers and address customers' ongoing needs (Day, 1994; Slater and Narver, 1998; Arrigo, 2012). Both are rigorously operating in the online shopping market with strong growth in size and magnitude in recent years (Farber, 2016). This trend signifies the needs for both companies to continue their technology innovation and develop capabilities of market sensing, client linking and technology monitoring so as to enable their delivery of quality customer service, development of new products and services and distribution of profits and wealth with various stake-holders (Day, 1994; Arrigo, 2012; Moustaghfir and Schiuma, 2013; Gordon, 2014; Yue, 2015; Capri, 2017).

Whilst both companies with their respective CEOs having the same goal of promoting small businesses and creating jobs and wealth for people with ordinary backgrounds, the methods to achieve such a goal vary. Based on the earlier literature review, Table 10.2 summarizes four key areas of differences with reference to two firms' choice of open innovation process and practice, respective target of capability development and varied outcome of capacity building.

Differences in open innovation process

It is evident that Alibaba and SHOP.COM have both blended some features of three core processes of open innovation. However, predominantly SHOP.COM/ Market America tends to show more of using the outside-in open innovation process whereby the company closely monitors the external environment to source knowledge and technologies from its stakeholders (Bellantuono et al., 2013), though the dual process is also evident. The key stakeholders of SHOP.COM are hundreds of thousands of their committed online shop consultants/independent unfranchise business owners and millions of customers worldwide. As mentioned

Table 10.2 Comparison of open innovation and capability between Alibaba and SHOP.COM

Differences in	Alibaba	SHOP.COM/Market America
Open innovation process	Coupled process; Focuses on building an entrepreneurial ecosystem	Dual process; Focuses on building an unfranchise business development system
Open innovation practice	C2C and/or B2C Strategic interfirm alliance; Collaborative innovation	B2B and/or B2C An innovation mall or network community + an elite circle
Target of capability development	Firm-focused; Inside-out capability; Collaborative ability	Customer-oriented; Inside-out and outside-in capability; Connection ability
Outcome of capacity building	Organizational learning; Further developing more diversified and modular firms without brands and specified products	Learning organization; Combination of vertical organization's structure within the boundary of unfranchise business system with brands and recognizable products and services

earlier, Market America was initially built by James and Loren Ridinger with seven people as the core of the company. In the early 2000s, as the old transaction site backed by either Microsoft or Google could no longer meet its ever-growing performances, Market America finally decided to buy off the internet portal SHOP.COM owned by Microsoft to expand its market from face-to-face direct sales to internet-based marketing to facilitate the rising demands of customers' preference for online shopping. In recent years, new market knowledge and improvement of internet technologies were largely sourced from online shop consultants and global customers. Therefore, the dual process of open innovation adopted by SHOP.COM has a unique focus on building an unfranchise business development system, with a clear aim of developing quality products based on market demands and empowering the independent business owners to create a new online economy by changing the way people shop.

In contrast, Alibaba, as claimed repeatedly by its founder Jack Ma, is to focus on building an innovative eco-business system so as to absorb old or traditional ways of doing business with reinvented new technologies and partnerships. Therefore, it appears that Alibaba would have also adopted the coupled open innovation process whereby it combines both outside-in and inside-out processes as the company works with complementary global partners as listed earlier.

Differences in open innovation practice

Distinctively, Alibaba's online business provides a platform or portal to allow online transactions between sellers and buyers, in an innovative form of C2C (customer to customer) or B2C (business to customer). As a result, Alibaba has no control over the qualities of the products and/or services sold on their portal (World Economic Forum, 2017). Thus, Alibaba's open innovation practices were reflected in its strong interfirm collaboration, with several joint venture investments in complementary partners such as eBay's listing tools Auctiva and Vendio, Google's AppScale, and HDS. In addition, Alibaba has established a strategic interfirm alliance with several trading, banking, ICT and industry associations in countries located across four continents to leverage their databases of customers, distributors and suppliers with aims to source and distribute complementary products with cost- and time-efficient delivery modes (Capri, 2017). Alibaba provides a good example of successfully using collaborative innovation (Lee et al., 2010; An et al., 2014) to serve its expanding global market and to meet customers' needs.

The effort made by SHOP.COM/Market America to meet customers' needs is largely mirrored from its collaborative exercises through building both open and closed partnerships (Pisano and Verganti, 2008). SHOP.COM portal allows online transactions between business to business (B2B) via its unique unfranchise business development system, as well as between business owners to worldwide customers who enjoy social shopping online (B2C). As a result, a network community was born to share experiences of products and services openly among unfranchise business owners and customers, and to seek advice for problems and directions as it happens in an open mall (see Table 10.1). SHOP.COM does this by standardized and systemized training and developing an elite group, whereby multi-level distributors move up and around the achievement ladders within the multi-level marketing scheme. These top performers are called specialized consultants or out-licensed (unfranchised) business owners. Any unfranchised shop owner has opportunities to learn and improve themselves in any and/or all majors through the Market America University and become professionals in the business, such as the TLS (transition lifestyle) program, Motives cosmetics pro-gramme, etc. The process of adopting open innovation practices in SHOP.COM is typically involved with not only internal employees but also external independent unfranchise business owners and customers.

Targeting at different capability development

Market-oriented firms such as Alibaba and SHOP.COM must have certain distinctive capabilities so as to deliver a high level of customer service, create new products and services, and generate benefits, profits and wealth for their various stakeholders (Day, 1994; Moustaghfir and Schiuma, 2013). In comparison of capability development, the nature, size, structure and culture of these two companies are considered. It is particularly found that the target of capability development is quite different from the two cases. Whilst Alibaba addresses the firm-focused capability development, SHOP.COM's capability development is very much focused on capability building of its customers (see Table 10.2).

Because its nature of business is internet-based product marketing, SHOP.COM heavily relies on its global customers' interests and feedback on online social shopping in order to generate the awareness and happiness of using its products and services. As a consequence, SHOP.COM would have to devote large amount of time and energy to support and train its customers, especially its elite group of employees and online shop consultants (unfranchised business owners) who make forefront contacts with their respective clients. A relatively small size of the firm (a total of 750 employees so far) means that developing the outside-in customers' capability is crucially important as it would help SHOP.COM to build strong relationships with external distributors and suppliers (Arrigo, 2012) and instigate close connection with customers around the globe. The organizational structure of SHOP.COM is clearly direct marketing, without necessary reporting relationships between superior and subordinates as it would occur in a conventional organization, therefore minimum control, 100 percent profit sharing within the organization and a decentralized decision-making mechanism allow free information sharing and knowledge creation among employees, customers, distributors and suppliers (Anand and Walsh, 2016). A strong culture of making customer contacts and building network community typically embodied in internet-based marketing companies, such as SHOP.COM, suggests that the firm's core competency is closely aligned with connecting ability.

Alibaba was initially established as a high-tech online marketplace firm that aimed at servicing small businesses to do business online. Alibaba does not hold particular products but its million-odd suppliers and distributors can use its internet portals Taobao (AliExpress) and Tmall to sell and market their respective products and services worldwide. In the very beginning of its establishment, Alibaba looked for strong collaboration with big firms such as Softbank, Goldman Sachs to secure its financial resources to build Alibaba Online platform, with further US$75 millions' investment from its global partner General Atlantic in 2009 to develop its presence in the global internet and technology sector (De La Merced, 2014). Therefore, the nature of Alibaba group determines that its internal capabilities development is firm-focused. With a strong size of 45,000 employees worldwide, Alibaba has a stronger focus on building inside-out capabilities, whereby various competencies such as R&D, technology development and human resource management would be the key target of Alibaba and its various associated companies to develop internally. In addition, because of its mission to serve small businesses and make online business easier, understanding of manufacturing, supply chain and logistics management process linked to the spanning process of delivering quality customer service, developing new products and designing pricing and purchasing methods are the compact skills Alibaba would have to acquire in order to keep close pace with external market changes. The structure of Alibaba represents one of those typical modular organizations whereby a conglomerate group of firms collaborate and function in an interdependent manner. Culture of Alibaba is best described by its CEO Jack Ma as an entrepreneurial ecosystem. Despite the ongoing debate on what constitutes an entrepreneurial ecosystem (see Isenberg, 2014), the idea of Ma's ecosystem advocates a strong sense of collaboration and interdependence of economic, social and environmental systems, under which Alibaba's various associated companies co-exist, co-innovate and co-create common organizational values (see also Lee et al., 2012). Therefore, collaborative ability and attitude would be mostly desired by Alibaba as it would require its employees to continue seeking collaborative relationships with various global partners to create new knowledge and generate innovative performance.

Outcome of capacity building

Because of different industry nature, firm size, structure and culture, the choices of different open innovation process and practice have led to two firms' targeting on different sets of capability development, which in turn would likely direct to different outcome of organizational capacity building, defined as the 'process of developing and strengthening the skills, instincts, abilities, processes and resources that organizations and communities need to survive, adapt, and thrive in the fast-changing world' (Eade, 1997, p. 26).

Here it is found that as a result of organizational capacity building, Alibaba addressed the importance of organizational learning between, among and across its various associated companies to combine internal and external knowledge to generate knowledge creation and open innovation (Moustaghfir and Schiuma, 2013). It is envisaged that more diversified firms as well as many small and medium-sized business owners and entrepreneurs would join Alibaba's eco-business system for years to come as it continues to facilitate open innovation, knowledge sharing and transfer through organizational learning and collaborative capability building.

In comparison, it appears that SHOP.COM/Market America has built a strong learning organization whereby it has similarly facilitated its organizational learning to combine internal and external knowledge, and its B2C and B2Borganizational structure. Nonetheless, such organizational learning would be within its boundary of the unfranchise business system to create, retain and transfer knowledge via its purposively developed customers network community and elite group of online shop consultants. It does not go beyond one single organization's territory. Products and services, though, can be sourced from many providers and suppliers, are unique and recognizable, as training is solely conducted by the company itself. IT and Product Quality Assurance are the two most critical departments in the company, and the company has a total control of product/service quality over its exclusively branded products, which is rather different from Alibaba. The goal of SHOP.COM/Market America is to help ordinary people succeed in the unfranchise business via offering up-to-date products and services to satisfy their preferred customers' needs and enhance the total purchasing power in order to create a stronger and, eventually, depression-free economy.

Conclusion

The chapter has drawn the insights from the resource and knowledge-based theory of the firms, and discussed the benefits of utilizing the open innovation approach for market-oriented firms for continuing knowledge creation and innovation in the changing global marketplace. Several open innovation processes and practices, in addition to the competencies and capabilities required for knowledge management were outlined.

The comparison of two internet-based online marketing firms, Alibaba Group and SHOP.COM/Market America, was conducted to draw out some similarities and differences of adopting varied open innovation processes and practices. It is argued that due to the nature of business, size, structure and culture, market-based firms may target at developing different sets of skills and capabilities for open innovation and knowledge creation. Consequently, the organizational capacity building may also vary as firms seek to either develop a modular of firms without brands and specified products (i.e. Alibaba Group) with an emphasis on organizational learning among and across its modular firms; or establish itself as a distinctive learning organization with reputable brands and recognizable products (i.e. SHOP.COM).

Several implications to other market-based firms can be drawn from this comparative case analysis. First, the choice of open innovation process and practice is dependent on the firm's size, structure and culture. Second, knowledge sharing and problem solving between internal and external stakeholders for further innovation and capability building rely upon the firm's orientation towards either enhancing organizational learning over an open ecosystem or building a learning organization within a boundary-defined entity. Third, an extension of building customer-based capability to facilitate open innovation and knowledge creation is a new concept adopted by SHOP.COM, and an aspiration to generate a depression-free online economy could be modelled to other market-based firms. However, further research should be conducted to identify the specific methods on how to achieve this goal. Fourth, a greater control of product/service quality through an open innovation system and further development of mechanism to facilitate such control may be the key focus for market-based firms in order to maintain and sustain their market share and reputation. SHOP.COM provides an exemplar example of quality control, which Alibaba could learn from.

Lastly but not least, it is important to notice that coopetition, co-innovation and complementary strategies (Lee et al., 2012; Ritala, 2012) can be implemented between and among rival companies such as illustrated in the current two cases. The idea of collaboration and coopetition between business owners and global customers (B2C), between business and business (B2B) and among customers (C2C) is itself novel. Market-based firms may like to take this idea, and utilize various open innovation channels to achieve their business success.

An online-based economy has come of age. Market-based firms must utilize open innovation to create new knowledge so as to better connect and collaborate with their customers and suppliers. It is perhaps the only way to help maintain and sustain the global online and depression-free economy for future.

References

An, X.-M., Deng, H.-P., Chao, L., and Bai, W.-L. (2014). Knowledge management in supporting collaborative innovation community capacity building. *Journal of Knowledge Management*, 18(3), 574–590.
Anand, A., and Walsh, I. (2016). Should knowledge be shared generously? Tracing insights from past to present and describing a model. *Journal of Knowledge Management*, 20(4), 713–730.
Argote, L. (2011). Organizational learning research: Past, present and future. *Management Learning*, 42(4), 439–446.
Arora, A., and Gambardella, A. (1990). Complementarity and external linkages: The strategies of the large firms in biotechnology. *Journal of Industrial Economics*, 38(4), 361–379.
Arrigo, E. (2012). Alliances, open innovation and outside-in management. *Symphonya. Emerging Issues in Management*, 2, 53–65.
Barney, J.B. (1991). Firm resources and sustained competitive advantage. *Journal of Management*, 17, 99–120.
Barney, J.B. (2001). Resource-based theories of competitive advantage: A ten-year retrospective on the resource-based view. *Journal of Management*, 6, 643–650.
Bellantuono, N., Pontrandolfo, P., and Scozzi, B. (2013). Different practices for open innovation: A context-based approach. *Journal of Knowledge Management*, 17(4), 558–568.
Bianchi, M., Cavaliere, A., Chiaroni, D., Frattini, F. and Chiesa, V. (2011). Organizational modes for open innovation in the bio-pharmaceutical industry: An exploratory analysis, *Technovation*, 31(1), 22–33.

Booton, J. (2017, January 17), Alibaba promises Trump it'll create a million U.S. jobs, but don't believe it. *Marketwatch.* Retrieved from: www.marketwatch.com/ story/alibaba-promises-trump-1-million-jobs-but-dont-believe-it-2017-01-09 [[Accessed 4 May 17].

Capri, A. (2017, January 12). Alibaba: Can a Chinese e-commerce company save the American dream? *Forbes.* Retrieved from: www.forbes.com/sites/alexcapri/ 2017/01/12/alibaba-can-a-chinese-e-commerce-company-save-the-american- dream-trump-jack-ma/#3e68ceef2fe3 [Accessed 20 March 2017].

Chesbrough, H. (2003). The logic of open innovation: Managing intellectual prop- erty. *California Management Review*, 45(3), 33–58.

Chesbrough, H. (2006). Open innovation: A new paradigm for understanding indus- trial innovation. In H. Chesbrough, W. Vanhaverbeke and J. West (eds), *Open Innovation. Researching a New Paradigm*, New York: Oxford University Press, pp. 1–12.

Chesbrough, H., Vanhaverbeke, W. and West, J. (2006). *Open Innovation: Research- ing a New Paradigm*. Oxford: Oxford University Press.

Chesbrough, H. (2012). Open innovation. Where we've been and where we're going. *Research Technology Management*, 55(4), 20–27.

Darroch, J., and McNaughton, R. (2002). Examining the link between knowledge management practices and types of innovation. *Journal of Intellectual Capital*, 3(3), 210–222.

Day, G.M. (1994). The capabilities of market-driven organizations. *Journal of Mar- keting*, 58, 37–52.

De La Merced, M.J. (2014, September 24). Silver Lake reaps a golden return on its Alibaba stake after the I.P.O. *The New York Times.* Retrieved from: https:// dealbook.nytimes.com/2014/09/21/silver-lake-reaps-a-golden-return-on-its- alibaba-stake-after-the-i-p-o/?_r=1 [Accessed 6 May 2017].

Díaz-Díaz, N.L., and de Saá Pérez, P. (2014). The interaction between external and internal knowledge sources: An open innovation view. *Journal of Knowledge Man- agement*, 18(2), 430–446.

Eade, D. (1997). *Capacity-Building: An Approach to People-Centred Development*. Oxfam.

Enkel, E., Gassmann, O., and Chesbrough, H. (2009). Open R&D and open innova- tion: Exploring the phenomenon. *R&D Management*, 39(4), 311–316.

Farber, M. (2016, June 8). Consumers are now doing most of their shopping online. *Fortune.* Retrieved from: http://fortune.com/2016/06/08/online-shopping- increases/ [Accessed 5 May 2017].

Fritsch, M., and Lukas, R. (2001). Who cooperates on R&D? *Research Policy*, 30, 297–312.

Gallego, J., Rubalcaba, L., and Suárez, C. (2013). Knowledge for innovation in Europe: The role of external knowledge on firms' cooperation strategies. *Journal of Business Research*, 66, 2034–2041.

Gassmann, O., Enkel, E., and Chesbrough, H. (2010). The future of open innova- tion. *R&D Management*, 40(3), 213–221.

Gordon, J. (2014, September 22). US businesses benefit from Alibaba's global expansion. *Featured in:* Asia, China. Retrieved from: www.asiamattersforamerica. org/china/us-businesses-benefit-from-alibabas-global-expansion [Accessed 20 March 2017].

Grant, R.M. (1996a). Prospering in dynamically competitive environments: Organi- zational capability as knowledge integration. *Organization Science*, 7(4), 357–387.

Grant, R.M. (1996b). Towards a knowledge-based theory of the firm. *Strategic Management Journal*, 17, 109–122.

Grant, R.M., and Baden-Fuller, C. (1995, August 17). A knowledge-based theory of the interfirm collaboration. *Academy of Management Proceedings*, 17–21.

Grönlund, J., Sjödin, D.R., and Frishammar, J. (2010). Open innovation and the stage-gate process: A revised model for new product development. *California Management Review*, 52(3), 106–131.

Gulati, R. (1998). Alliances and networks. *Strategic Management Journal*, 19(4), 293–317.

Hamel, G., and Prahalad, C.K. (1994). *Competing for the Future*. Boston: Harvard Business School Press.

Huizingh, E.K.R. (2011). Open innovation: State of the art and future perspectives. *Technovation*, 31(1), 2–9.

Inauen, M., and Schenker-Wicki, A. (2012). Fostering radical innovations with open innovation. *European Journal of Innovation Management*, 15(2), 212–231.

Isenberg, D. (2014, May 12). What an entrepreneurial ecosystem is? *Harvard Business Review*. Retrieved from: https://hbr.org/2014/05/what-an-entrepreneurial-ecosystem-actually-is [Accessed 6 May 2017].

Kogut, B. and Zander, U. (1992). Knowledge of the firm, combinative capabilities, and the replication of technology. *Organization Science*, 3(3), 383–397.

Laursen, K., and Salter, A. (2006). Open for innovation: The role of openness in explaining innovation performance among UK manufacturing firms. *Strategic Management Journal*, 27(2), 131–150.

Lee, S., Park, G., Yoon, B. and Park, J. (2010). Open innovation in SMEs – an intermediated network model. *Research Policy*, 39(2), 290–300.

Lee, S.M., Olson, D.L., and Trimi, S. (2012). Co-innovation: Convergenomics, collaboration, and cocreation for organizational values. *Management Decision*, 50(5), 817–831.

Lichtenthaler, U. (2011). Open innovation: Past research, current debates, and future directions. *Academy of Management Perspectives*, 25(1), 75–93.

Morgan, N.A., Vorhies, D.W., and Mason, C.H. (2009). Market orientation, marketing capabilities and firm performance. *Strategic Management Journal*, 30(8), 909–920.

Mortara, L. and Minshall, T. (2011). How do large multinational companies implement open innovation?. *Technovation*, 31(11), 586–597.

Moustaghfir, K., and Schiuma, G. (2013). Guest editorial: Knowledge, learning and innovation: research and perspectives. *Journal of Knowledge Management*, 17(4), 495–510.

Pisano, G.P. and Verganti, R. (2008). Which kind of collaboration is right for you? *Harvard Business Review*, 86(12), 78–86.

Ritala, P. (2012). Coopetition strategy – When is it successful? Empirical evidence on innovation and market performance. *British Journal of Management*, 23, 307–324.

Senge, P.M. (1990). *The Fifth Discipline*. London: Century Business.

Slater, S.F., and Narver, J.C. (1998). Customer-led and market-oriented: Let's not confuse the two. *Strategic Management Journal*, 19, 1001–1006.

Sobrero, M. and Roberts, E.B. (2002). Strategic management of supplier-manufacturer relations in new product development. *Research Policy*, 31(1), 159–182.

Song, J., Almeida, P., and Wu, G. (2003). Learning-by-hiring: Mobility and knowledge transfer? *Management Science*, 49(4), 351–365.

Spithoven, A., Clarysse, B. and Knockaert, M. (2010). Building absorptive capacity to organize inbound open innovation in traditional industries. *Technovation*, 30(1), 130–141.

Taminiau, Y., Smit, W., and de Lange, A. (2009). Innovation in management consulting firms through informal knowledge sharing. *Journal of Knowledge Management*, 13(1), 42–55.

Teece, D.J., Pisano, G., and Shuen, A. (1997). Dynamic capabilities and strategic management. *Strategic Management Journal*, 18(7), 509–533.

Tseng, C.-Y., Pai, D.C., and Hung, C.-H. (2011). Knowledge absorptive capacity and innovation performance in KIBS. *Journal of Knowledge Management*, 15(6), 971–983.

Van de Vrande, V., de Jong, J.P.J., Vanhaverbeke, W. and de Rochemont, M. (2009). Open innovation in SMEs: Trends, motives and management challenges, *Technovation*, 29(6–7), 423–437.

Wauters, R. (2010, December 15). Market America acquires Bill Gates-backed shopping site shop.com. *TechCrunch*. Retrieved from: https://techcrunch.com/2010/12/15/market-america-acquires-bill-gates-backed-shopping-site-shop-com/ [Accessed 4 May 2017].

Wernerfelt, B. (1984). A resource-based view of the firm. *Strategic Management Journal*, 5(2), 171–180.

World Economic Forum. (2017). Davos 2017 – An insight, an idea with Jack Ma. Retrieved from: www.youtube.com/watch?v=WsQ7ysVt-0A [Accessed 20 April 2017].

Wright, P.M., Dunford, B.B., and Snell, S.A. (2001). Human resources and the resource-based view of the firm. *Journal of Management*, 27(6), 701–721.

Yue, W. (2015, March 5). To boost China sales, Amazon tries Alibaba partnership. *Forbes*. Retrieved from: www.forbes.com/sites/ywang/2015/03/05/to-boost-china-sales-amazon-tries-alibaba-partnership/#5e86a06050c2 [Accessed 20 March 2017].

Zhou, K.Z., and Wu, F. (2010). Technological capability, strategic flexibility, and product innovation. *Strategic Management Journal*, 31(5), 547–561.

Websites indicating several examples of Alibaba's partnership and collaboration with various organizations around the world

Microsoft and Alibaba show strong cloud results:
www.investopedia.com/news/microsoft-alibaba-show-strong-cloud-results/
Check the site for partnership between AXA and Alibaba:
www.businessinsider.com/how-axa-could-leverage-its-new-partnership-with-alibaba-2016-8/?r=AU&IR=T
Coupa and Alibaba's partnership:
www.coupa.com/newsworthy/press-releases/coupa-announces-partnership-with-alibaba-com-providing-access-to-millions-of-global-suppliers/
Mars and Alibaba partnership:
www.prnewswire.com/news-releases/mars-and-alibaba-group-launch-global-strategic-business-partnership-300291933.html
Alibaba partnering with WCA:
www.wcaworld.com/eng/news.asp?id=1225

Alibaba partner with Aust Post:
    www.abc.net.au/news/2014-05-28/alibaba-australia-post-deal/5484458
Alibaba group – Aliyun – partnership with technology companies:
    www.alibabagroup.com/en/news/article?news=p160809a
Alibaba with IOC:
    www.olympic.org/news/ioc-and-alibaba-group-launch-historic-long-term-
    partnership-as-alibaba-becomes-worldwide-olympic-partner-through-2028
Alibaba's global service partners:
    https://activity.alibaba.com/ggs/Alibaba_Global_Service_Partners.html
Check this site again to compare different business models of Alibaba and Amazon:
    www.investopedia.com/articles/investing/061215/difference-between-amazon-
    and-alibabas-business-models.asp

11 Collaborative innovation

A viable strategy to solve complex transformational social issues in sport?

Anne Tjønndal

Introduction

Sport organizations are increasingly confronted with complex challenges and wicked problems, such as practices of social exclusion, gender inequality and discrimination; doping; corruption; and other significant ethical issues. Many of such social issues and policy problems are complex and contested and they are called 'wicked' for a good reason (e.g. Bueren et al., 2003). They are persistent despite considerable efforts to solve them. This is especially true of social exclusion problems in sporting practices and organizations (Tjønndal, 2018). While combating such issues in sport has been part of the political agenda of major international sport organizations such as the International Olympic Committee (IOC). the International Boxing Association (AIBA) and the International Football Association (FIFA), for several decades (e.g. IOC, 2015; AIBA, 2016; FIFA, 2016), the sports sector does not seem to be able to solve such challenges on its own.

Recent studies have shown that social inequality in sport participation has increased the last ten years (Strandbu et al., 2017). Another example of how such social issues manifest in sport deals with mega-sporting events such as the Olympic Games. There is a growing body of research suggesting that mega-events like the FIFA World Cup and the Olympic Games reproduce social inequality via elitism, commercialization, corruption, problematic forms of nationalism and negative local impacts on host cities (Bernard and Busse, 2006; Travers, 2011; Vanwynsberghe et al., 2012; Gaffney, 2010, 2012). This chapter discusses collaborative innovation as a possible solution to such 'wicked problems' in sport.

Reviewing the literature on sport innovation, there is little research on how collaborative innovation can solve complex social issues in sport. Research on combating social exclusion often focuses on work and education as empirical fields (Birkelund et al., 2014; Hansen, 2011; Heggen, 2003). Work and education are important areas for social inclusion, but other social areas are also significant for combating exclusion (Fangen, 2009). The promotion of social inclusion through sport has received increased attention in various disadvantaged groups (McConkey et al., 2012). There is also a broad body of knowledge on how social exclusion effects participation in sport (e.g. Collins, 2014; Spaaij et al., 2014). In general, there is a widespread belief that sport has the power to make society more equal, socially cohesive and peaceful, but the idea of sport as an agent of personal and social change has, of course, not gone unchallenged (Spaaij, 2009). While sport programmes have the potential to promote inclusion, sport does not automatically create a more equal society. In many cases, the inequalities of society are simply reproduced in sport (Spaaij et al., 2014).

Through collaborative innovation processes with multiple stakeholders, sport organizations can create greater feelings of shared ownership and responsibility for the outcome of new ideas and innovations. In this way, collaborative innovations also facilitate easier implementation phases in the real world (Sørensen and Torfing, 2012; Torfing, 2012). Studies of collaborative innovation in public sector services illustrate that collaborative innovation can facilitate new and creative solutions to complex social issues and wicked policy problems (Sørensen and Waldorff, 2014; Bjørgo et al., 2015). Studies on collaborative innovation have, however, mainly focused on public and private sector (Bommert, 2010; Sirianni, 2009; Eggers and Singh, 2009), but little of this research deals with social inclusion (Milbourne et al., 2003).

Some researchers have argued that some of the reasons that policy makers and public sector organizations are not able to solve complex social issues related to exclusion is because policy makers have too little knowledge about the problems they seek to solve (Koppenjan and Klijn, 2004; Torfing et al., 2012). Collaboration between multiple stakeholders and across sectors is therefore viewed as an important factor in developing new and innovative solutions to complex social issues (Seippel, 2002; Mulgan and Albury, 2003; Nambisan, 2008). How sport organizations work towards solving such social issues does however need more empirical attention (Enjolras and Wollebæk, 2010). In other words, we have little knowledge about how sport organizations work to solve issues of exclusion, what works, and what does not work.

In sport, innovation occurs at all levels, and shapes the development of elite and grassroots sports, volunteer sport organizations and commercialized sports leagues. While the phenomenon of sport innovation is not new, the research on this field is still emerging. Ratten and Ferriera (2016) argue that there is little unified knowledge of what sport innovation and sport entrepreneurship is, and that the theoretical development of the research needs further development. Innovation is often linked to new technology and new products (Moore and Hartley, 2008; Hartley, 2005). While these innovations are also found in the context of sport (Tjønndal, 2016a), this is a very limited understanding of what innovation in sport is and can be. Sport innovation might just as well be processes – often described as 'improvement', 'reform', 'change' or 'new ideas' (Sørensen and Torfing, 2011). This chapter seeks to contribute to the growing knowledge base on sport innovation by investigating collaborative innovation in sport. More specifically, this chapter explains the relationship between innovation and sport, and demonstrates how sport innovation can be enhanced through collaboration.

Innovation in sport

Sport is inherently innovative because of its capacity to adapt, evolve and change based on social, political and technological trends. While people may choose to participate in sport for a number of reasons, such as fun, leisure, fitness or social reasons, an inherent ambition and part of the ethos of sport, is to improve performance (Guttmann, 2004). Athletes strive for new records, new championships and new victories. Hence, modern sport has a 'natural drive' to innovate. In elite sport, competition can act as an innovation driver. Historically, the joy of play has also been a driver for sport innovation, especially in terms of development of new sporting activities. In other words, innovation as a phenomenon is nothing new to sport. Rather, it represents new ideas and changes to sport organizations, coaching, sport events, performance and competitive advantages in elite sport. In recent years, market and commercialism has also fueled many sport innovations. Examples of this includes changes to rules and regulations in sport in order to attract more supporters and fans, creating larger streams of revenue. Some of these market-fuelled changes have been highly controversial, such as regulations on the size and shape of female volleyball players' competition outfits, inherently to 'attract a higher number of male supporters' (Tjønndal, 2016b; 2016a).

There are different types of innovation that occur in sport including social innovation, technological innovation, commercial innovation, community-based innovation and organizational innovation (Tjønndal, 2017, 2018). Social innovation arises when sport organizations or individuals (such as athletes and coaches) are faced with social issues that requires creative and new ideas to solve. In this way, social innovation encourages solutions to complex social issues in sport contexts. Organizations and individuals are involved in social innovation by contributing to society in a positive manner through sport. Social innovations are often complex and time-consuming processes. The use of martial art as a tool to achieve gender and development objectives in Uganda through the global 'Girl Effect' campaign is an example of social innovation in sport (Hayhurst, 2014). Technological innovation occurs through advances in technology. Advances in modern technology over the past decade have innovated the way people participate in sport in a number of ways. In the reviewed literature, most studies dealing with technological sport-based innovations are related to advances in performance enhancement (Johnson, 2010), sport medicine (Ellis et al., 2011) improvements in measuring athletic performance (Sheridan, 2007), rehabilitation (van der Woude et al., 2006) and new adaptions to sporting equipment. New and improved sport equipment and athletic gear can change and improve how existing sports are practiced (Balmer et al., 2012). In other words, they can contribute to large-scale institutional changes in sport. However, technological innovation also affects how people participate in sport in other ways. For instance, the use of the internet has created a completely new way of participating in sport through e-sport, fantasy sport leagues and online betting.

Commercial innovation appears when businesses are involved in creating change in sport. These sport-based innovations can be product innovations (Fuller et al., 2007), processed-based (Liang, 2013) or both (Hyysalo, 2009). Commercial innovations by large international corporations involved in sport often relate to the way sports products and processes are marketed (Fredberg and Piller, 2011). In professional sport, commercial innovation occurs through risk-filled activities involving market capitalization, competition, credibility and business activities (Ratten, 2011a, 2011b, 2011c; Goldsby et al., 2005). An example of commercial innovation in the literature is the Parris et al. (2014) study of female professional wakeboarders' management of sponsorship and branding. Community-based innovation involves social responsibility and entrepreneurship in which individuals and sport organizations partner with local community groups to encourage working towards a common goal (Hoeber et al., 2015; Hoeber and Hoeber, 2012; Groves, 2011). This can often be related to social issues and social sport innovations. An example of a community-based sport innovation in the reviewed literature is Okayasu and Morais' (2016) paper on innovation, entrepreneurship and community development in Japan. Organizational innovation occurs when sport organizations and government institutions pursue projects of institutional change (Miragaia and Ferreira, 2016; Winand et al., 2013). Within the context of sport, there are a number of institutions that have changed the way sport organizations are structured (Winand and Hoeber, 2016). Examples of sport organizations that are involved in innovation are the International Olympic Committee (IOC) and Federation Internationale de Football Association (FIFA). As global sport organizations such as the Olympic Committee have a great deal of influence and power in how sport is viewed in society, it is important for them to be up to date with new developments in international sport. A way in which the Olympic Committee has done this is through the inclusion of new sports as Olympic disciplines such as taekwondo and beach volleyball. Studies of organizational innovation in sport can also concern teacher education in physical education, such as Pill et al.'s (2012) article on research-based innovation in Australian teacher education.

Innovation plays a vital role in the development of sport. Through new ideas, change and technological advancement innovation shapes how sport is played and organized. Sport-based innovation can occur as emergence of new sports, new athletic gear and equipment or new rules and regulations in sport. It could be as development of sport as an activity, by appealing to marginalized groups in society (e.g. people with various types of disabilities, elderly, immigrant women) or new methods of including and motivating people to participate in sport (e.g. government campaigns for public health and daily physical activity). Sport-based innovation could also be new ways of organizing sport (e.g. spectator involvement, financing and funding, new sport organizations and organizing systems). Lastly, sport innovation could be unethical, creating new ways of cheating (e.g. development of new performance enhancing drugs). By better understanding the diversity of sport innovation, researchers, sport policy makers and other professionals can better develop appropriate responses to resolving the intractable problems modern sport faces today.

Collaborative innovation

Innovation is often described as the introduction of new technologies or new products (Moore and Hartley, 2008; Hartley, 2005), but the innovations developed in sport organizations are rarely of this nature (Tjønndal, 2016b). Rather, the innovations in sport organizations are more often changes described as 'improvement', 'reform' or 'new ideas' (Tjønndal, 2016a). Such innovations can be defined as:

> Proactive processes that seek to solve problems and challenges, develop new possibilities and ideas, and implement and spread creative solutions that disrupt outdated practices and policies in a specific context.
>
> (Torfing et al., 2014, p. 19)

Such organizational innovation processes are often developed because of a challenge or social issues that cannot be solved through existing practices. These innovation processes are always chaotic and complex (Torfing, 2012). Similar to public sector organizations, through collaborative innovation efforts, the solution of social issues in sport can be perceived as a joint responsibility between stakeholders (Hartley et al., 2013). In this context, collaboration is defined as:

> A process, where two or more partners work together to create value, and throughout this processes exchange experiences, resources, competences and ideas, that both change the collaborators perceptions, ideas and identities.
>
> (Roberts and Bradley, 1991, p. 77)

Collaboration does not require all partners to be in complete agreement, but can be viewed as a process of work and development that deals with stakeholders from different backgrounds, with different experiences, ideas, interests and competences (Gray, 1989; Torfing et al., 2014). Collaborative innovations can involve a variety of different stakeholders (Sørensen and Torfing, 2011), such as sport organizations, public sector actors, private sector actors, researchers, athletes, coaches and volunteer organizations.

Collaborative innovation is built on several theoretical standpoints. Theories of 'network governance', which value the role collaboration and networks play in working towards finding innovative solutions to complex social issues are central here (Koppenjan and Klijn, 2004). Theoretical perspectives on learning and change through interactions and collaborative processes are also central to collaborative innovation theory (Lave and Wegner, 1991). Collaborative innovation is also derived from management-theories of innovation in private sector businesses where the focus is often on 'social innovations' (Phills et al., 2008), 'co-creation' (Bason, 2007; Prahalad and Ramaswamy, 2004) or 'open innovation' (Chesbrough, 2003). However, collaborative innovation differs from all the innovation strategies mentioned here (Torfing, 2013). Collaborative innovation is different from 'leadership-driven', 'employee-driven' or 'user-driven' innovation strategies by not promoting individual entrepreneurs as the key driving force behind innovative solutions (Torfing et al., 2014). While entrepreneurship theory and research often focuses on 'innovation champions' or 'heroes' (Ratten, 2015), collaborative innovation highlights innovation as a collaborative effort across sectors, organizations and individuals (Torfing et al., 2014).

This innovation strategy also differs from 'social innovation', where innovation is understood as something primarily created in volunteer organizations and sectors (Tjønndal, 2018). Collaboration between public, private and volunteer stakeholder are often downplayed in theories of social innovation (Bommert, 2010). Lastly, collaborative innovation differs from 'open innovation' (Chesbrough, 2003), where public organizations are highlighted as 'innovation champions'. In contrast to these innovation strategies, collaborative innovation is a relational strategy that highlights the creative and productive space that is created when stakeholders from different sectors and organizations come together to work towards a common goal (Ansell and Gash, 2008). However, there is little knowledge on collaborative innovation in sport. Previous research on collaborative innovation often focuses on innovation in public sector services (Hartley et al., 2013; Sørensen, 2012; Torfing, 2012, 2013).

Sport innovation through collaboration

While innovation is often defined by catch phrases like 'new ideas that work' (Mulgan and Albury, 2003) or 'new stuff that is made useful' (McKeown, 2008), these definitions does not clarify what the concept of innovation is. Building on Sørensen and Torfing's (2011) definition, innovation involves an open (and often unpredictable) process that is based on intentional actions through which actors aim to solve problems or improve the current state of things (Kingdon, 1984). Hence, the result can often become a mix of both intended and unintended outcomes.

Secondly, innovation aims to bring about particular types of changes (e.g. Hall, 1993). Innovation involves the production of qualitative (rather than quantitative) changes (Slappendel, 1996). However, there is no objective way to measure what amount of qualitative change qualifies as an innovation (Sørensen and Torfing, 2011).

Third, Sørensen and Torfing's (2011) definition insists that innovation is always relative to a specific context. In other words, while innovation brings about something new, the new is not necessarily novel to the world. It can merely be perceived as new in a particular organization or context (Zaltman et al., 1973; Tjønndal, 2016a, 2016b, 2017a).

Finally, while innovation carries a positive connotation, the definition used here does not include a normative perspective. This means that the consequences of innovation can be good, bad or neutral (Hartley, 2005). Successful innovations are successful when they lead to a desirable result in the eyes of the stakeholders. Ideally, the outcome of sport innovations should correspond with the preferences of sport organizations, making life easier for athletes, coaches, leaders and officials in sport, create higher athletic performances or higher enjoyment of participation in sport. In real life, however, sport organizations, athletes, coaches, referees and leisure participants often evaluate the outcomes of sport innovations in different, and sometimes conflicting, ways. This reflects the fact that sport innovation can serve different purposes. As such, sport innovation can be aimed at elite sport, for instance by improving elite level performance or improving competitive athletic gear. It can also be aimed at grass-roots sport, improving the accessibility of participating in sport as leisure and/or health-promoting activities. These represent two distinctly different objectives of sport innovations, and as such there are naturally crucial trade-offs between these different objectives.

Innovation is a nonlinear and complex process. However, we can identify five phases of innovation processes in sport (Figure 11.1).

Encountering the problem

The first phase of any innovation process in sport is about identifying a challenge or problem and discovering the need to change or improve existing policies and practices in sport.

Generating ideas for solutions

This phase involves the gathering, development and presentation of ideas that might solve the challenge at hand. The generation of ideas for solutions presupposes the identification of problems in sport, the opportunities gained from solving them and the clarification of shared goals and values between stakeholders. This phase also implies the questioning of long-held assumptions in specific sporting contexts.

Selection of ideas

While the generation of ideas may lead to a variety of possible solutions to a specific problem, the selection of ideas involves decisions about which one of these ideas are worth pursuing. Ideally, these ideas should be bold and transformative, but at the same time flexible, feasible and broadly accepted among stakeholders (Sørensen and Torfing, 2011). Negotiation, compromise and conflict settlement between collaborating parts are key features of this innovation phase.

Implementing new sporting practices

This involves the conversion of ideas into new procedures and practices in sport and sport organizations. The implementation phase is a difficult part of the innovation process and many things can go wrong (Hartley et al., 2013). This phase requires leadership, the construction of joint ownership and the creation of positive incentives. Sport innovators must be prepared to deal with unforeseen hiccups and temporary setbacks in this part of the innovation process.

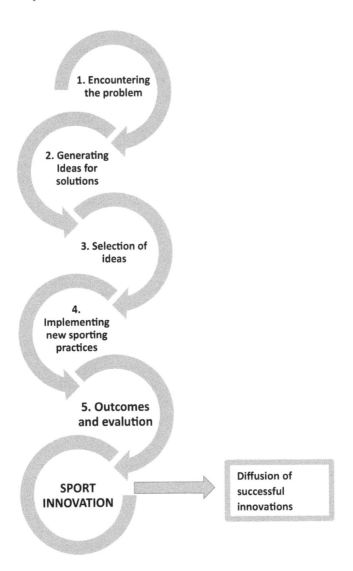

Figure 11.1 The innovation process in sport

Outcomes and evaluation

The final phase involves the evaluation of the innovation process and the innovation outcomes. Here it is important to evaluate if the sport innovation achieved the desired outcomes (e.g. if the innovation process has contributed to a solution to the encountered problem). It is also important to be honest and open about unintended (and perhaps undesired) outcomes as a result of the innovation process.

Finally, if the sport innovation has been deemed successful, an outcome of the innovation process is the diffusion of successful sport innovation processes. This implies the spreading of innovation throughout an organization or from one organization to another. This also involves overcoming standard objections related to change, such as 'we have always done it in this way' or 'we tried to change it before, but it didn't work'.

The innovation phases will not appear in this order. Collaborative innovation implies a complex and chaotic process where the different phases are often combined, integrated and rearranged (Torfing et. al., 2012). However, all five phases represents key factors in the innovation processes in sport.

Sørensen and Torfing (2011) claim that the innovation process can be strengthened through collaboration 'between relevant and affected actors from the public and private sector' (p. 852). Collaborating with other actors about 'the problem' (phase 1) and the need to solve it can generate a joint sense of responsibility in creating innovative solutions. Sharing these challenges with other actors also allows for exchange of challenges and problems between sport organizations where unknown similarities might be discovered. Secondly, the generation of ideas on how to solve these problems thrives when different actors share experiences and ideas through collaboration. Thirdly, the selection of ideas is improved when different collaborators with different knowledge and perspectives participate in assessing the potential and risks of working with competing ideas. Fourth, the implementation of new sporting practices is enhanced when collaboration creates a common ownership to these new and creative initiatives. This also reduces implementation resistance (Sørensen and Waldorf, 2014). Collaboration in the implementation phase also helps to mobilize resources, ensure flexible adjustments along the way and compensate eventual loses in the process (Sørensen and Torfing, 2011). Finally, the diffusion of successful innovation practices in sport is propelled by the formation of professional and social networks. Networks with 'strong ties' have a short reach but provide strong mutual support, whereas networks with 'weak ties' have longer reach but a lower level of support (Granovetter, 1977).

The positive impact of collaboration on the innovation process is confirmed by studies of innovation in private sector and by empirical studies of public sector innovation (Sørensen and Torfing, 2012, 2013). Many qualitative case studies have confirmed the positive impact of collaboration on public innovation (e.g. Roberts and Bradley, 1991; Dente et al., 2005). Roberts and Bradley (1991) highlight that collaboration has a positive impact on public policy innovation. However, studies on the impact of collaboration on innovation in sport is an underdeveloped field. There is little empirical knowledge on how collaboration affects innovation processes in sporting contexts. Given that the nature of innovation processes is highly context specific, further empirical research on sport innovation should investigate the impact of collaboration on the different phases of innovation processes in sport.

Furthermore, just as athletes, coaches and leaders will not always collaborate, collaboration will not always produce sport innovation. For instance, repeated collaboration in closed and stable networks that over time have developed (more or less) the same worldviews will tend to prevent innovation and stifle creativity (Skilton and Dooley, 2010). Unequal relations of power in collaborative arenas may prevent certain groups of actors from voicing their opinion and bringing new ideas to the table (Tjønndal, 2017). Networks sometimes create problems when trying to implement innovations because of the heightened level of uncertainty and the lack of institutionalization that can both diminish efficiency and trust (O'Toole, 1997). Lastly, the diffusion of innovations can be prevented by lack of communication that might occur when people collaborate with others whom they feel are too different from themselves (Burt, 1992).

Despite such challenges, with the right management and communication, collaboration can be a crucial source of innovation in the sports sector (Tjønndal, 2016a, 2016b, 2017). In public sector innovation literature there are proposed some different strategies for collaboration that may spur innovation. Eggers and Singh (2009) distinguish five collaborative strategies. (1) *The cultivation strategy* aims to facilitate collaboration between different individuals, so that they can exchange and develop new ideas and test them in their everyday working life; (2) *the replication strategy* aims to foster collaborative relationships between organizations to identify, translate, adapt and implement their best and most successful innovations; (3) *the partnership strategy* aims to develop and test new and creative ideas through collaboration between sectors, which have different rule and resource bases; (4) *the network strategy* aims to facilitate the exchange of ideas, mutual learning, and joint action through horizontal interaction between relevant and affected actors who have different kinds of expertise; (5) *the open-source strategy* aims to produce innovation by using the internet to invite unknown co-creators from around the world to help solve a specific problem. The choice between these different collaboration strategies depends on the time and place, the character of the innovation challenge, and the experiences and capacities of the public agency aiming to facilitate collaborative innovation.

Conclusion

Sport is inherently innovative because of its capacity to adapt, evolve and change based on social, political and technological trends. Innovation plays a vital role in the development of sport. Through new ideas, change and technological advancement innovation shapes how sport is played and organized. In other words, innovation affects the role of sport in society. In this chapter I have argued against the increasing tendencies to highlight the role of entrepreneurs and innovation champions in sport and instead draw attention to the large and relatively unexplored potential for enhancing sport innovation through collaboration between multiple stakeholders. As such, I have claimed that multiactor collaboration may facilitate the co-creation of new and transformative ideas and forge joint ownership to these ideas so that they may be implemented in practice and produce outcomes that are deemed valuable and desirable by key stakeholders. To sustain this claim, I have demonstrated how collaboration may strengthen all parts of the innovation processes and pointed out some central strategies for facilitating collaborative innovation in sport.

To expand and reinforce this new collaborative approach to sport innovation, there is a need for a broad range of empirical studies of collaborative innovation in different sporting contexts. The insights gained through various empirical studies will be a valuable tool for producing situated knowledge of what works in particular sporting contexts. Such situated knowledge will be greatly appreciated by local, regional and international stakeholders involved in collaborative innovation in sport. Furthermore, knowledge on how and in what ways collaboration across sectors can enhance sport organizations' innovation ability to solve complex social issues is greatly needed. As international governing bodies of sport do not appear to be able to solve wicked problems of social exclusion on their own, one can assume that collaboration with stakeholders in public and private sectors might represent the key to innovative solutions to such issues in modern sport. However, there is too little empirical knowledge about what collaborative innovation strategies work to solve issues of exclusion in sport.

My aim in writing this article has been to contribute to the growing literature on sport innovation. While collaborative innovation is an established research field on its own, the majority of this research focuses on public sector services and organizations. Within sport, the innovation literature is dominated by studies on entrepreneurs and innovation champions – a theoretical perspective that highlights the innovation efforts of individuals. Here I have argued that collaboration between multiple actors can enhance the innovation process and that such collaborative practices might also be necessary if modern sport organizations are to solve complex challenges connected to social exclusion and inequality.

Innovation represents complex processes that often lead to both intended and unintended outcomes. Working towards innovative solutions to social exclusion and wicked problems in sport it will be important to evaluate the innovation outcomes of collaborative practices between stakeholders. Innovation often carries a positive connotation, but the consequences of innovation can be both good, bad and neutral. Therefore, it will be important in future empirical studies of collaborative innovation efforts to solve social issues in sport to review the risks and consequences of sport innovation processes.

References

Ansell, C., and Gash, A. (2008). Collaborative governance in theory and practice. *Journal of Public Administration Research and Theory*, 18(4), 543–571.

AIBA. (2016). AIBA statutes. Retrieved from: http://d152tffy3gbaeg.cloudfront.net/2015/02/AIBA-Statutes.pdf [Accessed 5 October 2016].

Balmer, N., Pleasence, P., and Nevill, A. (2012). Evolution and revolution: Gauging the impact of technological and technical innovation on Olympic performance. *Journal of Sports Sciences*, 30(11), 1075–1083.

Bason, C. (2007). *Velfærdsinnovation. Ledelse av nytænkning i den offentlige sector* [Innovation. Leadership and new ideas in public sector]. København: Børsen Forlag.

Bernard, A.B., and Busse, M.R. (2006). Who wins the Olympic Games: Economic resources and medal totals. *The Review of Economics and Statistics*, 86(1), 413–417.

Birkelund, G.E., Rogstad, J., Heggebø, K., Aspøy, T.M., and Bjelland, H.F. (2014). Diskriminering i arbeidslivet – Resultater fra randomiserte felteksperiment i Oslo, Stavanger, Bergen og Trondheim [Discrimination in working life – results from a randomized experiment in Oslo, Stavanger, Bergen and Trondheim]. *Sosiologisk tidsskrift*, 04(2014), 352–382.

Bjørgo, F., Johans, S., and Hutchinson, G.S. (2015). Gjensidige problemer og samarbeidsdrevet innovasjon. I O.J. Andersen, L. Gårseth-Nesbakk og T. Bondas (red.), *Innovasjoner i offentlig tjenesteyting – Vågal reise med behov for allierte*. Bergen: Fagbokforlaget, 106–124.

Bommert, B. (2010). Collaborative innovation in the public sector. *International Public Management Review*, 11(1), 15–33.

Bueren, E., Klijn, E.H., and Koppenjan, J.F. (2003). Dealing with wicked problems in networks: Analyzing an environmental debate from a network perspective. *Journal of Public Administration Research and Theory*, 13(2), 193–212.

Burt, R.S. (1992). *Structural Holes*. Cambridge, MA: Harvard University Press.

Chesbrough, H.W. (2003). *Open Innovation: The New Imperative for Creating and Profiting from Technology*. Boston: Harvard Business School Press.

Collins, M. (2014). *Sport and Social Exclusion*. Oxon: Routledge.

Dente, B., Bobbio, L., og Spada, A. (2005). Government or Governance of Urban Innovation? *DISP The Planning Review*, 41(162), 1–22.

Eggers, B., and Singh, S. (2009). *The Public Innovators Playbook*. Washington, DC: Harvard Kennedy School of Government.

Ellis, H.B., Briggs, K.K., and Philippon, M.J. (2011). Innovation in hip arthroscopy: Is hip arthritis preventable in the athlete? *British Journal of Sports Medicine*, 45, 253–258.

Enjolras, B., and Wollebæk, D. (2010). *Frivillige organisasjoner, sosial utjevning og inkludering*. Oslo: Senter for forskning på sivilsamfunn og frivillig sektor.

Fangen, K. (2009). Sosial ekskludering av unge med innvandrerbakgrunn – den relasjonelle, stedlige og politiske dimensjon. *Tidsskrift for ungdomsforskning*, 9(2), 91–112.

Fredberg, T., and Piller, F.T. (2011). The paradox of tie strength in customer relationship for innovation: A longitudinal case study in the sports industry. *R&D Management*, 41(5), 470–484.

Fuller, J., Jawecki, G., and Muhlbacher, H. (2007). Innovation creation by online basketball communities. *Journal of Business Research*, 60, 60–71.

FIFA. (2016). FIFA statutes. Retrieved from: http://resources.fifa.com/mm/document/affederation/generic/02/78/29/07/fifastatutsweben_neutral.pdf [Accessed 18 June 2017].

Gaffney, C. (2010). Mega-events and socio-spatial dynamics in Rio de Janeiro, 1919–2016. *Journal of Latin American Geography*, 9(1), 7–29.

Gaffney, C. (2012). Between discourse and reality: The un-sustainability of mega-event planning. *Sustainability*, 5(9), 3926–3940.

Goldsby, M., Kuratko, D., and Bishop, J. (2005). Entrepreneurship and fitness: An examination of rigourous exercise and goal attainment among small business owners. *Journal of Small Business Management*, 43(1), 78–92.

Granovetter, M.S. (1977). The strength of Weak Ties. Social Networks, pp. 347-367.

Gray, B. (1989). *Collaborating: Finding Common Ground for Multiparty Problems.* San Francisco: Jossey-Bass.

Groves, R.M. (2011). New age athletes as social entrepreneurs: Proposing a philanthropic paradigm shift and creative use of limited liability company joint ventures. *Wake Forest Journal of Business & Intellectual Property*, 11, 212–242.

Guttmann, A. (2004). *From Ritual to Record: The Nature of Modern Sports.* New York: Columbia University Press.

Hall, P. (1993). Policy paradigms, social learning and the state: The case of economic policymaking in Britain. *Comparative Politics*, 25, 275–296.

Hansen, M.N. (2011). Finnes det en talentreserve? Betydningen av klassebakgrunn og karakter for oppnådd utdanning. *Søkelys på arbeidslivet*, 03(2011), 173–189.

Hartley, J. (2005). Innovation in governance and public services: Past and present. *Public Money and Management*, 25(1), 27–34.

Hartley, J., Sørensen, E., and Torfing, J. (2013). Collaborative innovation: Viable alternative to market competition and organizational entrepreneurship. *Public Administration Review*, 73(6), 821–830.

Hayhurst, L.M.C. (2014). The 'Girl Effect' and martial arts: Social entrepreneurship and sport, gender and development in Uganda. *Gender, Place & Culture*, 21(3), 297–315.

Heggen, K. (2003). An introduction to the main concepts: Marginalization and social exclusion. I K. Heggen (red.), *Marginalization and Social Exclusion*. Ålesund: Møreforskning.

Hoeber, L., Doherty, A., Hoeber, O., and Wolfe, R. (2015). The nature of innovation in community sport organizations. *European Sport Management Quarterly*, 15(5), 518–534.

Hoeber, L., and Hoeber, O. (2012). Determinants of an innovation process: A case study of technological innovation in a community sport organization. *Journal of Sport Management*, 26, 213–223.

Hyysalo, S. (2009). User innovation and everyday practices: Micro-innovation in sports industry development. *R&D Management*, 39(3), 247–258.

IOC. (2015). Olympic charter. Retrieved from: https://stillmed.olympic.org/Documents/olympic_charter_en.pdf [Accessed 1 November 2016].

Johnson, R.J. (2010). New innovations in sports medicine: Good for the patient or good for the pocketbook? *Current Sports Medicine Reports*, 9(4), 191–193.

Kingdon, J.W. (1984). *Agendas, Alternatives, and Public Policies.* Boston: Little, Brown.

Koppenjan, J. and E.H. Klijn (2004) *Managing Uncertainties in Networks: A Network Approach to Problem Solving and Decision Making.* London: Routledge.

Lave, J., and Wegner, E. (1991). *Situated Learning: Legitimate Peripheral Participation.* Cambridge: University of Cambridge Press.

Liang, L. (2013). Television, technology and creativity in the production of a sports mega event. *Media, Culture & Society*, 35(4), 472–488.

McConkey, R., Dowling, S., Hassan, D., and Menke, S. (2012). Promoting social inclusion through Unified Sports for youth with intellectual disabilities: a five-nation study. *Journal of Intellectual Disability Research*, 57(10), 923–935.

McKeown, M. (2008). *The Truth About Innovation.* London: Prentice Hall.

Miragaia, D., and Ferreira, J.J. (2016). Consumer behavior analysis: An innovation approach in non-profit sports organizations. In V. Ratten and J. Ferreira (eds.), *Sport Entrepreneurship and Innovation*. London: Routledge.

Milbourne, L., Macrae, S., and Maguire, M. (2003). Collaborative solutions or new policy problems: Exploring multi-agency partnerships in education and health work. *Journal of Education Policy*, 18(1), 19–35.

Moore, M., and Hartley, J. (2008). Innovations in governance. *Public Management Review*, 10(1), 3–20.

Mulgan, G., and Albury, D. (2003). *Innovation in the Public Sector.* London: Cabinet Office.

Nambisan, S. (2008). *Transforming Government Through Collaborative Innovation.* Washington, DC: Harvard Kennedy School of Government.

Okayasu, I., and Morais, D.B. (2016). Sport entrepreneurship and community development in Japan. In V. Ratten and J. Ferreira (eds.), *Sport Entrepreneurship and Innovation.* London: Routledge.

O'Toole, L.J. (1997). Implementing public innovations in network settings. *Administration & Society*, 29, 115–138.

Parris, D.L., Trolio, M.L., Bouchet, A., and Peachey, J.W. (2014). Action sports athletes as entrepreneurs: Female professional wakeboarders, sponsorship and branding. *Sport Management Review*, 17, 530–545.

Phills, J.A., Diegelmeier, K., and Miller, D.T. (2008). Rediscovering social innovation. *Stanford Social Innovation Review*, 6(4), Article 12.

Pill, S., Penney, D., and Swabey, K. (2012). Rethinking sport teaching in physical education: A case study of research based innovation in teacher education. *Australian Journal of Teacher Education*, 37(8), 118–137.

Prahalad, C.K., and Ramaswamy, V. (2004). *The Future of Competition: Co-Creating Unique Value with Customers.* Boston: Harvard Business School Press.

Ratten, V. (2011a). Sport-based entrepreneurship: Towards a new theory of entrepreneurship and sport management. *International Entrepreneurship Management Journal*, 7, 57–69.

Ratten, V. (2011b). A social perspective of sports-based entrepreneurship. *International Journal of Entrepreneurship and Small Business*, 12(3), 314–326.

Ratten, V. (2011c). Social entrepreneurship and innovation in sports. *International Journal of Social Entrepreneurship and Innovation*, 1(1), 42–54.

Ratten, V. (2015). Athletes as entrepreneurs: The role of social capital and leadership ability. *International Journal of Entrepreneurship and Small Business*, 25(4), 442–455.

Ratten, V., and Ferriera, J. (2016). Sport entrepreneurship and innovation: Concepts and theory. In V. Ratten and J. Ferreira (eds.), *Sport Entrepreneurship and Innovation.* London: Routledge, pp. 1–13.

Roberts, N.C., and Bradley, R.T. (1991). Stakeholder collaboration and innovation. *Journal of Applied Behavioural Science*, 27(2), 209–227.

Seippel, Ø. (2002). *Idrett og sosial integrasjon.* Oslo: Institutt for samfunnsforskning, rapport 2002, 9.

Sheridan, H. (2007). Evaluating technical and technological innovations in sport – Why fair play isn't enough. *Journal of Sport and Social Issues*, 31(2), 179–194.

Sirianni, C. (2009). *Investing in Democracy: Engaging Citizens in Collaborative Governance.* Washington, DC: Brookings Institution Press.

Skilton, P.F., and Dooley, K. (2010). The effects of repeat collaboration on creative abrasion. *Academy of Management Review*, 35, 118–134.

Slappendel, C. (1996). Perspectives on innovation in organizations. *Organization Studies*, 17, 107–129.

Spaaij, R. (2009). The social impact of sport: Diversities, complexities and contexts. *Sport in Society*, 12(9), 1109–1117.

Spaaij, R., Magee, J., and Jeanes, R. (2014). *Sport and Social Exclusion in Global Society.* London: Routledge.

Stranbu, Å., Gulløy, E., Andersen, P.L., Seippel, Ø., and Dalen, H.B. (2017). Ungdom, idrett og klasse: Fortid, samtid og framtid [Youth, sport and social class: past, present and future]. *Norsk sosiologisk tidsskrift*, 1(2), 132–151.

Sørensen, E. (2012). Measuring the accountability of collaborative innovation. *The innovation Journal: The Public Sector Innovation Journal*, 17(1), Article 9.

Sørensen, E., and Torfing, J. (2011). Enhancing collaborative innovation in the public sector. *Administration and Society*, 43(8), 842–868.

Sørensen, E., and Torfing, J. (2012). Collaborative innovation in the public sector. *The Innovation Journal: The Public Sector Innovation Journal*, 17(1), 1–14.

Sørensen, E., and Waldorff, S.B. (2014). Collaborative policy innovation: Problems and potential. *The Innovation Journal: The Public Sector Innovation Journal*, 19(3), Article 2.

Tjønndal, A. (2016a). Sport, innovation and strategic management: A systematic literature review. *Brazilian Business Review*, 13(special issue), 38–56.

Tjønndal, A. (2016b). Innovation for social inclusion in sport. In V. Ratten and J. Ferreira (eds.), *Sport Entrepreneurship and Innovation.* London: Routledge, 42–59.

Tjønndal, A. (2017). 'I don't think they realise how good we are': Innovation, inclusion and exclusion in women's Olympic boxing. *International Review for the Sociology of Sport.* doi:10.1177/1012690217715642.

Tjønndal, A. (2018). Sport innovation: Developing a typology. *The European Journal for Sport and Society*, 15(1), 1-17.

Torfing, J. (2012). Samarbejdsdrevet innovation i den offentlige sektor: Drivkræfter, barrierer og behovet for innovationsledelse. *Scandinavian Journal of Public Administration*, 16(1), 27–47.

Torfing, J. (2013). Collaborative innovation in the public sector. In S.P. Osborne og L. Brown (eds.), *Handbook of Innovation in Public Services.* Cheltenham: Edward Elgar.

Torfing, J., Peter, G., Pierre, J., and Sørensen, E. (2012). *Interactive Governance. Advancing the Paradigm.* Oxford: Oxford University Press.

Torfing, J., Sørensen, E., and Aagaard, P. (2014). Samarbejdsdrevet innovation i praksis: en Introduktion. I P. Aagaard, E. Sørensen og J. Torfing (red.), *Samarbejdsdrevet innovation i praksis.* København: Jurist- og Økonomiforbundets Forlag.

Travers, A. (2011). Women's ski jumping, the 2010 Olympic Games, and the deafening silence of sex segregation, whiteness, and wealth. *Journal of Sport & Social Issues*, 35(2), 126–145.

van der Woude, L.H.V., de Groot, S., and Janssen, T.W.J. (2006). Manual wheelchairs: Research and innovation in rehabilitation, sports, daily life and health. *Medical Engineering & Physics*, 28, 905–915.

Vanwynsberghe, R., Surborg, B., and Wyly, E. (2012). When the games come to town: Neoliberalism, mega-events and social inclusion in the Vancouver 2010 Winter Olympic Games. *International Journal of Urban and Regional Research*, 37(6), 2074–2093.

Winand, M., and Hoeber, L. (2016). Innovation capability of non-profit sport organizations. In V. Ratten and J.J. Ferreira (eds.), *Sport Entrepreneurship and Innovation*. London: Routledge.

Winand, M., Vos, S., Zintz, T., and Scheerder, J. (2013). Determinants of service innovation: A typology of sports federations. *International Journal of Sport Management and Marketing*, 13(1), 55–73.

Zaltman, G., Duncan, R., and Holbek, J. (1973). *Innovations and Organizations*. New York: Wiley.

12 The future for transformational entrepreneurship

Vanessa Ratten and Paul Jones

Introduction

Transformational entrepreneurship involves business ventures that have a profound change in how they influence and affect society (Farinha et al., 2017). In recent years, there has been more attention placed on transformational entrepreneurship due to the interest in social causes, philanthropy, environmental responsibility, global equality and disadvantaged communities. Whilst traditional views of entrepreneurship conceptualize it as innovation, risk taking and competitiveness, transformational forms of entrepreneurship consider its social effects as being more important. To best study transformational entrepreneurship it is useful to consider it as having an economic and societal dimension.

Transformational entrepreneurs need to have the knowledge and contacts to be successful. This involves having the appropriate networks in order to manage the change. Transformational entrepreneurs utilize networks to build relationships so that a significant task can be completed. This means telling stakeholders about the benefits of the business idea for individuals and communities. To do this there needs to be a monitoring of expectations from stakeholders in order to make the end result better. Transformational entrepreneurs offer their commitment to the marketing of a project by establishing good communication mechanisms. There is normally a great deal of time taken by transformational entrepreneurs to get the idea from the inception to commercialization stage. This is due to credibility being required to make tasks handled in a responsible and efficient manner. Often volunteers are part of the process of transformation as they can help with tasks.

Transformational entrepreneurship provides a unique approach to solving societal problems that need to be addressed in the community. There is a gradual recognition of the need to focus on solving societal issues as a catalyst for economic growth (Miragaia et al., 2017). The key characteristics of transformational entrepreneurship are the fast approach in terms of finance, marketing and time to solving social problems. There has been more discussion about the term transformational in terms of how it involves entrepreneurial behaviour. Transformational entrepreneurship is premised on the idea that major innovative ideas are needed to solve socially related problems (Ashforth and Mael, 1989). The observed activities of transformational entrepreneurs blur the boundaries between making money and enabling social change. The core reason for transformational entrepreneurship is to make a positive impact.

Importance of transformational entrepreneurship

Transformational entrepreneurs have a positive attitude towards uncertainty as they look to possibilities about the future. There are also more lifestyle entrepreneurs that are seeking to balance work/life issues by engaging in potentially transformational projects. Often personal reasons impact an entrepreneur's ability to be transformational due to their connection or empathy with an issue (Ratten and Dana, 2017). This makes an entrepreneur take advantage of areas for development that they think they can change. The perception of an idea in terms of its impact on society will affect transformational entrepreneurship rates. Entrepreneurs also need to be creative with how they launch a business venture (Ratten and Ferreira, 2017). The internationalization of the global economy has had positive effects but it also has created new market needs in terms of focusing on local business opportunities (Carroll, 1979).

Much transformational entrepreneurship has come from economic or social adversity existing in a community. Some people have a tendency towards transformational entrepreneurship due to their willingness to engage in social change. Thus, it is important to bring ideas together in new ways that lead to transformational entrepreneurship. There is confusion in the meaning of transformational entrepreneurship due to its diverse meanings and different cultural connotations. Culturally sustainable entrepreneurship involves enhancing the values of society by encouraging an entrepreneurial mindset (Gerguri-Rashiti et al., 2017).

Transformational entrepreneurship is linked to social activism due to its ability to advocate for change and aid in solving social issues. There is an interest in ways to alleviate poverty in society and bring about more efficient business practices. Researchers have been increasingly encouraged to study more societal or social elements of entrepreneurship. There is an acceptance that transformational entrepreneurship is an interesting sub area of entrepreneurship. There has been progress on developing the field of transformational entrepreneurship but it is still uneven and fragmented. The reason for transformational entrepreneurship is growing in significance and is being distinguished from more well-researched topics such as social entrepreneurship. This is due to the focus on major societal changes that coincide with technological progress. There has been a long-standing view that social entrepreneurship is transformational but more recently this has changed with the realization that big changes are needed in the global economy. As a result, transformational entrepreneurship investigates how issues such as global warming, poverty and social inequality can be changed. This allows a comparison between different institutional and socio-economic contexts.

Moving forward: future topics about transformational entrepreneurship

The topic of transformational entrepreneurship is growing in popularity and will likely lead to more researchers focusing on this area due to its practical significance. To advance the body of knowledge on transformational entrepreneurship there needs to be more academic and practical work. The interrelationships between change, innovation and society are unique and require more research about their antecedents. The way to advance the field of transformational entrepreneurship is to include more methodologically complex studies. Given the challenges encountered by transformational entrepreneurs, a more balanced representation of their difficulties and successes is needed. This could include multi-level analysis of the effect transformation has on entrepreneurs, communities and societies. In addition, relational analysis that focuses on the micro level analysis of transformational entrepreneurship is required. This could look into resource mobilization for transformational entrepreneurship and the role of social networks in performance outcomes (Ratten and Tajeddini, 2017).

More research is required on analysing the resources needed that enable better transformational results and the reasons behind success rates. Studies need to be conducted on transformational entrepreneurs to gain more information on their motivations and attitudes. This includes focusing on the managerial level in terms of the delegation of tasks and organization of the transformation. This would help to garner more information on the support required for transformational entrepreneurship. In addition, the role of human resource management in the process would aid in understanding how transformation entrepreneurship occurs in society.

There are many opportunities to conduct research on transformational entrepreneurship due to its early stage of development. Future transformational entrepreneurship research needs to provide for better methodological rigour and contextual positioning. Research about transformational entrepreneurship is still in its infancy so the chapters in this book represent significant additions to the literature. More research is required on transformational entrepreneurship to add to the expansive literature in general entrepreneurship studies and to cumulatively contribute to the development of future studies. There needs to be more connection to the existing theories to capture the heterogeneity of transformational entrepreneurship. Additional research needs to answer how to capture transformational entrepreneurship that is connected to previous research.

Transformational entrepreneurship is a scholarly community that needs to align with other sub-disciplines in the entrepreneurship literature. There are both direct and indirect ways for future research on transformational entrepreneurship to add to the existing body of knowledge. This can be done by directly focusing on transformational entrepreneurship as a theoretical framework or area of inquiry but also indirectly by using it as an antecedent or performance outcome in studies. There are many more research avenues needed for transformational entrepreneurship to progress but this represents a fertile area of inquiry. Table 12.1 presents some themes and research requirements for future research suggestions about transformational entrepreneurship.

New methodological approaches

More longitudinal studies about transformational entrepreneurship will provide a better understanding about how it progresses in society. This will help to build a better understanding about the role of different stakeholders in the

Table 12.1 Future research agenda

Theme	Research requirements
Clarifying the concept of transformational entrepreneurship	More conceptual clarity about the definition, nature and role of transformational entrepreneurship in society
	Detailed analysis of the different stages of transformational entrepreneurship
	Comparative research about different issues of transformational entrepreneurship
Outcomes of transformational entrepreneurship	Factors affecting the impact of transformational entrepreneurship
	Multifaceted analysis about the micro, meso and macro dimensions of transformational entrepreneurship
	Opportunities for further development and refinement of transformational entrepreneurship
Development of transformational entrepreneurship	Complexity of the transformational entrepreneurship at the practical and managerial level
	Resource needs to support and integrate transformational entrepreneurship

transformational process. In addition, more comparative analysis of transformational entrepreneurship in different international contexts is required. This would help to see if transformational entrepreneurship is more prevalent in developing countries due to the need for major societal change or if there is a no difference based on economic environment. As there has been a tendency to view transformational entrepreneurship as a developing world phenomenon it would be useful for future research to evaluate this perception. This would help to analyse the environmental context in which transformational entrepreneurship occurs to see how it is affected by income and education levels.

There needs to be more research attention on understanding the different types of transformational entrepreneurship. Some forms of change are continual and develop over a longer time period, whilst others quickly enter the marketplace. Thus, the frequency and impact of transformational entrepreneurship needs to be evaluated in more depth by future researchers. This would help to see if there are specific economic or seasonal factors that influence the level of transformation. Case study data about the role of government or aid agencies in the transformation will help to yield better results. In addition, the transformation might occur differently depending on whether it is a grassroots initiative or strategic development. More qualitative work is needed to unpack how transformational entrepreneurship works at different levels of society. There is a need to understand how transformational entrepreneurship differs at the local, regional and international levels. The current absence of knowledge about the multiple levels of change requires innovative methodological approaches.

There is a current research gap on transformational entrepreneurship in terms of contrasting and analyzing different international examples. This book contributes to the field of transformational entrepreneurship by consolidating research and demonstrating different examples. There is a need for more attention on how the private sector compares to the non-profit sector in terms of bringing about transformational entrepreneurship. It is well known that most forms of transformational entrepreneurship develop in the non-profit or social sector but it is less known about the role of the private sector.

There needs to be more empirical research with cross-country data analysis to improve our understanding of transformational entrepreneurship. This is vital given the increased interest in it and to make it more relevant in the general entrepreneurship and international business literature. Answering the question of how transformational entrepreneurship changes due to different international contexts would be a good starting point for future research. Further refinement of the transformational entrepreneurship phenomenon is needed so as to identify its unique characteristics. Research on transformational entrepreneurship is still fragmented and diverse in topic, which makes it hard to develop a coherent body of knowledge. Thus, there needs to be more consideration about the level of transformational entrepreneurship. This could include looking into incremental versus radical forms to see the difference in application. Whilst transformational entrepreneurship implies radical change there can still be smaller changes that have a profound effect on society.

Implications for policy

This book has several implications for policy initiatives and developments. Due to unequal power relationships and inequality in developing countries, more research is required on facilitating transformational entrepreneurship. This can be done with the help of international aid agencies that can develop grants programmes tailored to help transformational entrepreneurs. More attention is required on the different forms of entrepreneurship to extend our understanding about the way transformation occurs. In addition, international aid agencies and non-government entities need to develop appropriate strategies to facilitate transformational entrepreneurship. There are further explorations about transformational entrepreneurship that contribute to our understanding of the topic.

Transformational entrepreneurship is a societal priority and necessitates further examination in the literature. Future research could explore how transformational entrepreneurship differs between developed and developing countries and how different industry contexts utilize it. There needs to be more work on understanding how emerging technologies are influencing transformational entrepreneurship. This is important as the global innovation ecosystem is changing so transformational entrepreneurship has the potential to alter societal conditions. Transformational entrepreneurship can be studied from a variety of aspects including individual, community, firm, global, household, industry, nation and regional.

Conclusion

In conclusion, transformational entrepreneurship is more than a buzz word but a significant sub-topic within the general entrepreneurship and sociology literature. It is an accepted stream of research, but further research is required to understand its strategic applicability. A possible explanation for the recent surge in interest on transformational entrepreneurship is that the literature on social and sustainable entrepreneurship is at the maturity stage. Transformational entrepreneurship offers a compelling rational for developing a new approach to social and sustainability policy. This chapter has provided insights into transformational entrepreneurship and how it is practiced in society. Transformational entrepreneurship is a vital area of entrepreneurship that needs to be studied in more detail. This book will extend the research on transformational entrepreneurship by providing new ideas for future research.

References

Ashforth, B.E., and Mael, F.A. (1989). Social identity theory and the organization. *Academy of Management Review*, 14(1), 20–39.

Carroll, A. (1979). A three-dimensional conceptual model of corporate performance. *Academy of Management Review*, 4(4), 497–505.

Farinha, L., Ferreira, J., Nunes, S., and Ratten, V. (2017). Conditions supporting entrepreneurship and sustainable growth. *International Journal of Social Ecology and Sustainable Development*, 8(3), 67–86.

Gërguri-Rashiti, S., Ramadani, V., Abazi-Alili, H., Dana, L.-P., and Ratten, V. (2017). ICT, innovation and firm performance: The transition economies context. *Thunderbird International Business Review*, 59(1), 93–102.

Miragaia, D., Ferreira, J., and Ratten, V. (2017). Sport event sponsorship and policy: A social entrepreneurship and corporate social responsibility perspective. *International Journal of Sport Policy and Politics*, 29(4), 613–623.

Ratten, V., and Dana, L.-P. (2017). Sustainable entrepreneurship, family farms and the dairy industry. *International Journal of Social Ecology and Sustainable Development*, 8(3), 114–129.

Ratten, V., and Ferreira, J. (2017). Entrepreneurship, innovation and sport policy: Implications for future research. *International Journal of Sport Policy and Politics*, 29(4), 575–577.

Ratten, V., and Tajeddini, K. (2017). Innovativeness in family firms: An internationalization approach. *Review of International Business and Strategy*, 27(2), 217–230.

Index